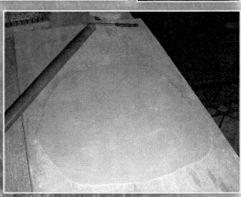

BEYOND THE
PASTA

Recipes, Language & Life with an Italian Family

MARK LESLIE

GEMELLI PRESS

Published by Gemelli Press LLC
9600 Stone Avenue North
Seattle, Washington 98103

Cover design and typesetting by
Enterline Design Services LLC

ISBN: 978-0-9821023-6-7
Library of Congress Control Number: 2010934593

Printed in the United States of America.
To order additional copies of this book
or for more information please visit:
www.gemellipress.com

GEMELLI PRESS

Per Nonna, Alessandra, Lillo, Marianna e Francesca—
Con tanto affetto

CONTENTS

PROLOGUE

S ome passionate love affairs are easily forgotten, others are only remembered as passing fancies or are over before they ever truly begin, but some are so instantaneously intense and wrought with pure, unbridled emotion that they can forever alter your life. I have had two such love affairs in my life and the one led to the other.

It began with my first trip to Italy in September 2001. This trip was not going to be a guided tour; instead it was a self-catered vacation—a thrilling idea: to have the freedom to navigate the country and the culture with no guides, only my partner Richard and our mothers. "Wait a minute—a love affair began while on vacation with your mothers and partner?" Yes, and it was a love affair of the heart, too, but not the kind you are imagining.

Driving down into Florence from the Tuscan hills we could see over the entire city—a vast sea of red brick and white stucco buildings capped with terra-cotta rooftops, pierced by the spires and domes of churches.

The most famous is the dome of the Cathedral of Santa Maria del Fiore—Filippo Brunelleschi's "Duomo." It appears as an island in the midst of this bustling sea.

While outside the *Duomo*, I broke away from Richard and our mothers to photograph its exterior. Whether you are Catholic or not, it is impossible not to be drawn to the *Duomo*—its dome and bell tower are masterpieces. The tri-colored marble façade is heavily carved with filigree and biblical figures, and its angels are mesmerizing. They are not the tranquil Victorian feminine figures that one associates with the word "angel." Here they are male, aggressively lunging from the carved designs. The faces and bodies of these Renaissance angels are full of purpose, with a fierce determination to carry out God's wrath upon the sinner. Their glaring eyes and angry postures proclaim to both believers and non-believers that they are a force to be reckoned with. God's army, carved in stone, was policing all who passed by and entered their domain.

I had taken my last photo when I noticed a woman approach Richard and our mothers. I walked over and she reintroduced herself as a UNICEF employee and told us, in a proper British accent, "The World Trade Towers, the Pentagon, and the White House have been destroyed. I just saw it on CNN." She left us as quickly as she had approached—we stood dumbfounded.

"What should we do?"

"It sounds like a hoax. Like something out of Orson Welles' *War of the Worlds*."

"It's impossible. She was trying to scam money out of us by saying she was from a reputable charity and then telling us something horrible had happened back home."

An angry angel caught my eye.

In complete disbelief, and without knowing what to do, we half-heartedly continued our visit to the *Duomo's* baptistry. Inside, golden mosaics cover the octagonal domed ceiling. At that moment, the enormous mosaic of a Byzantine Christ sitting with welcoming, outstretched arms, proudly displaying the nail wounds of his ultimate gift, struck me as profound. America had been attacked, yet there we were safely looking up at the heavens—golden visions of angels, saints and martyrs—all the while being embraced by this golden Christ. My senses were reeling: it was difficult to reconcile the image of merciful salvation before my eyes with the news of unmerciful destruction still ringing in my ears.

Heading back out to the streets of Florence to clear our heads, we spent the next hour making our way back to the car. As we passed parked police cars, their radios were reporting something important, but since it was all in Italian, we could only make out city names—"Washington," "Oklahoma City," "New York." We looked into tobacco shops and cafés for other Americans or a TV, with no success. Suddenly we seemed to be the last English-speaking people in Florence. It was impossible to focus on the beauty of the city—with each passing minute I was increasingly distracted by the woman's words echoing in my head. Driving out of Florence at evening rush hour, we noticed the flags on the Florentine buildings had been lowered to half-staff.

It was a silent drive into the darkening Italian night toward our "home" in southern Tuscany. The only conversation was when the car's headlights caught some nocturnal wildlife: large owls perching on fences or flying across the road, a deer or wild boar running ahead in a field, a pair of large porcupines, quills up, waddling across the road. We commented about how exciting it was to see such beautiful animals, but as soon as one passed, we fell back into our silence. I was trying not to imagine the things we had been told—and trying harder still not to believe them.

We stopped for dinner at a roadside *trattoria* that was owned and operated by a thirty-something couple in a little town near Montalcino. The husband cooked, while the wife was the hostess and waitress. She seated us in the small dining room where there was only one other table of customers, an older couple, seated in the back corner. Upon hearing our accents, they introduced themselves—they were Americans, too, and explained that they had seen all the CNN footage of the day's events on their hotel room's TV. They clarified the misinformation we had been given outside the *Duomo* and confirmed what had happened back home.

Dinner was served: simple pastas with homemade ragù sauces, steak cooked rare and to perfection, thinly sliced and drizzled with local olive oil. It was just what we needed—Italian comfort food. I was comforted more by what our hostess said to us after dinner.

"I am-a so saurry," she said in very broken English.

Thinking she was apologizing for the meal, I said, "The food was wonderful. *Buonissimo!* Absolutely nothing to be sorry about." Our appetites were small, given the circumstances, so I felt I needed to overly compensate for our apparent lack of interest in the meal—though what I did taste was delicious.

"No, no, no. I am-a so saurry for-a you and ... aaah ... your country. I hope you did-a not have any *famiglia* or friends in-a New York. My heart, it ... aaah ... breaks ... it breaks for you and I will-a pray for all your country and all of the world tonight. I am-a so saurry."

My heart was breaking, too, and, even though I was sitting across the table from my mother, I felt orphaned. We were all on the verge of falling apart, and I struggled to hold it together for fear of never being able to recover. This Tuscan woman's concern for me—for us and for our country—held me up when all I wanted to do was collapse. Her expression of grace, which some might have considered mere empathy, resonated as so unselfishly pure to my wounded and unguarded soul that, for lack of better words, I fell in love—not literally in love with this woman, but I fell in love with the depth of her compassion, which seemed to go beyond herself and reveal the very essence of her country, too. Unknowingly, she had touched my soul and I was forever changed.

The drive the last hour south was perfectly quiet—even the romping wildlife had ceased to spark conversation. It was almost 11:30 p.m. when we parked outside the ancient stone wall of Proceno, our "home." As we walked through the gate we stopped at the town's shrine to the Madonna, a small plaque of the Virgin Mary, containing a candle. On previous after-dinner strolls through Proceno, we noticed that the shrine's candle was never lit and the city flag, which daily flew above the image of Mary, was always removed by nightfall. Now, in front of us, the candle was lit and the flag hung at half-staff.

We wept.

————

In the early spring of 2005, I was watching a television program about Italy. The host was visiting a cooking school in Parma. Still aching to return to the country I fell in love with in 2001, my brain started reeling with thoughts of learning to cook in Italy. I jumped on the Internet hunting for Italian cooking schools. I skimmed over schools and private courses until a course offered in Siena caught my eye. The other courses were associated with professional chefs and restaurants, professional training schools or involved taking lessons from a retired food writer or critic. The Dante Alighieri Society in Siena offered many full immersion courses where a student could take cooking and language lessons at a school while living with an Italian family. However, there was one very particular course where a student could, alone, live with a family and learn from the grandmother (*nonna* in Italian), the professor of cooking, and the mother, the professor of language. It seemed perfect—but was I up for the adventure of living with a family and trying to learn their language? The more I researched it, the more it called to me.

The course, "Italian and Cooking," could be booked in one-week increments up to a maximum of eight. Wow, two months seemed terrifying and yet, how short and insufficient a single week sounded—what could I possibly learn in seven days? My previous trip to Italy was ten days in length and, though I had tried to learn as much Italian as possible before I went, it really only amounted to *"ciao"* and the usual pathetic tourist sayings: *Vorrei una bottiglia d'aqua, per favore* —I would like a bottle of water, please; *Grazie* —thank you; *una tavola per quattro persone* —a table for four people.

I wanted to be conversational and there is nothing more conversational than a familial environment. I had concerns though: Would we get along? Would I understand them? Hell, would they understand me? At 41, was I too old to learn something new? And the one that haunted me the most: Would Richard mind my going to Italy for a month without him?

Missing work wasn't an issue. I work in professional theatre and I was going to be between shows for the month of August, so my schedule was clear. Four weeks seemed the perfect amount of time—longer than the usual vacation, but not so long as to make Richard feel like he was being completely abandoned while I went off to play in a foreign country. It wasn't easy for Richard to agree to the idea of me going to Italy without him, however, in all relationships there is a give and take and he was unselfish enough to let me indulge myself.

The details in this book are taken from my daily journal of the twenty-eight days I spent with the Stefani family in Viterbo, Italy, in August 2005—my second love affair and a time as life altering, but more joyfully so, as Florence had been four years earlier.

DAY ONE (Il Primo Giorno)

Benvenuti a Viterbo!—Welcome to Viterbo!

I am safely in Viterbo, Italy, after being dropped off at the airport by a rather green-eyed monster—I could tell Richard was more than a little envious as we said our good-byes. I had endured an exhausting series of flights from Atlanta to La Guardia with a transfer to JFK, before finally landing at Leonardo da Vinci International in Rome. My early morning arrival had given me time to sightsee before the afternoon train to Viterbo, so I hunted for a bag check at the Stazione Termini, the main train station in Rome. Who wants to schlep luggage while sightseeing?

Checking my bags turned into my first Italian adventure. I quickly learned that no one in Italy moves fast in the morning—particularly on a Sunday. After hauling my bags across the station's enormous main level and down two flights of stairs, I was surprised to see a line so early at the check-in counter. While taking my place at the end of the line, I noticed some Asian tourists were having issues with their luggage at the counter. All I could figure out from the pointing and loud talking (the Italian workers and the Asian tourists did not speak a common language) was that there seemed to be something wrong with the check-in computer and their bags. It looked as if we were going to be here a while. The line grew longer with each passing minute and, oddly, most of the people getting into line were not foreigners, but Italians.

After thirty minutes without progress, impatient Italian wives started prodding their husbands to go find out why the line wasn't moving. The more the men tried to resist, the more insistent the women became. Sometimes in pairs and sometimes alone, these poor scolded husbands would go up to the counter, like schoolboys on their way to the principal's office. When the workers explained the situation—involving many hand gestures and loud exclamations—all the men, on both sides of the counter, would shake their heads in agreement that something was indeed wrong. The root of the problem was that no one knew exactly what was wrong, so no one knew what to do to fix it.

In Italy more is said with hand gestures, grunts and gasps than with actual words. It is more artful to grunt *"Bah"* and shake your hand up in the air—a combination of a pope's wave and a homecoming queen's wave on her float. This gesture, along with *"Bah,"* tells a person you don't believe they are telling you the truth or that their answer is not good enough. It is a beautiful thing to watch, unlike the rude hand gestures Americans imagine Italians stereotypically using.

After much head scratching, waves and *bah*'s, the husbands, having no more information now than they started with, made their way sheepishly back to their wives. As they passed me, they would shrug their shoulders and say, *"Eh,"* implying, "Well, it is Sunday. What can we do?" I smiled back as if I, too, a self-proclaimed Italian citizen for the month of August, understood all that had transpired at the counter and agreed—*"Eh."*

Ninety minutes later my bags were checked, and I set off to visit the Esquilino neighborhood near the train station—a section of Rome that I had never seen before. I walked south toward the Basilica di Santa Maria Maggiore and quietly slipped in to listen to a bit of the mass already in progress. I am not Catholic, but I enjoy some "smells and bells"—a church service where the clergy swing smoking incense burners and ring bells to announce important moments in the liturgy. I do like a pageant.

I stopped at every church I passed to catch a glimpse of their service. In Rome there is a church on every corner and in between there is *una gelateria*—an ice cream shop. Of course I had to stop and have gelato. Gelato is made from milk, not cream like its American counterpart. This causes the gelato to be smoother and softer in texture, though not any less fattening. It was around 10:00 a.m.—still breakfast time, I assured myself—and isn't milk a good thing to have for breakfast? I'm afraid of what a month of eating gelato will do to me, but I am up for the punishment. I spent the next couple of hours either walking around with a gelato in my hand or on my knees in church asking to be pardoned for the sin of gluttony.

It is easy to lose track of time in Rome; the city itself has forgotten time with the ancient and modern worlds so intertwined. I was lost in thought in front of a portion of an ancient Roman aqueduct when I was suddenly jolted me back to the present, panicked about how long it might take to retrieve my luggage. I cut my sightseeing short and hurried back to the Termini—needlessly—it only took five minutes to reclaim my bags. Oh well, it gave me some time to buy my train ticket to Viterbo and prepare myself to change trains at a small station on the outskirts of Rome. Riding the rails is not an everyday event for me; there are no commuter trains where I live in Alabama. The last time I had to change trains in a foreign country I ended up on a train heading west when I needed to be heading east. Taking the subway in New York or the "L" in Chicago, also fills me with dread. I'm not sure where this fear comes from. When I was a child my mother and I often took the train from San Diego, where we lived while my Dad was stationed in the Navy, to visit family in Chicago. Nothing terrifying ever happened on those trips, except once, when a particularly mean train steward yelled at me for making so many trips to refill my paper cup at the water fountain in the club car. Hmm, maybe I am afraid of getting on the wrong train and not being allowed to drink water?

Anyway, my nervousness about changing trains, coupled with my lack of language skills, forced me to focus on each approaching train. No doubt I looked like a crazy person standing on the platform as I checked the train schedule posted on the wall, walked over to look up and down the track and checked the tickets in my hand—repeating the cycle over and over again every few minutes. Each approaching train, whether mine or not, had me standing at the edge of the platform asking every conductor who stepped off if this was the train to Viterbo. I was a nervous wreck by the time my train arrived—I made the connection with no problem. Surviving here for a month might be possible after all, if my nerves can handle it. I found an empty seat, opened a window, sat back and read some of the research on Viterbo I had done after enrolling in the program.

Viterbo is an ancient city 70 miles northwest of Rome in the northern section of Lazio. For most Americans, Tuscany is the most famous region of Italy. Lazio is the region just south of Tuscany and, for most Italians, Rome and Viterbo are the most famous cities in Lazio. The Etruscans originally inhabited the territory of Viterbo in 800 BC. The Romans overtook the Etruscans 500 years later and started building settlements there. Emperor Cassius built a roadway, named Via Cassia in his honor, connecting Viterbo to Rome, which is still a highly trafficked route today. The old city wall surrounding Viterbo was built in AD 776. It is 60 feet tall and made entirely of large stacked stones. In the 12th and 13th centuries, Viterbo was home to many popes, and local folklore claims that Viterbo is the place where the first conclave was created and held to elect a new pope.

The train stopped and the woman next to me woke me from my nap to tell me that this was my stop. *"Grazie, signora. Grazie." "Certo, signore."*

Alessandra Stefani, my language teacher and mother of the family, was meeting me at the train station in Viterbo, so I waited for the platform to clear. I figured we would end up being the last people standing there after the train pulled away. Sure enough, there she was, but she wasn't alone—a second woman waited with her. Alessandra approached me first. She is a tall woman in her late forties, a brunette with blonde highlights, and very fashionably dressed in linen pants and tailored shirt. All women in Italy are fashionably styled until they attain *nonna*—grandmother—status. It is a status not determined by age, but by the individual woman herself. Once she decides to make the switch, she instantly becomes dowdy: a simple skirt and blouse, a cardigan sweater, eyeglasses on a chain and comfortable shoes—from Superman to Clark Kent in the blink of an eye, trusting in the knowledge that under her mild-mannered cardigan still lurks the man of steel.

"Buonasera, mi chiamo Alessandra e le presento mia mamma, Nonna."
—"Hello, I'm Alessandra and this is my mother, Nonna."

"Piacere, Marco," —"Nice to meet you, Mark,"— Nonna said.

"Il piacere è il mio," —"The pleasure is mine,"— I said, shaking her hand and then Alessandra's.

I was proud of myself for remembering one of my few tourist phrases and it seemed to impress them. Nonna was going to be my cooking teacher. I was grinning ear-to-ear, flanked by my teachers, as we headed to the car. There was such a rush of adrenaline that I had the urge to stop every passerby and say, "I'm in Italy. I am finally in Italy and these are my new professors. Isn't this cool?!"—or maybe I was just feeling the heat. It is *caldo*—hot— in Viterbo. Unlike the American South, there is no air conditioning here— none in the train, train stations, churches or *gelaterie*. It reminded me of my childhood in northern Illinois where in late August the whole family would sit in front of a single box fan trying to remain comfortable while panting like dogs. Little did I know how well my midwestern upbringing would prepare me for an Italian August.

Since I was the guest, Alessandra insisted that I sit in the front passenger seat while she climbed into the back. Nonna drove home because Alessandra has never learned to drive. The three of us were packed into the little white car, windows down, whizzing through traffic around the ancient city wall of Viterbo. Nonna has a lead foot and whips around like a taxi driver. She is 79 years old and takes no prisoners when driving. It was great fun!

"Rallenta, mamma!" —"Mamma, slow down!"— Alessandra would yell from the back seat, keeping her hand on top of her head in an effort to preserve her hairstyle. Nonna would slow down momentarily, but just as quickly return to her race car pace, leaving the slower drivers in her wake. Nonna is not the stereotypical cardigan-wearing grandmother. She is an energetic, modern grandmother with things to do and places to go. She is much shorter than her daughter, with the spark of a mischievous elf in her eye. Nonna is definitely a character. I can only imagine what our time in the kitchen will be like together. I cannot wait to learn how to cook from her.

We arrived at the house in the suburbs of Viterbo, about a mile from the city center—a large three-story "L"-shaped stucco structure with a classic Italian terra-cotta tiled roof. The stucco is painted a light raspberry color. Alessandra told me that it is one of the oldest houses in the neighborhood, dating from the early 1900s. The Stefanis own the whole structure but only live in the foot of the "L." The other section of the house is divided into two large apartments that are rented out and have their own separate entrances. The house sits on a piece of property that is walled and gated at the corner of two streets. Across the street is an elementary school and next to that is an auto mechanics shop. On the opposite street there is a large apartment complex. There is nothing ancient or stereotypically romantic about this Italian neighborhood. The Stefanis' yard is filled with fruit trees—yellow plum, persimmon, apple, fig—and roses line the walk to the front door. Once inside, two of the family's dogs, Tequila and Brighitta, greeted me with a resounding canine fanfare. Tequila is a large white Italian version of a Golden Retriever. He is not quite a year old and, though he is large, he is still a puppy. Brighitta, a much older dog, is a white West Highland Terrier.

Alessandra escorted me up to my room on the third floor—its own little apartment, minus a kitchen, that I have all to myself. The sitting room is furnished with a sofa and chairs, bookcases, desk, and even a weight bench. The bathroom, with marble floors and a large tub, is spacious. There is a large bedroom furnished with an antique bedroom suite. Most importantly, the bedroom has an oscillating fan—HOORAY! There are no windows on the third floor, but every room has at least one, if not two, skylights. I may not be able to see out, but I can see up. Alessandra left me to get settled in, unpacked and cleaned up before *la cena*—dinner.

When I came down for *la cena*, I was introduced to the rest of the family.

"Marco, le presento mio marito Angelo," —"Mark, this is my husband Angelo,"— Alessandra said.

As we shook hands, he reached up with his left and rubbed my shaved head, laughed and then rubbed his own. Our identical haircuts quickly broke the ice. Angelo wasn't the only one to manhandle me right off the bat. When I was introduced to their daughters, Marianna and Francesca, each of the girls grabbed one of my biceps.

"Ooo, belle braccia," —"Oh, nice arms,"— Marianna said, squeezing my left, while Francesca squeezed the right and said, *"Sei molto muscoloso."* —"You are very muscular."

I regularly go to the gym, so I have a muscular build and the girls were blatant in acknowledging it. It made me blush.

"Sei un facchino," —"You are a *facchino*,"— Nonna said, while the rest of them nodded their heads. I had no clue what she was talking about, so I just smiled and blushed more.

Alessandra went on to explain that Marianna worked at a gym. "Great," I thought, but when I asked if it was possible for me to go while I was here for the month, I was quickly disappointed.

"Marianna's gym is closed for vacation the entire month of August," Alessandra said.

There were lots of smiles as we sat down at the table for my first dinner with my new Italian family. We jumped right into what was a slightly awkward situation for me. They are more accustomed to having strangers at their table than I am to sitting at a stranger's table. In moments like this I become unusually shy, fearful of coming on too strong only to commit a social faux pas and seem like a jackass—an American jackass. I was very aware that I was not only representing myself, but also my whole country!

I am notorious for putting my foot in my mouth. I was raised in northern Illinois, but I have lived in the Deep South for the past eighteen years. At one of the first Southern cocktail parties I attended with Richard, I was nervous being so far from my comfort zone. A smartly dressed, blue-haired, matronly woman approached me, introduced herself as "Mrs. Dr. So-and-So Somebody Blobbity-blob," and upon hearing my name asked, "And who are your people?" Well, I had never heard a question like this before—"My people? What did she mean by that? I don't own any people," I thought to myself. In the confusion of the moment, looking at this blue-blooded Southern lady, my mind immediately jumped to images of slavery. Feeling the pressure of a new social circle, without thinking, I replied, "Oh, I don't own any slaves." Her face soured and she glared at me as if I had just peed on her curtains and, in a huff, she abruptly turned and muttered "damn Yankee" as she walked away. Rather innocently, I had inserted my foot squarely into my mouth—and eaten it up to the knee! Later, I found out what she was actually asking me: "Who is your family—what social and economic circle do you come from?" Had I understood that as her question, I probably still would have answered her in the same way. In either case, I went from fish-out-of-water to jackass in a split second, and I certainly don't want to repeat that experience now. Open mouth—insert foot! I wonder what the Italian phrase is for that? I hope I never learn it.

The girls got the conversation going once we were settled. I assumed that it was the usual type of family dinner chat since I could not understand a word. I had been awake for about 36 hours straight, so I was exhilarated and exhausted at the same time. Alessandra, the only one in the family who speaks English, would translate and keep me included in what was being said. She always started by asking if I understood what the conversation was about. One time, I told her that I thought Angelo and Marianna were talking about either cabbage—*cavolo*—or a horse—*cavallo*. She translated for the family and everyone got a big kick out of that. Lots of laughter at my expense, but isn't that what family dinner conversation usually is? I do know some random Italian words, but sometimes I can't always remember their exact meaning, proving, I guess, that I don't really know those words after all. Angelo and Marianna were talking about training Marianna's horse—not training her cabbage. The family has a little farm with some cows and two horses, one for each of the girls. Alessandra said that Marianna is an exceptional rider and we will have to take a trip to the farm one day. At least the conversation was about horses at the farm and not the possible jackass at the table.

I was more than happy to sit, listen and absorb the atmosphere. Marianna and Francesca would argue about things, as sisters do. There was much disagreement between the daughters and their parents. Nonna would chime in and everyone would say *"Bah,"* shake their hands and laugh or argue more. They are a good-hearted, generous, caring, loving family, and they argue as much as they laugh. I am very happy to be in a house where I will be openly and honestly exposed to the everyday family life of a foreign culture, something one rarely experiences as a tourist.

Next came the food. We had what I would consider a classic Italian dinner for a warm summer's night: *antipasti* consisting of prosciutto, assorted salami, cantaloupe, figs and rustic bread. The first course was a *frittata con zucchine*—zucchini omelet, which Nonna had started preparing as soon as we arrived at the house. That was followed by a course of three different pecorino cheeses. Pecorino is a sheep's milk cheese (*pecora* is the Italian word for sheep): one was a very soft, young pecorino; the second was a local pecorino, which was firm but not hard; the third was dry and hard. The cheeses were served with honey, fresh yellow plums from the tree out in the yard and large pieces of an unusual flat bread. The flat bread comes in 18-inch round sheets stacked in a large paper wrapper. Each sheet is dry like a cracker. Alessandra took a couple of the sheets of bread, broke them into large pieces and then soaked them in water until they were pliable. Once soft, the water was gently squeezed from the bread. On this bread, Alessandra would layer plum slices, pecorino and a drizzle of honey before rolling it up like a small burrito. Nonna had also made fresh yellow plum marmalade earlier that evening before dinner, and she brought that out to go with the cheese as well. After watching her for two seconds, I can tell she is a talented cook and that I am going to learn a lot from her—and, for that matter, from everyone seated at the table. Angelo proudly served a white wine, *"Est! Est! Est!"* produced in this region of Viterbo.

I was finished politely stuffing myself when Angelo brought out an orange-flavored liqueur Alessandra had made, dubbed *Arancello d'Alessandra*. It was very similar to *limoncello*, a popular Italian lemon-flavored liqueur that is sweet, strong and served cold. Both are for after-dinner sipping to aid with digestion. Even though Angelo only poured a shot into a small glass, it was too strong to knock back like I would do with tequila or whiskey.

Dinner in Italy occurs much later than in America and goes on for longer. We started at 8:30 p.m. and it lasted two hours. From reading what we ate it may seem like a lot of food, but the servings were small, and dinner consisted of fresh and cool food for a hot summer's night. With my brain overloading from new sensations and sheer exhaustion setting in, a simple dinner with clean tastes was exactly what I needed—and a couple of sipping-shots of the *arancello* didn't hurt either!

Frittata con Zucchine e Cipolla

Zucchini and Onion Frittata

Zucchini, like most squash, has a high water content. When shopping for this dish, choose small to medium-sized ones rather than one large zucchini, because the larger they grow, the more water and <u>less flavor</u> they have.

2 tablespoons sunflower oil (extra virgin olive oil may be substituted)

1 small-medium onion, finely minced

1 clove garlic, finely minced

¾ cup water, divided

3 medium zucchini (about ¾ pound), sliced into ¼-inch rounds

½ teaspoon salt

¼ teaspoon freshly ground black pepper

6 eggs, beaten

½ cup freshly grated Parmigiano-Reggiano cheese

Heat the oil in a 10-inch nonstick skillet over medium heat. When the oil is hot, add the onion and garlic. Cook for one minute, stirring constantly. Add a ¼ cup of the water and cook for 2 to 3 minutes until the water has almost evaporated. Add another ¼ cup water and cook an additional 2 to 3 minutes until the water has, once again, almost evaporated. Stir in the zucchini rounds, salt, pepper and the remaining ¼ cup water. Lower the heat, cover and simmer, stirring occasionally, until the zucchini is soft, 10 to 12 minutes.

Meanwhile, beat the eggs in a medium bowl and stir in the Parmigiano-Reggiano.

When the zucchini is soft but still retains its shape, remove the cover, return the heat to medium and cook until the excess moisture has evaporated, 4 to 6 minutes. Stir in the beaten egg mixture, making sure the zucchini and onions are evenly distributed. Cook until the bottom of the frittata starts to lightly brown and the top begins to set up, 4 to 6 minutes. With a spatula, loosen the edges of the frittata from the sides of the pan and with a quick firm shake, flip the frittata over in one whole piece.* Cook the second side 2 to 3 minutes, until the bottom is lightly browned.

Invert the finished frittata (or if inverting seems scary, you can slide the frittata) onto a serving plate, cut into wedges and serve warm or at room temperature.

Serves 8 as an appetizer, or 4 as an entrée.

Note: If flipping the frittata seems daunting, place a dinner plate over the frittata and turn the pan over, inverting the frittata onto the plate. Slide the frittata back into the pan and finish cooking the second side. A third way to finish the second side of the frittata is to place it under a broiler: Preheat the broiler and when the bottom of the frittata is lightly browned and the top is still loose, place the pan under the broiler until the top is set and browned, 3 to 4 minutes. Nonna flipped hers effortlessly. I still tend to put mine under a broiler.

DAY TWO (Il Giorno Due)

I was too exhausted and stuffed full of the first day's events, sights, sounds and tastes to dream. I was out like a light—and wide awake at 5:00 a.m. with all kinds of thoughts swimming in my head. I wondered what my Italian hosts thought of their new American houseguest. It was hard to get back to sleep. Did I make a good impression last night? Did I eat enough? Did I eat too much? I hope I didn't insult their hospitality. I tossed in bed until 6:30, when I dropped deeply back to sleep only to awaken suddenly, panicked, at 7:30 and rushed to get downstairs by 8:00 for *colazione*—breakfast.

For breakfast we had toast with Nonna's plum marmalade, some freshly made sweet biscotti with raisins (more like soft cookies than hard biscotti), tea and *melone*—cantaloupe.

Nonna grabbed her purse and keys, pinched me on the back of my arm, and nodded her head toward the front door. In a flash we were out in the car and heading to run errands.

We whipped into the parking lot of a small grocery. Nonna got out and headed to a cart rack, but my attention was drawn to an Indian gentleman outside the store selling things out of a shopping cart. He had brooms, feather dusters, cleaning chemicals and other small household items for sale. I could not tell if he was associated with the store or if he was just hawking his wares outside the entrance. He tried to sell Nonna something as we passed, but she was having none of it, which made me think he had nothing to do with the store.

With a cart securely in hand, we shopped Nonna's list. At the register the checkout clerk asked, *"Busta?"* (Pronounced "BOO-stah.") In Italy you have to pay for your *busta*—grocery bag. They are exactly like the plastic grocery bags we get back in the States. Every *nonna* usually answers the clerk, *"No, grazie,"* because out in the car is a collection of grocery bags from previous trips to the store. They are not going to pay for new shopping bags every trip. *Nonne* are frugal and resourceful; nothing is used only once and nothing is ever wasted.

"Busta?" asked the clerk.

"No, grazie," Nonna said.

We left the store with our unbagged groceries still loose in the cart—the store does not allow used *buste* to be brought inside. Nonna keeps her stash of plastic bags inside the trunk. While we were bagging our groceries at the rear of the car I thought to myself, "Why don't you be a good person and take the cart back to the rack for Nonna? Wouldn't that make a good impression on my first shopping trip by showing her what a considerate and helpful person I am?"

"Nonna, per favore." I pointed at the empty cart and then at the rack across the parking lot.

"Si, si, certo, Marco. Grazie."

I got near the rack, pushed the cart in from a distance and went back to the car, congratulating myself for being such a good little helper—*Bravo, Marco!*

"*Marco, dov'è il soldo?*" Nonna asked, when I got in the car.

"*Che soldo, Nonna?*" I didn't know what she was talking about. Why was she asking me where the coin was?

"*Nel carrello. Marco, c'è un soldo nel carrello.*"

"*Non ti capisco. Mi dispiace, Nonna,*" —"I don't understand. I'm sorry, Nonna,"— I said, shrugging my shoulders.

Immediately, she was out of the car and heading towards the rack. I followed.

"*Marco, quale carrello? Quale carrello?*" she said, pointing repeatedly at the rack.

"*Ummm ... quì* —here?"

I pointed to the third row of carts in the rack, where I had pushed our cart. It was now obvious that I had done something wrong—maybe I should have pushed it into the first row? I quickly looked to see if a sign was posted with directions. Nope. Thinking that my first answer of "*quì*" sounded too unsure, out of guilt I started shouting, "*Quì Nonna! QUÌ! QUÌ! QUÌ!*" I was hoping my authoritative tone might cleanse me of my unknown sin at the cart rack. Nope. All I did was return a cart; what could I have gotten wrong?

Nonna started pulling on the carts in the third row. I now noticed a locking mechanism on the handle, which I had not seen before, that locked the carts to each other. Nonna demonstrated that you have to put a 2-euro coin in the mechanism on the handle and push it in to unlock the cart from the others. More importantly, Nonna demonstrated that when returning the cart you needed to relock it so the mechanism pops open giving back your original 2-euro coin. I didn't know about this, so I didn't relock the cart when I returned it. Our cart and coin were gone—the next shopper must have taken it, or maybe the Indian gentleman had helped himself to my ignorant generosity. I had my suspicions. He stood grinning ear to ear as Nonna explained to me the workings of the cart rack. Regardless of where the coin ended up, I just cost Nonna two euro.

"*Nonna, mi dispiace molto!*" I kept apologizing over and over as we walked back to the car.

"*Marco, non è niente. Non c'è problema.*"

She was being nice, but I felt horrible. I <u>still</u> feel horrible! My first morning in Viterbo—and two euro down the drain! I wonder what the Italian word is for "jackass?"

"Marco, what is wrong?" Alessandra asked me, as I walked in the house.

"Nonna will tell you. *Mi dispiace, Alessandra.*" Nonna explained my mix-up with the cart and the lost coin.

"*Marco, non è niente. Non c'è problema,*" Alessandra said, trying to comfort me.

"*Disastro, Marco. Era un disastro!*"—"Disaster, Mark. It was a disaster!"—Nonna said, winking at me, trying to make me laugh by exaggerating the situation. I smiled and she gave me a little hug to reassure me that it truly was not a problem.

We unpacked the groceries and I started my first cooking lesson with Nonna. We began preparing things for *il pranzo*—lunch. Her first culinary trick was to show me how to de-bone a chicken while still leaving it whole. The process made me think of what an alien from outer space might do to a cow in a field in Iowa: remove the bones without ever cutting the cow open. I might just sleep with one eye open after seeing her expertise with a small paring knife.

Nonna is a very patient and thoughtful teacher. She does speak a word or two of English but nothing more than "okay," "here," "you," and "more." She never resorts to using the English words until it appears obvious that I am completely lost. It is going to make for an interesting learning experience.

Our lesson started with lots of pointing and "*Guarda!*"—"Watch!"— or "*Capito?*"—"Understand?" The whole "extraterrestrial" skeletal extracting process took about twenty minutes. It involved making a series of cuts around the ends of the drumsticks, breaking joints and slowly extracting the bones from the flesh without ever cutting the carcass into pieces. For those who are squeamish, remember that in order to understand food, you have to get your hands into it. I am very comfortable in a kitchen and am confident enough to jump right in and get my hands dirty. Cooking is more than just taste. It is about using all of your senses throughout the entire process—that is how a *nonna* cooks. Nonna is a master of chicken anatomy and, although I might not be bashful in the kitchen, she certainly intimidated me with her skills.

We stuffed the whole boneless chicken with a meatball, or meatloaf, mixture of veal and turkey. After stuffing the chicken with half of the mixture, we closed up the neck and tail with toothpicks. It was seared briefly in sunflower oil, and then white wine and water were added. It braised on top of the stove in a covered pot for over an hour. Next, we used the remaining stuffing mixture to make meatballs, rolled in bread crumbs and fried in sunflower oil.

Nonna then made a simple *sugo*—sauce. She started the *sugo* by sautéing minced onions in hot sunflower oil, letting them cook for a minute before adding a small amount of water to the pan. She says that sautéing in oil alone makes the onions hard to digest and they brown too much, making them bitter. The added water slows the cooking process and allows the onions to mellow in flavor. It is a concept that I had never thought about before. To the onions she adds canned whole tomatoes, crushing them with her hands, a little tomato sauce, wine, minced garlic, salt and pepper. She didn't add any other spices to this *sugo*. The fried meatballs were added to the *sugo* and they simmered together on the stovetop.

Next, she started a *torta di patate*—potato casserole—to be eaten later for dinner. A bottom layer of mashed potatoes is topped with a layer of chopped prosciutto, salami (both leftover from last night's *antipasti* ... remember, a *nonna* never wastes a thing!) and cubed Parmigiano-Reggiano (the authentic Parmesan cheese). That layer is topped with more mashed potatoes. The entire *torta* is sprinkled with bread crumbs and dotted with dabs of butter. Nonna set it aside until later in the afternoon to be baked— not in the refrigerator, but in the unheated toaster oven. Refrigeration seems to be reserved for the things that absolutely have to be kept cold. I am not sure yet what qualifies an item for the privilege of being in the refrigerator, but I'm keeping an eye on that.

With that done, I was off to the dining room for my first Italian language lesson while the chicken braised and the meatballs stewed. Yikes! I can tell you that at that moment I felt a lot like the chicken and meatballs! Cooking concepts I understand, being somewhat of a foodie, but now I had to LEARN. It hit me that this is school and no longer a cute little vacation. I really want to do well and seem somewhat intelligent to Alessandra.

The lesson went well, but I still felt stupid and slow. Learning a new language at 41 is a bit challenging. It would help if I could remember the parts of speech—what is imperfect indicative tense? What are reflexive verbs, past participles and gerunds? Why didn't my junior high teachers make sure that I paid better attention so I would be a better language student at 41? Luckily, Alessandra is very nice, complimentary and has a lot of patience. It is great to have a one-on-one teaching experience. I liked having a private tutor. Regardless of her endless patience, however, I found I was pressuring myself to be a quick study. I continually reminded myself that I am not supposed to know Italian before I learn it.

We finished the lesson at 1:30 p.m. Lunchtime! I was ravenous. Learning is hard work. Angelo and the girls came home for lunch—with Nonna's cooking waiting on the table, why go out? Both of the daughters live at home. Marianna, the eldest at twenty-four, is moving out next week into a new apartment complex in Viterbo with her boyfriend, Marco. Marianna has dark, short-cropped hair and is shorter than her mother. In a way that I cannot quite put my finger on, she resembles Nonna. Always sportily dressed, she is a vibrant person, and her smile is infectious. Francesca is a little taller and slightly thinner than Marianna, with long, beautiful dark hair. Although she wears glasses, you can see her large chestnut eyes shining through the lenses. Francesca is a giggly schoolgirl of nineteen and her mother is always telling her to speak slowly because, to quote Alessandra, "Her Italian is not very good, and even I have a hard time understanding her because she talks too fast." I have to agree. When Francesca speaks I can never hear where one word ends and the next begins. Marianna speaks beautifully. She has great diction, and it is a joy not only to hear her speak, but to watch her speak. With Italian, you always pronounce <u>all</u> of the letters in the word. The only silent letter is "h"; otherwise, each and every letter gets pronounced. For example, *ciao*—hello and goodbye—is pronounced "chee-ah-ow." It is starting to feel that the way to succeed in speaking Italian is to chew the words. Every syllable, every bite!

After our two-hour lunch, we all headed up to our rooms for a mid-afternoon siesta. (The family's bedrooms are on the second floor, behind a door I have yet to venture beyond.) I am starting to enjoy the concept of the siesta. It was great to have a little rest before returning to my afternoon language lesson from 4:30-6:30. Learning the language is challenging but I'm really enjoying it. I am going to go home with a much better knowledge of the language—and some great recipes, too. Learning is not just occurring over the stovetop or in the dining room. It is happening every second, all around me. I am starting to notice the way Italian society works in the home. It is still very male-driven in the sense that Angelo and I are served first, our wine is poured first, and our plates are removed for us. In America, we tend to serve women first when bringing a plate to the table or pouring a glass of wine. I wonder how long it will take before I am spoiled by this kind of treatment?

We had guests for dinner—Alessandra's nephew, Nicola, was in town with his friend, Jimmy. Nicola grew up in the northern Italian town of Genova. Jimmy is from a small town in the French Alps. They go to university together in France near Jimmy's hometown and they are both nineteen. They are on summer vacation and spending the break in and around Viterbo for the entire month of August. Nicola is a little stocky and very laid back; Jimmy is his polar opposite—thin and twitchy. Alessandra's family does not like Jimmy; in fact, the family has come to have a certain disdain for him. Jimmy and Nicola stayed with the family last Christmas, and it seems that all

Jimmy talked about was "French this" and "French that," and "in France this is better because...." He would eat Nonna's cooking and say that it was good, "but my grandmother makes something like this that is much better." The family quickly tired of hearing about the unequaled virtues of France. Also, to make matters worse, Jimmy continually made passes at Francesca. I am surprised she let him live.

The conversation around the table was vigorous. Visiting family usually increases the pace and energy of dinner conversation. My ability to converse in Italian is still very limited, so I was eating and listening mostly. Jimmy only speaks a little Italian, too. Nicola, who is fluent in both Italian and French, but speaks no English, translates for Jimmy when needed. It was fun not to be the only one who didn't speak the language, although Italian and French are similar enough that there were things Jimmy could understand by default. It wasn't until after dinner that I was subjected to Jimmy's nationalism. I was actually a little surprised that he waited until we were alone in the kitchen before he started in with his questions. Jimmy wanted me to speak only in English so he could hear it and practice speaking, too. In his broken, but not bad English, he started asking a barrage of questions without letting me answer one before starting the next.

"Why aren't you learning French? Don't you like the French language? Is it too hard for you? You should be learning French, not Italian. Italian is much easier than French. You would be more challenged to learn French."

Of course, he did not really speak Italian either, so how would he know? I am sure he believes speaking Italian is beneath him. Trying to be politic, I said that I visited Italy before France and that is why I was interested in Italian. I also told him I had three years of French in high school but wanted to try something else. When I told him about my one trip to Paris, he was very eager to know what I thought of the city and the French people. Again, I was politic and changed the conversation back to his studies at university. I wanted to tell Jimmy that, although I enjoyed Paris and Parisians, Italy is where my heart is. The Parisians I encountered were very nice and warm.

I never experienced the "rude Frenchman" that many American tourists seem to encounter. Worrying it might spur him on to talk more about the superiority of France and considering I was standing in the kitchen of a most gracious and hospitable Italian family, I thought it best not to prod the young Frenchman. I could understand Jimmy's sense of nationalism at age nineteen, but he was in Italy and the family had just fed him dinner at their table. Jimmy has a lot to learn about being a gracious and appreciative guest.

Allora, stasera alle ventidue—So, tonight at 10:00 p.m....

Nicola and Jimmy said their goodbyes. Marianna and Francesca went out with friends, but they cleverly waited until Nicola and Jimmy had left before announcing their plans. I think Francesca was worried that Jimmy would have wanted to tag along. Nelo (Angelo's nickname—I guess it is short for Angelo) and Alessandra decided to take me into Viterbo to see the town at night and to have gelato. *"Mi piace gelato molto!"* —"I like gelato a lot!"— I said. Nonna stayed at home. She was not up for a late evening on the town.

The three of us climbed into Nelo's car, and as we pulled away, I told them about Jimmy's kitchen interrogation. Alessandra translated for Nelo since he doesn't speak any English. They had a good laugh.

"Francia, Francia, Francia!" Nelo exclaimed.

"Sempre Francia!" —"Always France!"— was Alessandra's reply.

"Povero Jimmy!" —"Poor Jimmy!"— I said, joining in.

Windows down, we howled with laughter all the way toward the city center. Alessandra, from the back seat with her hand on her hair and wiping tears of laughter from her eyes, leaned forward to tell me a brief history of Viterbo. How wonderful to have my own personal tour guide and a driver.

Yesterday, when I arrived in Viterbo I only saw part of the stone wall, lined with parapets, encircling the ancient city center. Tonight as we approached it I could see the large Porta Fiorentina ahead. This was the ancient northern gate in the city wall that opened toward Florence. We drove through the *porta* into the Piazza della Rocca and circled the town square a couple of times before finding a parking spot and jumping out into the nightlife.

The *piazza* was alive with people of all ages—grandparents, families with young children, teens and young professionals. Most were strolling, but some were watching a beach soccer game. During the summer a ton of sand is hauled into this particular *piazza* creating a beach-like soccer field surrounded by a tall net. The field, more like a court, is less than half the size of a regulation soccer field. Two teams consisting of five men each (one goalie and four others) play a scaled-down version of soccer in the sand. It reminded me very much of American beach volleyball. Sections of bleachers are set up on both sides of the field, and the teams play barefoot. In winter, in the same location, they put up an ice rink where everyone can come and skate. Nelo said he is very proud of the city for making the effort to bring free activities into the historic center.

After stopping for a moment to let Nelo see what was happening with the soccer game (I don't understand the game of soccer), we took a *passeggiata*—a stroll—around Viterbo. It is an amazing city full of history. When the black plague was killing off the people of Rome, the pope moved out to Viterbo, which then had a larger population than Rome. Viterbo was also a stop on the pilgrimage route to Rome from the rest of Europe. This explains why there are a lot of old hotels scattered inside the ancient walls and why so many things bear the name of Saint Pellegrino, including the *Piazza di San Pellegrino, Via di San Pellegrino*, and *La Fontana di San Pellegrino. Pellegrino* is the Italian word for pilgrim.

The more we walked around, the more beautiful the city became—it was magical. The motorized noises of the day stop, replaced with the wafting conversations from the many open windows. Sometimes the conversations are full of laughter, sometimes of anger, but they are always in the beautiful tones of the Italian language, full of passion and emotion. There are people of all ages out walking. The sound of shoes clicking or scuffing on cobblestone streets adds a nocturnal rhythm underscoring the lyrical conversations floating out on the humid evening air. Our *passeggiata* would take us down a narrow street or around a corner where socializing *nonne e nonni*—grandmas and grandpas—sat crammed together on a bench, no doubt similar to the American South before the invention of air conditioning, with neighbors sitting out at night discussing the matters of the day or windows wide open exposing the private workings of each household. In some strange way all of these sounds were very peaceful and comforting. Even if a *piazza* had fifty people in it, it was peaceful. It could have been because each *piazza* has a different style of fountain in it, so there is always the sound of water in the evening air. Of course, there was nothing peaceful about the beach soccer game.

We passed many churches that had odd-looking pieces of stonework built into their walls. They made no sense to me. Nelo told me that old stone Etruscan coffins were broken down and used as building pieces. The builders of these centuries-old churches used whatever they could find whenever they could find it. Rhyme and reason were not as much of a construction influence as were luck and providence. We stopped at one church that had a carved relief of a bearded face embedded above the entrance. Alessandra said for hundreds of years this relief was believed to have been the face of Jesus. In truth, the church was built on top of an ancient pagan religious site, and the pagan images were used in the construction of the new Christian church. It is the face of Zeus, not Jesus, which is carved into the stone above the door. I love the idea that the carving still remains—no one has removed the pagan image from this Christian church.

Finally, we arrived at Nelo's favorite gelato shop. I couldn't believe how many people were at the *gelateria* at this hour on a Tuesday night. And it wasn't just young people; it was a wide range of ages. The oldest was a group of grandparents who were easily in their mid to late 80s—the Italian culture surprises me at every turn. It would be hard to find an ice cream shop in Smalltown, USA, with a group of senior citizens in it at 11:00 p.m. on a Tuesday night. The gelato was delicious, of course. *"Mi piace gelato molto!"* (That might just become my credo.) With gelatos in hand, we were back to our *passeggiata*.

On one street, we passed several old palaces. Because Viterbo had been home to several popes and many cardinals, their papal palaces and apartments remain, and over time they have been converted into single-family apartments. Remember, because of the heat, the windows were wide open so we got to peek inside. Yes, we were strolling, gelato-carrying Peeping Toms. Alessandra said that she had never seen into many of these apartments because the drapes were usually closed. Even though the palaces had been turned into apartments, the original frescoes still remained on many of the walls and ceilings. Some ceilings were frescoed with mythological figures and scenes, others were celestial in nature. One had a coffered ceiling with its beams gold leafed. Between the beams were brightly colored patterns and shapes. There was one that appeared to have a huge fresco of a garden painted on the wall—we could only see the top portion from the street below. I asked Alessandra if these frescoes and paintings were new. "No, because these apartments are historic, people are not allowed to paint over them or change them," she explained.

It was quite dangerous walking along the ancient cobblestone street with our heads turned upward looking into the second floor windows. We stumbled and tripped several times along that particular winding street. Before long, we had gone full circle and ended up stopping to watch the last five minutes of the beach soccer game. The red-shirted team won. *Bravi! Bravi!*

On the way home, Alessandra told me of a citywide festival in Viterbo where men—"100 strong men" ("*i Facchini*")—carry large stone blocks into town to much fanfare of drums and pageantry. They use the stones to build a tower 30 meters tall. All the lights in town are turned out except for the many colored lights on the tower. The festival—*La Macchina di Santa Rosa*—is in honor of Viterbo's patron saint and has been a Viterbo tradition for over 450 years. "How can they build a 100-foot tower with only one hundred stones?" I wondered. Alessandra said that, until about sixty years ago, the tower was built entirely from wood timbers. Wait—what happened to the stones? I guess, as with the face of Jesus/Zeus, does it really matter? *"Bellissimo, no?"*

Polpette

Meatballs / Stuffing for the Chicken

The secret to moist meatballs and stuffing is using stale or day-old bread. A frugal nonna wastes nothing, so when bread goes stale and becomes too hard to eat, it is sliced, reconstituted in water, squeezed dry and added as an extender, enabling Nonna to make a few more meatballs—and insuring they'll be moist when served.

2 slices Italian bread (½-inch slices of a Tuscan boule or similar bread)
½ cup plain dried bread crumbs
½ pound ground veal
½ pound ground turkey (or ground pork)
2 eggs
1 large clove garlic, finely minced
½ teaspoon freshly ground nutmeg
1 teaspoon salt
½ teaspoon freshly ground black pepper
Sunflower oil for frying (vegetable or canola oil can be substituted)
Sugo (see recipe below)
Freshly grated Parmigiano-Reggiano cheese for garnish

Put the slices of bread in a medium bowl and pour enough water over the bread to cover the slices. Place a teacup saucer on the bread slices to keep the bread submerged. Set aside to soak for 5 to 10 minutes.

Place the bread crumbs in a shallow dish and set aside. The meatballs will be rolled in the bread crumbs before frying.

Next place the veal, turkey, eggs, garlic, nutmeg, salt and pepper in a medium bowl. Remove the soaking bread from the water and, using your hands, squeeze the excess water out of the bread. Tear or crumble the bread into very small pieces and add to the meat mixture. Using your hands or a spoon, gently mix all the ingredients until well combined. Divide into 10 equal parts (roughly the size of a golf ball) and shape them between the palms of your hands into meatballs. Roll the shaped meatballs in the bread crumbs to coat.

Meanwhile, heat an inch of oil in a heavy medium-size frying pan over medium heat. When the oil is hot, fry the meatballs in batches, turning them to brown on all sides, about 5 minutes per batch. Place the meatballs on paper towels to drain. Add the drained meatballs to the simmering sauce (recipe below), partially cover the skillet and simmer together for 30 minutes, stirring occasionally. To serve, remove the meatballs from the sauce to a warmed platter, garnish with the Parmigiano-Reggiano and serve hot.

Sugo di Nonna

Nonna's Simple Sauce

About tomatoes: When fresh tomatoes are out of season, Italians turn to the next best thing—canned San Marzano tomatoes, because of their firm flesh and sweet taste. This recipe also calls for "strained tomatoes," which are simply whole tomatoes that have been put through a food mill to remove their skins and seeds. This differs from tomato sauce, which is often seasoned with salt, pepper and spices. In a pinch, tomato sauce can be substituted, but the finished sugo *will be far from authentic.*

2 tablespoons extra virgin olive oil

1 small-medium onion, finely minced

¼ cup water

2 large cloves garlic, finely minced

½ cup wine (Nonna used either red or white, whatever was left from the previous night's dinner)

1 (28-ounce) can whole peeled Italian tomatoes (preferably San Marzano
   tomatoes), placed in a bowl and crushed by hand, reserving all of the liquid

1 cup strained tomatoes, such as Pomi brand ★

½ teaspoon salt, or more to taste

¼ teaspoon freshly ground black pepper, or more to taste

1 tablespoon chopped fresh Italian flat-leaf parsley

1 pound pasta (spaghetti, bow tie, fettuccine, penne, or your favorite)

Heat the oil in a large skillet over medium-high heat. When the oil is hot, add the onion and sauté for a minute, stirring constantly. Add the water and cook until the water has almost evaporated, 2 to 3 minutes. Add the garlic and cook another minute. Add the wine and cook until the wine has reduced by half, stirring occasionally, another 2 to 3 minutes. Add the crushed tomatoes with all their juices, strained tomatoes, salt and pepper. Bring to a boil, then reduce the heat to low and simmer. (If using with the meatballs, add them at this point.)

Simmer the sauce for 20 to 25 minutes, stirring occasionally. Remove from the heat, adjust the seasoning with salt and pepper and stir in the parsley. To serve, remove the meatballs and plate as indicated in the recipe above.

To serve the *sugo*, prepare the pasta, cooked *al dente*—tender but firm to the bite—in plenty of boiling, salted water. Drain the pasta and add to the *sugo* skillet, tossing until the pasta is well coated. Garnish with freshly grated Parmigiano-Reggiano, Pecorino Romano or Grana Padano cheese. Serve hot with the meatballs as a side dish, or serve the meatballs separately as a second course.

★Note: Strained tomatoes can be readily found in most supermarkets in either the canned tomato or pasta aisles. Sometimes the product may be referred to by its Italian name "passato" and can be found either bottled or cartoned, as is the case with the Pomi brand.

DAY THREE (Il Giorno Tre)

lready on day three, Nonna and I have gotten into a routine when we leave the house to run the morning errands. She drives and I ride shotgun—the passenger window rolled down and my arm hanging out—both looking very chic in our sunglasses as we head first to the newspaper stand, then to a grocery store and lastly, to the recycling bins.

The newspaper stand is a small green shack on the side of the road in front of a large apartment building a mile south of the house. The newsstand is like any in a large metropolitan city in America. Besides buying a newspaper or magazine, one can buy small toys for children, books and DVD movies. Nonna whips off the road, stopping in a cloud of dust, to park right in front of the stand. I stay in the car while she thumbs over some magazines, a toy or two, and the movies. She only buys the local paper and one of Rome's large daily newspapers.

As for grocery stores, Nonna has three favorites. There is a small grocery store (where I lost the two euro), a medium-size grocery store, and then there is Le Clerc. Le Clerc is similar to a Wal-Mart superstore with its enormous food market. The seafood department sells swordfish heads—with the sword still attached! As with any superstore they also sell clothes, housewares, tools, etc. The medium-size store is where Nonna goes most often. The people who work there know her better than do the employees at the others. Besides sheer size, I haven't quite figured out what the difference in selection is between them, but I am sure Nonna has her reasons.

After the grocery store we swing by the large recycling bins. Recycling is huge in Italy. There are large bins all around town for people to drop off their recyclable items: paper, glass and plastics. Before we leave the house in the morning we always put the plastic shopping bags of recyclables into the trunk. It has become my job to sort the bags of empty wine bottles, plastic containers and newspapers into the material-appropriate, color-coded bins. We only discard the plastic shopping bags if they get torn or are nasty from being used so much. With the planet saved for the next generation, we head home to start cooking and teaching me Italian. That has become our routine, without fail.

This morning we went in search of *melanzane*—eggplant, but not just any eggplant—the perfect eggplant. In Italy, if it isn't very fresh or perfect, the *nonne* don't buy it. If you want to make an eggplant dish and the eggplant at the markets aren't amazing, then you just don't make the eggplant dish. Instead, you change it to whatever other vegetable looks amazing that day.

Three stores later, we returned with picture perfect eggplant. They were small and a rich, deep purple with completely unblemished skins. We used them for eggplant parmesan. Nonna makes hers with grilled eggplant, Parmigiano-Reggiano, mozzarella and a little *sugo*. We will have that for dinner. We also made meat rolls: cutlets of turkey and veal with a slice of speck (smoked prosciutto) and a sage leaf in the center and rolled up. They were rolled in a little flour, sautéed in sunflower oil and braised in some water, broth and a little white wine to make a sauce. We had the cutlets for lunch with a salad and some penne pasta in a mushroom and cream sauce. We were very busy in the kitchen this morning. These are definitely recipes to add to the list.

Colazione, in case you are wondering, was the same as yesterday. Well, almost the same. Yesterday, Nonna wanted to know what I ate for breakfast in America. I said that I usually have a bowl of cereal, so this morning there was a box of Italian corn flakes sitting on the table. It was a lot like Product 19, a cereal I happen to like. Nonna asked me if I liked my cereal with warm or cold milk. My answer was obvious.

Nonna is a very funny person. At 79, besides still driving, she has two cell phones (the queen of the text message), and heads a local Boy Scout troop. When we cook she never turns on the overhead light. In the morning the kitchen gets a decent amount of light, but later in the afternoon it becomes pretty dark. Yesterday, with the help of an Italian dictionary, I told her I was going to call her *la talpa*—the mole—because we work in the dark. She laughed, but said she didn't like that name. She thought she should be called a different nocturnal animal's name. I said, *"Il pipistrello."* —"The bat."— Her eyes turned upward while she considered it. *"La civetta,"* she said. —"The little owl."— She hooted and turned on a light.

My daily schedule is turning out to be: two hours of cooking and two hours of language class in the morning before lunch, lunch followed by a siesta, then another two hours of language in the late afternoon. I usually help Nonna with dinner or take a little break to start writing around 6:30. At day three I understand a little more. I am not sure I can repeat anything I hear but I am starting to recognize words in conversation and know what they mean. The language workbook's examples and exercises have a lot of European cities and people's names that I have never heard of, making the proper names in the CHOOSE FROM list a dilemma. When asked to fill in the blanks for the exercise: "___ is very big. ___ has many tourists."—it helps to know which proper names in the list are cities and which are people because the sentences read differently if, instead of choosing "Atlanta," you were to choose "Betty." Betty might be big but saying, "She has a lot of tourists" implies more about her occupation than her size. Alessandra laughed a lot during that particular set of exercises.

Stasera per la cena—tonight for dinner—we had the eggplant parmesan. *Buonissimo!* Unbelievably delicious! Grilling the eggplant before layering it in the dish made all the difference. In America, the dish is made with battered and fried eggplant before layering, but grilling it made it so much lighter. What a simple and tasty dish. The eggplant was followed by salad and slices of *melone*—cantaloupe. Italians tend to eat a much larger meal for *il pranzo* and a smaller meal for *la cena*, which is exactly how we ate today.

Penne con Panna e Funghi

Penne with Cream and Mushrooms

In the fall, when they are in season, porcini mushrooms reign supreme. Fat, squatty, and meaty, it is the mushroom one envisions a forest pixie or sprite perched upon. It is nearly impossible to find fresh porcinis in America, so the dried version is an acceptable necessity. Make sure to reserve the strained liquid after reconstituting them—the liquid provides an earthy undertone to this dish.

1 ounce dried porcini mushrooms

1 pound mixed fresh mushrooms (such as cremini, shiitake, chanterelle and white button mushrooms) cleaned and cut into a medium dice

⅓ cup extra virgin olive oil

1 medium onion, finely minced

2 cloves garlic, finely minced

½ cup dry white wine

1 teaspoon salt

½ teaspoon freshly ground black pepper

1 cup heavy cream

3 tablespoons chopped fresh Italian flat-leaf parsley

1 pound penne rigate pasta

1½ cups freshly grated Pecorino Romano or Grana Padano cheese, or more to taste

Place the dried porcinis in a small bowl and cover with 2 cups warm water, placing a teacup saucer on the mushrooms to keep them submerged. Soak for 15 to 20 minutes. Drain the porcinis, reserving the liquid. Chop the porcinis into a medium dice. Line a strainer with paper towels and strain the reserved liquid into a bowl. Set aside.

Add the diced porcini mushrooms to the diced fresh mushrooms and set aside.

Heat the oil in a large skillet over medium heat. When the oil is hot, add the onion and garlic and cook for one minute, stirring constantly. Add a ½ cup of the reserved porcini liquid and cook 4 to 5 minutes until the liquid has almost evaporated. Add the white wine and cook for 2 to 3 minutes until the wine has reduced by half. Raise the heat to medium high and add the mushrooms, salt and pepper. Cook the mushrooms, stirring frequently, until they are golden and have released their juices, about 5 to 7 minutes. Add the cream and the remaining reserved porcini liquid, bring to a boil and cook for 2 to 3 minutes to thicken. Remove from the heat.

Meanwhile, bring a large pot of water to a boil over high heat. Add 2 tablespoons salt, and stir in the penne rigate to the boiling water and cook, stirring occasionally until the pasta is *al dente*—tender but firm to the bite. Drain the pasta and add to the mushroom skillet. Turn the heat on medium and toss the pasta and the sauce together until they are well combined. Remove from the heat, stir in the parsley and garnish with the grated cheese.

Serves 6 to 8 people ... Italian-size portions.

This is a hearty dish that works well in the fall when there is a chill in the air and one starts to long for comfort food. It can be served alongside a meat entrée or served alone as a hearty vegetarian main course.

DAY FOUR (Il Giorno Quattro)

It has been raining off and on today and the temperature is dropping. Hurray! I may turn my bedroom fan on low tonight. *Allora, un gran temporale*—a large storm—is looming.

The most important thing I learned today was that I have been misunderstanding what they were calling Alessandra's husband, Angelo. **Lillo** (not Nelo) is his nickname, which is pronounced, "lee-low." See how well I am learning and understanding Italian? Yikes!

For my morning cooking lesson Nonna and I made *biscotti con grappa*—cookies with *grappa* and raisins. *Grappa* is a very strong liqueur made after the wine pressing process using the leftover grape skins, seeds and stems. (Again, Italians waste nothing.) The alcohol is cooked off and the *grappa* provides a very different grape flavor compared to the flavor of the raisins. Raisins have a concentrated sugar taste, while *grappa* has a more earthy or woodsy taste. It is a juxtaposition of tastes from technically the same food source: the grape. These biscotti are for after dinner but Nonna said I had to taste them now to make sure they turned out. I was happy to oblige. They would be best in the morning with a cup of coffee, or that is how I imagine Americans enjoying them. The corn meal gives them a muffin-like taste and they are not particularly sweet—we do like our cookies on the sweet side. Maybe I'll try making these as muffins when I get back home. I have yet to see a muffin anywhere in Italy.

Another thing we made for dinner tonight was zucchini stuffed with tuna and anchovies. I realize anchovies, in general, have gotten a bad rap in America; however, in this dish they add a delicious salty depth of flavor. The stuffing consisted of bread, eggs, parsley, anchovy paste and canned tuna in olive oil. Anyone who likes tuna will enjoy this dish. While I was in morning language class, Nonna stayed in the kitchen to make a *sugo* for lunch and again, did not put the prepared zucchini in the fridge. As with the eggplant parmesan yesterday and the potato casserole on Monday, the uncooked stuffed zucchini went into the toaster oven to store. When to actually refrigerate something is still a complete mystery to me.

For *il pranzo* we had *zampone*—a pig's leg (well, from the knee to the foot) that has had the leg bone removed. The foot bones still remain because they are too small and numerous to remove. The de-boned leg is then stuffed with a pork sausage-like substance. Usually only eaten at Christmas, it is something of a specialty—and not for the weak of heart! It is purchased fully prepared in a box. The box reminds me of the Christmas gift liquor boxes salesmen would give my father as a thank-you for his company's business—shiny blue foil with an embossed label, very regal looking. Those boxes contained Jack Daniels or Johnny Walker's best. Inside this box—a gold foil bag containing the *zampone*. The shiny gold bag is placed into a pot of water and ... boiled. Sound appetizing yet? I wasn't paying attention to how long the bag boiled but at the appropriate time it was removed and cut open to reveal the *zampone* in all its succulent splendor. Sliced into ¼-inch rounds it is something visually to ponder before mustering the courage to dig in. Two pieces of *zampone*, steaming and glistening in all of its juicy pork goodness, went onto my plate. I was secretly wishing for a shot of Jack Daniels instead. I think Lillo took four pieces to start.

It is an acquired taste, to say the least. Alessandra and her daughters will not eat it. It is too spicy for Nonna, or at least that is her excuse. I gave it my best shot. It is something I would consider eating again, but I can see why it is only brought to the table once a year. It is very rich. Lillo loves it and kept trying to get me to eat part of the foot. Seeing this part of the pig consumed is not an unusual sight for me. My mother's family would often eat pickled pig's feet on special occasions. What makes an occasion so special that it needs to be commemorated by sucking on the bones of a pig's foot? I have no clue, but pickled pig's feet have repulsed me since childhood. Lillo sat across the table sucking on and eating around the joints and bones of the foot. My grandfather had a similar style when attacking the pickled variety. Lillo kept trying to nudge me into trying it.

"Marco, è molto buono. Davvero!" —"Mark, it is very good. Really!"

"No, Marco. Non è buono!" Alessandra and the girls would insist.

Everyone laughed.

I looked to Nonna for guidance. She was smiling ear to ear as if to say, "I dare you." She never weighed in on the "to suck the foot or not" debate.

Alessandra and the girls won. I did not join Lillo in the experience of the foot, but stuck to the sausage-like slices of the lower leg that glistened on my plate. Luckily, this was not the only thing served for *il pranzo*. We also had bowtie pasta with a simple *sugo*. The customary two glasses of wine were not to be missed either. Lillo kept pouring throughout the meal and had another two glasses before retiring for his siesta. The Italians know how to live. The wine helped me finish my *zampone*. It certainly took the edge off!

I am truly having fun and we are getting along great. Nonna likes that I am not scared to jump right in and get my hands dirty in the kitchen. Alessandra and I certainly have had our share of laughs navigating the language. Lillo enjoys having another man in the house and at the table. I am only the third *l'uomo*—man—to take this course and the first American man. The first two men were *Giapponese*—Japanese—chefs and were here for a week each—as Nonna says, *"Eh,"* (with the appropriate hand gesture) implying, "What can you learn in a week?"

Nicola and Jimmy stopped in for a brief visit after lunch. Nonna has been whispering under her breath in a most distasteful tone, *"Francia, Francia, Francia,"* and then giggling. She is truly mischievous and I love her for it. *"Povero Jimmy!"* has become the family's new sentiment when discussing him … after he leaves, of course.

Whenever Nonna or Alessandra discovers I have never tried a particular food or dish, we inevitably end up making it. Two days ago I was asked if I had ever had bruschetta. I had and they wanted to know what type. I have had the classic chopped tomato and basil.

"Hai mangiato la bruschetta con acciughe?" —"Have you eaten bruschetta with *acciughe*?"

"Acciughe?" I thought someone had sneezed.

They explained that *acciughe* were anchovies and that there is a bruschetta made with mozzarella and *acciughe* (pronounced "a-chew-gay"). That was our *antipasta* tonight and it is now a new favorite.

In case you don't know, bruschetta is a slice of bread that is toasted or grilled before a topping is added. The classic bruschetta is a slice of grilled bread rubbed with a piece of garlic and topped with chopped tomato, basil, olive oil, sea salt and pepper. In America, you often hear bruschetta pronounced incorrectly. The word is not pronounced "brew-**shet**-ta." The correct Italian pronunciation is "brew-**sket**-ta." Think of how you pronounce the word "spaghetti." The "h" makes the "g" have a hard sound as in the word "get." The same is true for the "h" in "bruschetta." The "h" makes the "c" have a hard "k" sound as in "kept." "Brew-SKET-ta" only, please.

The stuffed zucchini were baked in the toaster oven and served for *il secondo*—the second course. They were as good as the bruschetta. Then the usual salad and slices of fruit (tonight it was *ananas*—pineapple) followed the zucchini. I now understand why Europeans eat their salads after the main course. It is a palate cleanser because the citric acid from the fruit refreshes your taste buds and gets them ready for the next course—dessert and coffee.

Alessandra made *caffè*—espresso—to go with the *biscotti con grappa*. I thought that was going to be the end of the evening, but oh no. Lillo and Alessandra grabbed me and off we headed to Viterbo. This time we walked around a different part of the city. *Bellissima!*

Here's another Italian lesson: If something is beautiful to look at you say *bellissimo* or *bellissima*, depending on whether the word for the thing you are looking at is masculine or feminine. If something tastes great you say *buonissimo* or *buonissima*. As with French and Spanish, words are either masculine or feminine. The Italian word for "city" is *la città*, which is feminine, so when describing how truly beautiful the city is you would say, "*Bellissima!*"

With a trip to Viterbo do you think my evening was over? Nope. I wondered why we didn't eat any gelato while walking around Viterbo, but I didn't want to say, "Hey, where's the gelato?" When we got back into the car, Lillo noticed the puzzled look on my face.

"*Non c'è problema, Marco. Adesso andiamoci a prendare un gelato!*" —"No problem, Mark. Now we're going for gelato!"

My face lit up because, as you know, "*Mi piace gelato molto!*"

We drove to the nearby town of Bagnaia, where the main *piazza* was full of people listening to—of all things—karaoke. In the heat of the summer Italians flock outside at night; town festivals are very popular in August. It took us about ten minutes to drive slowly around the *piazza* searching for a parking space before we gave up and drove back out a short distance, parked and walked back in, serenaded by karaoke. Alessandra said that Tequila and Brighitta could sing better. She was not exaggerating. Sadly, just as in America, it appears that people who get up and perform karaoke can never sing or are often drunk.

Bagnaia had been a poor medieval town; it did not have the money and, therefore, the splendor of Viterbo. We walked past the karaoke stage towards the main *gelateria* in Bagnaia. Alessandra covered an ear, looked at me and said, *"Mamma mia!"*—an elderly gentleman was on stage slaughtering a Bon Jovi song. *"Mamma mia!"* was an understatement. We got our gelatos as the crowd erupted in applause for Signor Bon Jovi. Lillo caught my eye and motioned with his head, "This way." We were off on another *passeggiata*.

The streets of Bagnaia are very narrow. A single compact car would narrowly miss the stoops and walls of the buildings on either side of the street—there is no way two cars could pass each other. The tight street became magical; as we strolled we could listen to all of the conversations happening inside the houses. Down the wider streets of our Viterbo *passeggiata* we only heard the tones of conversations, but here, the compactness of the Bagnaia streets made every word understandable. On a hot August night there were no secrets. With windows flung wide open and lace curtains fluttering in the hot evening breeze, everyone outside would hear a fight inside the house.

We came upon a small shop that was open late. Alessandra stayed outside while Lillo and I went down the steps into the shop. This little shop was actually a civic meeting room for the city of Bagnaia. It happened to have a photo exhibit because of tonight's festival. Inside there were a couple hundred old photos posted on bulletin boards that hung on the walls. Signs dated the photos from about 1905-1975, and other posted signs asked if you could find yourself or your friends in the photos. Some photos were large, some small, some black and white and others in color. There was a group of six *nonne* in the room. Arm in arm and standing shoulder to shoulder they were all pointing, talking and laughing about the photos. These ladies, while looking at the photos, were no longer elderly matrons of Bagnaia, but were once again sixteen-year-old schoolgirls giggling about a particularly handsome boy or some unfortunate girl's unfashionable outfit. Sometimes a photo of a sorrowful event would evoke sighs and sadden them almost to the point of tears. Each photo brought back memories for this group of small town grandmas. This was everyday Italian life up close and personal—exactly what I had hoped to experience by coming to live in Viterbo.

The variety of images fascinated me: kids one-arm saluting in Fascist clothes, old wedding photos, various town celebrations, a civic organization with its band, and farmers in fields. In one, a very lank and lean priest in a long black cassock, with mouth tightly pursed, sternly pointed a stick at a list written on a blackboard:

"SAY NO to indecent clothing!"

"NO to lurid movies!"

"NO to distasteful speech!"

The list went on....

The *nonne* howled with laughter when they got to this photo. They either knew of this priest or were among the children in the photo rigidly seated facing the blackboard.

Lillo struck up a conversation with these ladies. I never understood anything anyone was saying. He tried explaining to me what the ladies said about the photos, but I couldn't understand exactly what he meant. Part of me wished that he spoke even a little English, or that my Italian was just a little better, in the hope that even a few more understandable words between us could have helped me to make a connection with the *nonne*. Alessandra was not inside with us, so I was resigned to accept that maybe the experience was made more special because I couldn't understand.

Full of memories, new and old, gelato and off-key singing, we headed back to the car, Viterbo and bed.

Biscotti "Zaletti"

Grappa Cookies

Italians are not known for their "sweet" desserts or treats—maybe with the exception of gelato. We ate the zaletti *as snacks, but in America I think they would be better served as muffins. Feeling adventuresome? Turn these cookies into muffins by dividing the batter amongst muffin cups in your favorite muffin tins, bake until an inserted toothpick comes out clean and serve warm with butter. I think Nonna would approve.*

½ cup unsalted butter

¾ cup golden raisins

¾ cup raisins

2 cups plus 1 tablespoon all-purpose flour

1½ cups self-rising corn meal

¾ cup sugar

1 tablespoon baking powder

½ teaspoon salt

2 eggs, slightly beaten

2 tablespoons *grappa* ★

1½ teaspoons vanilla extract

1 cup whole milk

Preheat oven to 350 degrees. Line a baking sheet with parchment paper. In a small saucepan, melt the butter and set aside to cool.

In a small bowl, mix together the raisins and 1 tablespoon flour until the raisins are well coated. (This keeps the raisins from sticking together.) Set aside.

In a large bowl, stir together corn meal, 2 cups flour, sugar, baking powder and salt. Add the beaten eggs and the cooled, melted butter to the dry ingredients and beat well to combine. Beat in the *grappa* and vanilla thoroughly. Add ¼ cup of milk at a time, beating until combined between additions, until a cake batter-like consistency is reached. Stir in the raisins until evenly distributed.

Drop teaspoons of dough 2 inches apart onto the lined baking sheet. Bake until firm and very pale golden, 10 to 12 minutes. Remove at once to a wire rack. Makes 3 ½ to 4 dozen.

Distilled from the leftover grape stems and skins of the wine pressing process, grappa *is usually served as an after-dinner drink to aid in digestion. It can be found at a liquor store, usually with the other liqueurs.*

If you have an aversion to cooking with alcohol, substitute water or freshly squeezed lemon juice for the grappa.

Technically, these are not "biscotti" because they are only baked once. In Italian, "bis" means "twice" and "cotti" means "cooked." I'm not sure what they'd be called once baked as a muffin. I have never seen a muffin in Italy.

DAY FIVE (Il Giorno Cinque)

It seems that everything spoken here in Italy is repeated two or three times, much as it is in opera. Here are some situations I have noticed:

Whenever you see or talk to someone you know, *"Ciao, ciao."*

Whenever you answer a question, *"Si, si, si"* or *"No, no, no."*

Whenever you say goodbye on the phone, *"Ciao, ciao."*

Actually saying goodbye on the phone is a comedy routine.

"Ciao, ciao."

Pause—while the other person responds, *"Ciao, ciao."*

Then *"Ciao, ciao, ciao."*

Pause. Then the response back—*"Ciao, ciao, ciao."*

Back and forth goes the *"Ciao, ciao, ciao."*

With each successive *"Ciao, ciao, ciao"* your head gets closer and closer to the base of the phone until finally your free ear is on the base and with your last *"Ciao, ciao"* you hang up the receiver thus winning.

Whenever anyone leaves the house, *"Ciao, ciao, ciao."*

"Ciao, ciao," from everyone back and forth.

There must be twenty *"Ciao, ciao's"* before the door closes. It seems that getting in the last *"Ciao, ciao, ciao"* is key!

At *colazione* I asked Nonna if she knew how to make *amaretti*—almond cookies—one of my favorite Italian cookies. She said no. I couldn't believe it. She looked at me as if she had somehow disappointed me. I told her it was absolutely okay if we didn't make them. "Oh no, I want to try. Now, we have to make them!" she insisted.

Marianna has spent the past week slowly moving her things out of her bedroom and into her new apartment with her boyfriend, Marco. She is leaving the nest for the first time. There is as much joy about Marco and Marianna having their first apartment together in Viterbo as there is sadness over her leaving the house. There is a little parental trepidation, from both sets of parents, about their living together and not being married. In Italy, it is still the norm that children do not move out of their parents' house until they are married, so it is not unusual for a child be in her mid-20s and still living at home; Marco and Marianna are the exception, not the rule.

Francesca and Marianna came bounding downstairs during *colazione* with an overstuffed laundry basket each containing the last of Marianna's possessions. There was much hugging and kissing of Marianna as everyone headed towards the door. The *"Ciao, ciao"* chorus began and there was no counting them this morning. There was no feeling of contest today, just a cacophony of joy, sorrow, happiness, exhilaration, trepidation, sadness and laughter all wrapped in every *"Ciao."*

Nonna and I headed off to the market. We were again hunting *melanzane* along with some other items. It is interesting that in Italian grocery stores, you have to put on a plastic glove when you pick up produce. That goes for everything from potatoes to grapes to watermelons. Very hygienic, no? And yet, at the same time, eggs are not refrigerated in the store. The minimal use of refrigeration here has become a little unnerving. I haven't been ill or seen anyone else adversely affected by this, so obviously it isn't a problem, but it is still odd to me.

Back at the house we started putting together tonight's dinner. We made *crespelle*—crêpes—filled with a slice of *prosciutto cotto* and an equal-sized slice of mozzarella, each rolled and tucked as a single layer in a baking dish, and dotted with butter. There are two major types of prosciutto. *Prosciutto cotto* is just like the American version of cooked ham. *Cotto* means "cooked." *Prosciutto crudo* is made by covering the ham with salt, hanging it to air cure for several months. In truth, *prosciutto crudo* is never really cooked which is why it is called *crudo*—raw.

We made a potato and green bean *sformata*. Technically, *sformata* means "to take out of a mold" but, since we left it in the dish, I understood *sformata* to also mean "casserole." Mashed potatoes, cooked green beans and grated pecorino cheese were mixed together and placed in a buttered and breaded casserole dish. Unlike the *sformata* we made earlier in the week with the prosciutto, salami and cheese, this one is not layered. Once again, neither the *crespelle* nor the *sformata* were refrigerated before being baked—interesting.

For *il pranzo*, we made eggplant "meatballs." Small cubes of boiled, peeled eggplant are prepared like meatballs and fried in sunflower oil. I had never heard of such a thing. This is a perfect vegetarian dish. They were served in a simple *sugo*. And, if all of this wasn't enough to prepare before I headed off to the den for my language lesson, we also made a *risotto con zucchine*—zucchini risotto.

I am making some progress in language class. Will I be any better at speaking Italian when I leave? Not sure about that at the moment, but Alessandra and I are having fun. I find myself trying more and more (and failing more and more) to speak it and to learn more words, and verbs, and structure ... *Mamma mia!!*

It was just Nonna, Francesca and me for dinner tonight. Alessandra went out to dinner with a friend and Lillo had to work late. There were times at the table when it was *silenzio. MOLTO SILENZIO!* That was a good thing. It reminded me how much I rely on Alessandra for communication and understanding, when I really need to try and get beyond that. When Nonna and Francesca did speak it forced me to be brave and jump head first into Italian. Dinner tonight felt like an end-of-the-week pop quiz.

Earlier today at lunch, Francesca was not very happy because Alessandra would not give her permission to go on a weekend trip with Stefano, her new boyfriend, so as any 19-year-old girl still living at home would do, Francesca pouted. She pouted in grand fashion—in grand Italian fashion. There was sighing, sobbing and moments of extreme anger and hysterics. Alessandra held her ground, but Francesca used every angle and trick to get her mother to change her mind. I have no doubt that Francesca's performance could have inspired Puccini to write another great opera. When Francesca left the table in a mad flourish, Nonna said, *"Lei é un Scorpione,"* —"She is a Scorpio,"— and proceeded to make hand gestures for a scorpion. Her arm went up over her head and became the poisoned stinger, and then, in a quick stinging motion, her arm came down and struck the victim.

Francesca was feeling better by dinner. It seems that just before we sat down to eat she spoke with Stefano on the phone. He said that Alessandra was right in saying no because they had not been going out for that long. Stefano certainly is a wise boy, huh? For Francesca, one moment there is a great storm and the next the sun is shining bright. Such is life in this Italian house. All is well now. Of course, it took me all of dinner to understand why Francesca's mood had improved. Given the silence and my unease with the language, Nonna, the now pacified Scorpion, and I pleasantly survived dinner. I would only give myself a grade of "C" on tonight's quiz—I should have tried harder to communicate. Maybe week two will see a surge in my willingness to attempt communication regardless of success or failure.

Remember that when I write what people are saying in conversations, Alessandra is the <u>only</u> one who is speaking English. Even then, there are times when Alessandra's English isn't the best and I get confused. At times, I think she is talking about a woman only to find out later that the "she" in the story is actually Lillo. She willingly admits that she often gets "he" and "she" mixed up. I do understand a little more every day, and it is getting easier for me to get the gist of things in certain situations. Nonna might use an English word every now and then while cooking but absolutely no sentences. In fact, it is getting harder and harder for me to remember how to correctly spell English words because I want to use the Italian spelling. I find myself writing in a more Italian-style sentence structure. Checking to make sure that I am putting words in their correct order in a sentence is starting to become a necessity.

After dinner I took a long walk around the neighborhood to see what it is like. I have only seen the neighborhood in daylight from the passenger seat of the car when Nonna and I have been out shopping. It was a perfect evening for a walk. At dusk, it was *fresco*—cool—outside. There is an auto-mechanic shop across the street that doesn't look like a mechanic's garage in the American sense. There are no extra cars sitting around or loud tools. I haven't quite figured out exactly what gets repaired there. Since it is August, the garage is not open for regular business. Traditionally, August is when Italians close up shop for the entire month and go on vacation. Two blocks down the street there are several new apartment buildings going up in the neighborhood. I have been hearing some of that construction during the day.

My *passeggiata* gave me a chance to see into neighborhood yards and gain another view of Italian life. Two streets away there was a family having dinner in their yard. They had planted a small vineyard in the lot next to their house and in the middle of that a pavilion had been built. It was an old, metal roofed pavilion overgrown with grapevines just starting to drip with small, tight clusters of fruit. Surrounding the pavilion were neatly manicured rows of grapevines. Children and dogs were running and playing amongst the rows. In the pavilion, the adults sat at a large table covered with a white tablecloth, platters of food, water glasses, wine goblets and many open bottles. This party of Italians was enjoying the summer night.

No doubt the remnants of the summer feast now strewn about the table had been prepared by a *nonna* or two.

The men, comfortably dressed, sat back in their chairs drinking and smoking. The women were well dressed in linen outfits of all colors and styles. Sometimes a child would run to his mother demanding that some dispute with a friend be settled in his favor. Occasionally the dogs, too, would squabble and snarl. This was quickly sorted out by one of the men who would clap his hands and say, in a low, stern voice, *"Silenzio!"* I lingered in the road, soaking in the atmosphere. The setting sun behind the pavilion was turning the sky brilliant hot summer colors. If this moment had been captured on film no one would believe it was real. I walked until dark, admiring more gardens, lawns and homes. It was a splendid summer evening *passeggiata* through the neighborhood.

Ciao, ciao ... ciao, ciao, ciao!

Polpette di Melanzane

Eggplant Meatballs

Some may consider this recipe difficult—it isn't. It is short on ingredients but a little long in process—it is one of the few Italian recipes that requires some time to prepare. The secret to its success is in removing as much water from the cooked eggplant as possible. Eggplants are spongy and readily absorb liquids, especially water, so the more water that can be removed after cooking, the better. I have prepared these for friends that LOVE eggplant and for friends that are vegetarians—and blew their socks off with it!

3 large eggplants, approximately 3 ½ to 4 pounds

2 tablespoons plus ½ teaspoon salt

2 slices Italian bread (½-inch slices of a Tuscan boule or similar bread)

1 cup freshly grated Parmigiano-Reggiano or Grana Padano cheese

2 cloves garlic, finely minced

¼ cup chopped fresh Italian flat-leaf parsley

2 eggs, slightly beaten

½ teaspoon freshly ground black pepper

1 cup plain dried bread crumbs, plus a little more if needed

Sunflower oil to fry in (your favorite frying oil may be substituted)

Peel the eggplant, slice into ½-inch rounds and then cut into ½-inch cubes. Place the cubed eggplant in a large 6-quart pot. Add the 2 tablespoons of salt and stir to coat all the eggplant. Pour in enough water to cover the eggplant by 2 inches. Let the eggplant soak in the salted water for an hour, stirring every 15 minutes.

After the eggplant has soaked, place the pot over medium-high heat and bring to a boil. Boil the eggplant until thoroughly cooked, 10 minutes. Drain into a colander and remove the excess liquid by placing a plate on top of the eggplant and adding a weight to the plate (Nonna used a large can of tomatoes). Let the eggplant drain until cool.

Meanwhile, place the bread slices in a bowl and cover with water. Place a teacup saucer on the bread slices to help keep the bread under water. Set aside to soak for 5 to 10 minutes.

Place the drained and cooled eggplant in a large bowl. Remove the soaking bread from the water and, using your hands, squeeze out the excess water. Tear the bread into small pieces and add to the eggplant, along with the Parmigiano-Reggiano, garlic, parsley, eggs, salt and pepper. If the mixture is too soft, add a tablespoon of dry bread crumbs. Form the eggplant mixture between the palms of your hands into 1-inch diameter balls, and roll each ball *(polpette)* in the bread crumbs to coat.

Heat ½ inch of oil in a heavy medium-size frying pan over medium heat and, in batches, brown the *polpette* on all sides, about 4 to 6 minutes. Place on paper towels to drain. While still warm, sprinkle with salt to taste. May be served alone as an *antipasta* or covered with Nonna's Simple Sauce *(see page 32)* and served as a second course.

Makes about 32 *polpette*—6 to 8 servings.

Normally, Nonna would suggest using small- to medium-sized eggplant in a recipe; however, here, she used LARGE eggplants. I am not sure I know the reason why, other than it may have something to do with their being boiled, so the increased water content of a large eggplant wouldn't really matter. For all I know, large eggplants are less expensive in Italy, which would definitely give Nonna the incentive to go big!

DAY SIX (Il Giorno Sei)

I woke up this morning craving bacon and eggs. I'm not sure why, unless my body was tired of having the same old thing for breakfast, but I knew it wasn't going to be possible. For one thing, American-style bacon doesn't exist in Italy—*pancetta* is considered the Italian equivalent, but it bears no resemblance to what we would think of as bacon. Also, there is no culture of "start your day off with a good breakfast" here in Italy, so I didn't think I could ask Nonna to fry up some *pancetta* and make two eggs, over-easy, for me.

One of my earliest memories of food is of watching my grandma on my mom's side cooking eggs in bacon grease. It is a very specific memory for me—I was 5 years old, sitting on a bench seat in my grandparents' pickup truck camper. My grandpa was in the cab of the truck driving, while my grandmother and I were back in the camper. I remember sitting at the tiny table, staring out of the window behind me—under the blind that had been raised a crack, just enough for me to see the sun rising over endless green

Wisconsin farmland with perfectly straight rows of corn that seemed to ripple as we went speeding by. Across the table, my grandma stood at the propane stove cooking eggs in the grease left over from frying up bacon. The sound of the eggs popping and wheezing as they fried and the smell of the bacon filled my senses. That sound and smell was so comforting to me. My grandmother loved over-easy eggs and she always took great pride in being the one to expose all of us grandkids to dipping toast into our first fried egg "with the runny yolk." To this day, the smell of bacon frying immediately takes me back to that early morning camper ride.

Nonna had an appointment this morning with her doctor before he goes on vacation for the rest of August. She has an ulcer or something wrong with her stomach, because at least once a day she takes a large spoon of liquid medicine from a bottle kept in the *frigo*. I had my morning language *lezione* first instead of cooking right after *colazione*. It was a nice change of pace to switch up my morning routine. Nonna was back by the end of the language lesson, having been given the "a-okay" by her doctor, so we rolled up our sleeves and prepared three things *per il pranzo*.

We made an apple and pear strudel—*rotolo* (because it is rolled up). The dough was made with *grappa*. I am learning that a little *grappa* added to dessert *pasta* adds an almost nutty hint of grape flavor. The word *pasta* really refers to all types of dough, not just the kind used to make noodles. *Fettuccine*, *gnocchi*, *biscotti* and dessert crusts are made from *pasta*. When it was time to roll out the *pasta* we had made from scratch, Nonna disappeared into the pantry to haul out the pasta board. The pantry is a small room occupying the space under the staircase that leads to the second floor. The pantry's curtained doorway is only four feet high, so even Nonna, who maybe stands at five feet, has to stoop to go through. Inside, there are many shelves loaded with dry and canned food staples and, surprisingly, there is a stand-up freezer. I was wondering where all the meat for dinner had been coming from.

Stooped over with the pasta board in its cloth sack thrown over her shoulder, looking like *Babbo Natale*,—Santa Claus—Nonna appeared from the pantry. The well-used wooden board is much larger than a standard cutting board in America. Nonna also has an assortment of rolling pins in a separate cloth bag in the pantry. She has seven different rolling pins of varying lengths, thicknesses and types of wood, each used to make a particular type of pasta. The longer ones are used to roll out large sheets of pasta. Others have a slightly rough, grooved surface which adds texture to the pasta as it is being rolled out. The board and rolling pins are only used for making pasta. They never come in contact with anything besides dough and they are never cleaned with soap and water, which, according to Nonna, would ruin their surfaces. A metal scraper is used to remove any remaining dried dough stuck to the wood and a dry cloth wipes them clean before being put back into their sacks. This is the first time I have seen the pasta board and rolling pins; all the pasta we have eaten up to this point has been factory produced.

Contrary to popular belief, Italians do not make fresh pasta every day, nor do they only cook with extra virgin olive oil. I have been here six days and we have only eaten factory-produced pasta—the same boxed pasta we eat in America. So far, there has been no flour covered Nonna kneading and rolling out sheets of pasta in the Tuscan hills, while *"O Sole Mio"* is being sung by Pavarotti in the background with Lucille Ball stomping on grapes to make wine. Also, as it is in America, extra virgin olive oil is more expensive than other oils, so Nonna uses sunflower oil to fry everything in, and only uses extra virgin olive oil when the dish requires the fruity and peppery taste that the first cold-pressing of the olives produces. Two stereotypes crushed. I was surprised, too.

Getting back to the *rotolo* ... we used a long, skinny, smooth rolling pin for the strudel *pasta*. Preparing the filling is like making an apple pie. Nonna used apples, pears, sugar, cinnamon and small pats of butter. The filling tops the sheet of dough; it is rolled up and shaped like a horseshoe, placed on a cookie sheet and baked. *È molto semplice, no?*

Per il primo piatto—for the first course (always a pasta), we made *spaghetti con tonno*—spaghetti with tuna. It consists of spaghetti in a simple *sugo* of tomato sauce with onion, garlic and canned tuna (packed in olive oil). Before eating you add some dashes of bottled *piccante*—spicy—pepper sauce over the top of the spaghetti. Slender, tiny yellow-green peppers are packed tightly in a jar with vinegar. In Alabama, people like to sprinkle this type of pepper sauce on top of their collard greens. A couple of drops were all I used since I prefer only mildly *piccante* spaghetti. Lillo likes his *molto piccante*. The heat is what puts a little extra "somethin' somethin'" in the dish. In Italy, most seafood pasta dishes are *piccante* and never have cheese on them. The flavor of cheese competes with the subtle flavor of seafood.

Il secondo piatto era trota—the second course—was trout. The second course of an Italian meal is usually some type of protein. In case you were wondering, we didn't go down to the local stream to catch and clean trout— Nonna picked up the trout filets at the market on her way home from the doctor's. The salmon-colored trout filets were simply topped with ground fennel seed, salt, pepper, a sprig of fresh rosemary, slices of garlic and drizzled with olive oil. Placed on a baking sheet they were roasted in the oven.

On my first day in Viterbo, Alessandra and Nonna asked if there were any foods that I didn't like. *"Non mi piace ...* Brussels sprouts," was my immediate answer. Neither of them knew what I was talking about. Although Alessandra does speak English, she doesn't know every word.

"They are tiny, tiny cabbages clustered on stalks," I said.

"Ah, *cavolini*, Marco," said Alessandra. Naturally. The word for cabbage is *cavolo* so it made perfect sense that Brussels sprouts, looking like tiny— *ini*—cabbages, would be *cavolini*.

"Except for *cavolini*," I said, "I would eat anything, including octopus and calamari—squid." Nonna's eyes lit up.

Today she asked me again if I liked octopus and calamari. I told her about a great Greek restaurant in Chicago, The Parthenon, that serves wonderfully prepared octopus, and the calamari at Biba Caggiano's restaurant in Sacramento is the best I have ever tasted. Nonna loves calamari, too. I have never cooked squid before, but she said not to worry because she had a great recipe for stuffed squid.

I can tell my enthusiasm about food sets Nonna's mind to work. Conversations about one dish will lead to another and another and, before you know it, Nonna will say she has eight things she wants us to make. She doesn't have a set menu plan for students. In my case, she seems to be bouncing ideas off of me to see what I think. I am definitely going to be exposed to a wide variety of foods. The fact that I am here for more than a week allows her to make all kinds of different dishes. The only other male student discussed with regularity is the Japanese chef who was here last year. He went back to Japan and opened a restaurant where he serves a lot of dishes made from Nonna's recipes. He sent the family his restaurant's menu; Nonna pulled it out today and proudly showed me.

After my afternoon language *lezione* we made *mozzarella alla carrozza*— mozzarella in a carriage. A slice of mozzarella is topped with an anchovy and placed between two slices of bread. For those of you who are still fearful of anchovies you can leave it out. Nonna said that you may only make it two ways: either with mozzarella alone or mozzarella with anchovy. *"Solo, Marco, solo!"*—That was Nonna's command. For her, no other variations are possible. None. (I have seen a cook on television make it with mozzarella and basil. I am not sure Nonna would approve.) Once you have assembled this little cheese and anchovy *antipasta*, it is rolled in a beaten egg wash and pan fried in a small amount of sunflower oil. It becomes a savory sandwich of egg, hot melted mozzarella and anchovy. I think the slight saltiness of the anchovy is essential. I ate four—all with *acciughe*—anchovies.

For dinner, besides the *carrozza*, we had a platter of *prosciutto crudo*, *salumi*, *prosciutto cotto* and little sandwiches called *tramezzini*. When Alessandra first described them I thought the sandwiches were coming from a store called Tramezzini, but when Lillo brought them home they looked like something purchased from a cafeteria vending machine. They are crustless tea sandwiches packaged in plastic triangular shaped containers with a clear piece of plastic covering the cut end of the sandwich halves. There were three kinds: mayonnaise with bologna (Italian bologna, naturally), mayonnaise with a little tuna and mayonnaise with salami. The packages were opened and the sandwiches were cut into smaller triangles. Alessandra's family loves them—they went crazy over them—I couldn't believe it. They tasted okay but I could not see what all the fuss was about. Maybe for them it was the mayonnaise. I smiled and acted as if I had never had anything like this before—well, when in Italy. As usual, we finished with *l'insalata e l'ananas e il melone. Per il dolce, abbiamo mangiato delle fette di rotolo e poi dopo abbiamo bevuto il caffè*—for dessert, we ate slices of the *rotolo* and had coffee afterward.

Tonight's meal was one that you could eat all night long, picking at a little of this and a little of that. *Buonissimo!* After dinner, Marianna and Francesca went out to meet some friends. We older adults stayed at the table, talking and drinking Alessandra's *arancello*. I went upstairs and brought down my laptop to show Alessandra, Lillo and Nonna photos of my life back in Alabama.

"*Ooooo ... un bel cane, Marco. Come si chiama?*"—"A beautiful dog, Mark. What is its name?"— Alessandra asked.

"*Si chiama Agnes.*"

Nonna asked the next question, but I couldn't understand her, so Alessandra helped.

"She wants to know who is taking care of Agnes while you are here with us?"

There are those moments in life where the world stops and a thousand things rush through your mind. It is that nanosecond where, when faced with possible danger, everything becomes slow motion and you see yourself move through time and space. Here was the simplest question asked in a most innocent way and yet, for a moment, it paralyzed me.

"Um, my friend ... my friend Richard ... umm, *il mio amico Riccardo* is taking care of Agnes."

I heard myself speak and it saddened me—not sorrowful sad, but disappointed sad. I had just let myself down. Up to this point in my stay here I hadn't really said much about my personal life. I had mentioned my parents, a sibling and some friends, but whether conscious or not, I had not mentioned Richard, my partner of the past 16 years. It was natural for Nonna to be curious about my life. I had shopped with her, eaten her cooking, sat at her table, laughed with her and had started to develop a friendship with her—with everyone in the family— so why was her question so devastating to me? It wasn't; it was my very own homophobic answer—made in that unending nanosecond before I spoke it.

My answer should have been, "Richard, my partner of 16 years, is taking care of our dog, Agnes." But it wasn't. I got nervous about what a group of people that I had just started to develop a relationship with might think of me, about being gay in a Catholic country spiritually governed by the pope himself—only an hour away in Rome. I panicked and decided to take the path of least resistance, as I had done so often in the past, and in doing so in this moment—I lied about myself right in front of myself.

What is so terrifying about telling the truth? I forced myself to come out to my family years ago after divorcing my wife and moving in with Richard, because of a very similar moment in a Christmas dinner conversation. I sat at my grandparents' table surrounded by cousins, uncles and aunts, siblings and parents and my grandfather, who was seated to my right, innocently enough asked, "So Mark, how are the Southern women treating you?" I was trapped in that same unending nanosecond of indecision. I looked up at my mother's expression that said, "So, how are you going to get out of this one, Mr. Newly Out Homosexual Man?" To my grandfather, in front of my entire family, the people whom I deeply cherish, I said, "Oh, you know, they're okay," and then lamely chuckled. The lie devastated me for a week before I finally told the entire family—no more lies to the people I love. Also, I wanted to be able to talk about Richard, to talk in the "we" and not the "I."

Yet here I was, 16 years later, once again speaking in the "I" to people I have started to build a relationship with. Again I didn't claim Richard. Next week, or sometime in the future, I will have to tell the truth.

"*Il tuo amico Riccardo è molto gentile,*" —"Your friend Richard is very nice,"— Nonna said.

"*Sì, è vero,*" —It's true,"— I said. On the surface, it was nice of Richard to take care of Agnes while I was gone, but deeper than that he is nice for a million other reasons, not one of which I could bring myself to tell her right now. There was so much to claim by just saying the simple words "my partner," but uncourageously I dared not share one iota of that with Nonna, Lillo or Alessandra.

I went on to show them photos of my (our) house, the backyard rose parterre that Richard had painstakingly planted (the beauty of which I alone was now taking credit for), a photo of Richard asleep on the sofa late one Christmas Eve surrounded by mounds of opened gifts and discarded wrapping paper and bows (no comment) and photos of where I worked—a theatre that produces works by William Shakespeare.

"*Sei un attore?*" —"Are you an actor?"— Nonna asked.

"*No, mi dispiace, sono un* stage manager," I said.

I didn't know the Italian term for "stage manager," so I quickly grabbed the English/Italian dictionary that always lives on the sideboard next to the kitchen table.

"*Sono un direttore di scena.*" —"I am a scenic director." It was not an exact translation or description, but it was the best that I could come up with using the dictionary. It was even more difficult to explain to them exactly what I did as a *direttore di scena*. (It is even hard for me to explain it in English when people back home ask.) Alessandra tried to translate my job description to Lillo and Nonna but even she was having a hard time understanding what it is that I do. Lillo gave up and decided that I was *un direttore*—a director— and that was that. Why split hairs?

Seeing the photos on my computer tonight made me homesick and, once I was up in my room, I took out my rented international cell phone and called Richard. Even though it was late evening, given the time change I caught Richard in the middle of the afternoon at work. We couldn't talk long, but it was great to hear his voice and we quickly caught up on all the day's events in both countries. When I told Richard how much the Stefanis loved the images of our garden, he asked if I had told them how long and hard he had worked on it. My answer? How could I admit to Richard that I didn't have the courage to tell them that he was anything more to me than just a friend? I couldn't, so I lied. I told him what he wanted to hear, which was more than I could admit to them and far less than he deserved.

It had been an evening of much laughter and of getting to know one another—well, that was the outward appearance. I never really let them know much of the best of me. Inwardly, especially after calling Richard, I was sad, disappointed and a liar in two languages.

❦

Spaghetti con Tonno

Spaghetti with Tuna

I like canned tuna a lot; Richard despises it—and yet he enjoys this dish. Italians like their seafood spicy, and this dish is no exception. Nonna controlled the heat by only using a modest amount of peperoncini—*red pepper flakes. Lillo and I jacked up the heat by adding dashes of bottled pepper sauce on top of our plated pasta. I have maintained the amount of "heat" in the recipe as Nonna did. If you like it spicy hot, I suggest you hit the bottle!*

2 tablespoons extra virgin olive oil

1 small onion, finely minced

2 large cloves garlic, finely minced

½ teaspoon red pepper flakes, or more to taste

4 cups strained tomatoes, such as Pomi brand ★

1½ teaspoons salt, or more to taste

½ teaspoon freshly ground black pepper, or more to taste

3 (6-ounce) cans light meat tuna, packed in olive oil. Drain and discard the
   oil from one of the cans only. Use the entire contents, including the olive

oil, of the other two cans

¼ cup chopped fresh Italian flat-leaf parsley, plus more to garnish

1 pound spaghetti

Bottled pepper sauce (tabasco peppers in vinegar)

Heat the oil in a large skillet over medium heat. When the oil is hot, add the onion and cook until it starts to soften and turn golden, 4 to 5 minutes (if it starts to brown too quickly, add a tablespoon or two of water to slow the cooking process). Stir in the garlic and red pepper flakes, cooking briefly for 30 seconds. Add the strained tomatoes, salt and pepper, and stir until well combined. Cook until mixture starts to boil, then lower the heat to low.

Add the drained tuna to the skillet, along with the entire contents (including the oil) of the other two cans of tuna. Gently stir until the tuna is evenly distributed in the sauce, being careful not to break any chunks of tuna. Simmer on low for 15 to 20 minutes. Turn off the heat and stir in the parsley.

Meanwhile, bring a large pot of water to boil over high heat. Once boiling, add 2 tablespoons salt, then the spaghetti, stirring occasionally to insure it doesn't stick together. When it is *al dente*—tender, but firm to the bite—drain and add to the sauce, mixing well over low heat until the pasta is well combined. Adjust salt and pepper to taste. Garnish each serving with additional parsley and pass the bottled pepper sauce so people can raise the heat to their individual taste.

Makes 6 to 8 servings.

*Note: Strained tomatoes can be readily found in most supermarkets in either the canned tomato or pasta aisles. Sometimes the product may be referred to by its Italian name "passato" and can be found either bottled or cartoned, as is the case with the Pomi brand.

DAY SEVEN (Il Giorno Sette)

*O*ggi è sabato—Today is Saturday. (The names of the days of the week and months are not capitalized in Italian.) Saturdays and Sundays are off days, so I have no formal classes this weekend. Usually, students only spend one week here, making Saturday the departure day and Sunday the arrival day for the next student. I am in Italy for four weekends, so I am spending this weekend here, next weekend in Rome, the third weekend in Florence, and then I'll be flying out of Rome the last weekend. I figured the family would enjoy having their weekends to themselves. I don't need to be underfoot every waking moment.

Last evening's fun around the kitchen table gave us a good reason to sleep in this morning. *Colazione* was at 9:30 instead of the usual 8:00. It is the only meal where the food is exactly the same every day. Honestly, there is comfort in starting my wildly varying days with something that is always consistent. It has become a secure place from which to hold my breath and jump off into the rest of the day. So, comforted by monotony, Nonna and I headed out on our almost daily shopping run—even though I didn't have any classes today, I always want to go with Nonna.

Nothing traumatic has happened on our trips to the grocery stores since my first euro-losing excursion, but we always have some silly story to tell Alessandra the moment we walk back in the house. More often than not the stories involve me making some humorous blunder. The stories always end the same way: our three heads thrown back in a chorus of laughter and my admitting, *"Sono un idioto."* —Do I really need to translate?— One of them always replies, *"No Marco, sei geniale!"* —"No, Mark, you are clever!"

Clever or not, this morning's trip started with Nonna heading out the front door with a bag of recyclables in each hand, and I was right behind her. With my one recyclables-free hand, I reached back, grabbed the doorknob, and over my shoulder said, *"Ciao, Alessandra. Ciao!"*

"Ciao, ciao, Marco."

"Ciao, ciao, ciao."

"Ciao, Marco. Ciao, ciao!"

"Ciao, ciao, ciao. Ciao!" and I closed the front door. I won … I think.

The trunk was loaded with recycling and we were off. The newspaper stand was uneventful. The usual cloud of dust rose in the air as Nonna stopped and jumped out: two newspapers, a quick thumbing and disapproval of a gossip magazine while she waited for her change, and we were away before the dust settled.

At the medium-sized grocery Nonna got a cart. I paid attention this time as she placed a coin into the locking mechanism and pushed it in, freeing the cart from the rack. We headed in to buy all kinds of things. Today was a larger shopping day than usual because, in addition to getting ingredients for lunch and dinner, we needed to get ingredients for Marianna's *torta*. Tomorrow she turns twenty-five and there is going to be a celebration at the house; she has requested Nonna's special *torta* as her birthday cake.

"Busta?"

"No, grazie."

Then, it was out to the car, where we bagged our groceries. As Nonna was bagging the last item, I grabbed the cart and made a big point of saying, *"Oggi, riccordo il soldo."* —"Today, I remember the coin."

"Naturalmente, Marco," she said.

We both chuckled and I went to return the cart, while Nonna got in the car.

"Quanta costa per il carrello?" —"How much for the cart?"

"Due euro," I said.

A young woman with her boyfriend had approached me as I got to the cart rack just inside the doors. I hadn't put the cart away yet, so the coin was still inside the handle lock. The young woman searched in her change purse for a 2-euro coin while he rifled through his pockets. After several moments of searching, it looked as if neither of them had the correct coin.

"Avete due soldi?" —"Do you have two coins?"— I asked.

She reached in her change purse, handed me two 1-euro coins and I gave her the cart. They went into the store and I went to the car. The car was running when I got in, and as soon as the door closed, Nonna started backing out of the parking space and said, *"Dov'è il soldo, Marco?"*

"Ecco, Nonna." I put my hand out proudly displaying the two shiny 1-euro coins in my palm. Mid-reverse, she slammed on the brakes—stopping the car in the middle of the driving lane in front of the store's doors.

"Marco, cosa c'è che non va! Dov'è il soldo?" She took the coins from my hand.

"Nonna, è lo stesso. Due soldi per due euro. Lo stesso." I pointed at the two coins in her hand and held up a single finger.

"No, Marco, non è lo stesso. Ho usato una moneta da cinque cento lire." Her voice started getting louder and louder. *"Non è lo stesso! Era un soldo da cinque cento lire!! CINQUE CENTO LIRE!!!"*

The harder she tried to get me to understand what she was trying to say, the faster and more complicated her Italian became. I panicked—my brain immediately stopped translating. I could only think and speak in English. Now, she was yelling at me in Italian, and I was yelling right back in English. The harder I tried to explain to her that it was the same amount of money, the more frustrated she became.

"NONNA, IT'S THE SAME … THE SAME!! TWO 1-EURO COINS FOR ONE 2-EURO COIN!"

"NO, MARCO, NON È LO STESSO! CINQUE CENTO LIRE!" And with that, she threw on the parking brake and jumped out.

Trying desperately not to be misunderstood, I threw my door wide-open and jumped out too. We met each other at the rear of the car. I tried to think of an Italian word, ANY Italian word, to help explain myself.

"Nonna, there was a woman … a woman … una donna …."

"Dov'è la donna? Dov'è la donna? Marco, DOV'È LA DONNA?!"

"INSIDE, INSIDE, INSIDE!" I pointed as intensely as I answered. Like a hound after a fox, Nonna tore into the store with me running behind.

"Dov'è la donna? Dov'è la donna?" She was wildly turning in circles in the produce section looking around for a woman—any woman. I pointed out the young woman and Nonna, breathless, startled the poor unsuspecting couple as they were putting carrots into the cart.

There was much discussion back and forth before, turning the cart around, Nonna and the couple headed back toward the front doors. Feeling like an idiot, I walked behind the three, trying to feign innocence. I am sure it looked like ignorance. Every few steps the Italian trio would look back at me and shake their heads in disapproving judgement. What had I done?

At the cart rack, Nonna—now a magician—silently performed a "coin trick of a transaction" with the couple. She started by giving the woman back the two shiny 1-euro coins that came out of my palm. The woman said, "Grazie." Nonna then relocked the cart—groceries still in it—into the rack and removed her original coin from the lock as it popped opened. Next, Nonna pulled her coin purse out of her blouse pocket, opened it and put that coin into her purse. Deliberately reaching back into the coin purse she brought out another coin.

She showed the couple this 2-euro coin, placed it in the lock mechanism and unlocked the couple's cart from the rack. She gave the cart back to the couple and the boyfriend took the two shiny 1-euro coins from his girlfriend's hand and dropped them into Nonna's coin purse. With a click, the purse was closed and the performance was over. Nonna smiled, the couple pushed the cart back into the store and everyone was happy.

Nonna, now with the exact coins in her change purse that she refused to take from me moments ago, headed out the doors, turned back and looked at me as if to say, "Well? Are you coming?"

I headed out and saw the car—both doors wide open, still idling in park and blocking the drive in front of the store. In our fury over the cart we had forgotten all about the car. I am surprised no one took it. Back in the car, I didn't know what to say. I really wanted to say, "What in the hell was all the drama about?" but I don't know how to swear in Italian—I don't even know how to say "Darn!" or "Shoot!"

Instead, throwing my hands in the air, I looked her right in the eyes and said, "NONNA??!!" She knew what I was asking. Embarrassed, she opened her purse, took out a 2-euro coin and a 500-lire coin, and showed me that they were exactly the same size. Now I understood. Italy switched its currency from the lire to the euro in 2002 and at that point, lire became worthless. Today, Nonna used a worthless coin in the cart at the store—she used a slug—because she didn't want to take the chance that I would lose another two euro. It wouldn't matter if I lost the cart because the money in the handle was worthless. Nonna didn't trust me, and now I knew it— she was busted. I will give her the benefit of the doubt by saying that she did have my best interest at heart this morning—she stopped me from unknowingly cheating someone out of two euro; however, Nonna was much more embarrassed that I found out she didn't trust me with the cart.

She could see the light bulb turn on over my head as I realized what had happened. I looked at her ... and laughed. She laughed. Someone honked their horn behind us and brought us out of our little world—we were still sitting in front of the store blocking the drive. Laughing and shaking our heads, we drove to the recycling bins. She parked, and as I was about to get out, she grabbed my arm. I looked at her, *"Si?"* A Cheshire cat-like grin came across her face.

"Marco, in cucina sei geniale, ma al mercato sei STUPIDO!"

There was a beat of silence.

We both burst out laughing; tears were running down our faces we laughed so hard and long. It was the perfect thing to say, "Mark, in the kitchen you are clever, but at the store you are STUPID!" I continued laughing and crying as I put the recycling into the bins. We laughed all the way home.

Nonna and I are now best friends.

Back at the house, she gave me the recipe for the birthday *torta*. She didn't exactly hand me the written recipe. She allowed me to write it down as we made it. This may not sound out of the ordinary since I have been writing down every recipe we have cooked, but I am the first and <u>only</u> student to get this recipe. She has served this *torta* to students before and taken it to functions in the community; she has just never written the recipe down for anyone or allowed anyone outside the family to watch her make it. For those of you who cook, you know how special it is when someone gives you her top-secret recipe. I have been given the family's four-generation-old *torta* recipe. For me, this is a priceless gift.

The recipe comes from Nonna's great-grandmother. Nonna's grandmother made it for Nonna's wedding, and in this family it is still reserved for special occasions. It is a sweet crust filled with a lemon and sheep's milk ricotta cheese batter—similar to a cheesecake. The batter had a lightly sweet, tangy taste. I cannot wait until I taste the finished product tomorrow. Alessandra told me that Nonna wanted to give this recipe, this gift, to me because Nonna could tell we were kindred spirits when cooking in her kitchen. My eyes welled up with tears when she said that.

With Marianna's *torta* baking in the toaster oven we turned our energies towards getting lunch underway. We sautéed zucchini for *zucchine con farfalle*. What could be more basic than zucchini with bow tie pasta? While the zucchini cooked, the second course was started: chicken with green olives. Nonna started by cutting a chicken into about 14 pieces. It will go a long way in feeding the six of us. I hope this will give you an indication about the portion sizes in Italy. It must seem that we eat huge meals here, but the portion sizes are much smaller than in America. Three Nonna-sized pieces of chicken would amount to a single breast-sized American portion. If I actually ate three pieces of chicken, the family would look at me funny. One piece would be considered sufficient; two pieces more than filling; and three, well, downright gluttonous—a Thanksgiving dinner.

Instead of our usual siesta, Nonna, Alessandra and I set off for town. I wanted to get Marianna something for her birthday, and I hadn't seen the city center during daylight. There are actually two parties tomorrow. Besides her birthday luncheon at the house, Marianna and Marco are having a house warming party at their new apartment tomorrow night. I wanted to get something that was a combined birthday and housewarming gift. Alessandra said I wasn't expected to give anything, but I wanted to. I overheard Marianna tell Alessandra that she was concerned about not having a fruit bowl for their table at the new apartment. Fresh fruit is very important to this family—we have it every night after the salad. Alessandra told Marianna not to worry about having everything right away; she would acquire things as time went along. I think that a large decorative platter/fruit bowl is what I want to give as my gift.

Viterbo is as beautiful during the day as it is magical at night. Alessandra, Nonna and I strolled through *il centro*—the historic center—and went into several gift shops. Some were touristy, with the usual trappings of oil and vinegar sets, brightly colored terra-cotta plates, serving platters and small glass figurines. A couple of the shops were galleries. They had beautiful art pieces and magnificent works in Venetian glass, but alas, there was nothing I really liked or could afford.

As we were leaving one gallery, Nonna sighed and said, *"Francia, Francia, Francia."* Surprise, surprise! Nicola and Jimmy were in town, too. Nonna noticed them at the other end of the street before they had noticed us. Alessandra looked up from the shop window and said, "Marco, let's run for it!" She translated it for Nonna who agreed, *"Si, si."* Nonna turned in the opposite direction and took the classic Greek Olympic runner's pose as if running away. We laughed so loud that Nicola and Jimmy noticed us and headed our way. We chatted with them while we walked into a parking area toward their car. Jimmy spoke almost exclusively to me … in English. I think Alessandra and Nicola were catching up on family happenings. Nonna walked in front of us and would occasionally turn back and look at me as if to say, "Does Jimmy ever shut up about himself?" I would peer at her with my gaze saying, "Nonna, don't make me start laughing in his face!" Oblivious to this, Jimmy was babbling on about how last night three girls were all over him because he was French.

When we got to the car I wanted a picture of the four of them together. Nonna immediately grabbed Nicola, putting Jimmy on the opposite end of the photo next to Alessandra. I have a feeling Nonna would rather be stabbed than stand next to Jimmy and put her arm around him.

With Nicola and Jimmy gone, Alessandra said, *"Gelato?"*

"Si, si. Mi piace gelato molto!"

We all agreed that gelato would be the only way to recover from a surprise encounter with Jimmy. *"Povero Jimmy!"*

Three double-scoop cups later, we still hadn't found anything for Marianna. Nonna thought we should drive over to the other two shopping centers (the mall and Le Clerc). The mall was *PAZZO*—CRAZY! Considering the crowds, it seemed more like the day after Thanksgiving in America rather than a random Saturday in August. The mall proved to be a bust, but I found something at Le Clerc. A large, glazed Chinese platter—red and moss green with a pattern throughout. I loved that it wasn't something Italian. It was different from all of the typical Italian-looking things. Don't misunderstand me. If I was going to bring something home to someone in America there were a multitude of gift ideas, but why buy the typical Italian looking gift for an Italian?

On our way to the registers Alessandra stopped at the bakery section.

"*Mamma, pizza bianca?*"

"*No, grazie. Non è la migliore. C'è n'è un'altro.*" —"No thanks. It isn't the best. There is the other."

"*Vero mamma, ma l'altro mercato non apre adesso. Sonno chiusi per ferie.*" —"True, but the other market isn't open now. They are closed for vacation." And, with that, Alessandra reached down and picked up what appeared to be foccacia in a bakery bag.

Out in the car, Alessandra opened the bag, broke off a piece of this *pizza bianca*—white pizza—and handed it to me. The white pizzas that I have in America are usually a pizza with only white cheese on it, hence the name. But here, it was more like a foccacia—soft, thicker than a thin-crust pizza, a hint of salt, brushed with a little olive oil and nothing else. I said it was good, but Nonna insisted that there was better *pizza bianca* in Viterbo. She was so insistent that she refused to eat a piece when Alessandra offered some. That's how Nonna is—she never settles for anything less than the best. Alessandra is less exacting, and even though she agreed with Nonna, she thought it was important for me to taste the Le Clerc version so I could compare it to Nonna's favorite *pizza bianca*. I hope I get a chance to make the comparison.

We were home by 6:00 p.m. I was a little concerned about dinner since we hadn't been home to prepare anything. When we walked in the door Lillo announced that we were going out to dinner tonight. Nonna rarely goes out with us after the sun goes down. She doesn't go to bed early, but I think she enjoys a quiet evening home alone while we go out for fun. An hour later, after having showered and changed into something a little dressier, Francesca, Alessandra, Lillo and I piled into the car, windows down, and headed to Marta.

Marta is a small village on the southwestern shore of Lago di Bolsena, a crater lake in the northernmost part of Lazio roughly 30 minutes north of the house. The lake was formed by the collapse of an ancient volcano. There are two islands in the lake, created by underwater volcanic activity. Lillo said that ancient Roman records mentioned volcanic activity as late as the second century B.C. Luckily, it has been inactive since then.

Alessandra insisted that I sit in the front passenger seat while Lillo drove. I think Alessandra wanted to chat and gossip with Francesca in the back seat. This also forced me to carry on a conversation with Lillo. Alessandra is good about putting me in situations where I am forced to speak Italian.

Lillo is a patient man and goes out of his way to try and explain things when talking to me during meals around the kitchen table. When I start to look like a deer caught in the headlights, his hands come alive and start acting out the words that I don't understand. Because he speaks absolutely no English, he has mastered the use of hand gestures, even when driving, as a language tool to help illustrate what he is saying. If Lillo's explanations start to veer from the truth, or start to become exaggerated, Alessandra always chimes in with, *"Ehhhh."* This is not the same shoulder-shrugging expression—*"Eh"*—used to imply "Well, what can you do?" This *"Ehhhh"* is said with a more emphatic tone of correction indicating that Lillo has now entered the realm of untruth and exaggeration. It is the tone a mother would use upon walking into the kitchen and finding her son sneaking his hand into the cookie jar. When Alessandra does catch Lillo with *"Ehhhh,"* he looks at her, shrugs his shoulders, and says, *"Cosa?"* —"What?"— She corrects him and he concedes with a sly grin.

Along the way toward Marta, Lillo pointed out things of interest and explained what they were. Sometimes I succeeded in understanding, sometimes not. When hand gestures and steering the car became too precarious, Alessandra would quickly chime in from the back seat and translate.

I have discovered that when it sounds like Lillo has made a statement and I sort of understand what is being said I can encourage the conversation along by saying, *"Davvero?"* —"Really?"— *"Si, si, si, Marco... "*—launching Lillo into further detail. Sometimes the detail helps; more often than not it confuses me even more. My look of confusion restarts the entire conversational cycle of gestures and Alessandra's ultimate rescue with the translation, and in this instance also saving us from careening off the road into a ditch.

Suddenly, Lillo started waving out the window, yelling, *"Ciao, ciao, ciao!"* Alessandra and Francesca chimed in too. I started looking around to see who we knew on the side of the road, but no one was there. Lillo pointed to a field littered with grazing sheep. He explained that it is a tradition to wave and say hello to sheep when you encounter them. *"Marco, è buona fortuna."* —"Mark, it is good luck." I wasn't quite sure if he was pulling my leg or not, but by the time we had passed the third flock, I sheepishly—pardon the pun—joined in. I am sure we were quite a sight: four adults packed into Lillo's little car waving out of the windows and well-wishing herds of sheep as we sped down the road.

Marta was having its city festival in honor of its patron saint, *Santa Marta*. It was now dusk, and from our car, parked on the lakefront, I could see the islands, and much farther off in the distance I could see the opposite side of the lake and barely pick out some twinkling city lights.

"Lillo, che città è là?" I asked pointing towards the distant lights.

"Bolsena, Marco. È là...," pointing at a closer set of lights, *"Quella è Capodimonte."*

A very grand boardwalk, lit by lampposts and bordered on either side by trees, followed the shoreline. Lillo explained that this boardwalk went on for many kilometers and connected several smaller towns along Lago di Bolsena. We walked the wide boardwalk towards the town center. We passed many of the same things that you would find at a small town festival in America. Town organizations and clubs had booths set up selling a wide variety of things: fried fish, cooked sausages, roasted pig and desserts. Others were handing out information. There was a large pavilion with picnic tables and a band was playing songs both new and old. Most of the music, surprisingly, was American. There were also the usual arts and crafts vendors selling their wares. I thought we were going to eat at one of these booths but we kept walking past the food.

We soon arrived at a long stretch of hotels lining the lakefront, each with its own *ristorante*. We passed many before arriving at Lillo and Alessandra's favorite: Otello. I thought the restaurant's name—Othello—was rather symbolic considering that I am in theatre and have worked on productions of that Shakespeare title.

Lillo went in to ask if we could eat *al fresco*—outside. In Italy, every *ristorante* has dining outside under large umbrellas. Besides being enjoyable, there is a practical side to dining *al fresco*; since there is no air conditioning, dining outside in the fresh air keeps everyone from roasting inside. Tonight was perfect for dining outside.

Otello's was very busy and Alessandra was very concerned that it was going to be a long wait before we could be seated. Lillo soon came hopping back from inside with a devilish grin on his face. Immediately, we had the *maestro*—maitre d'—seating us ahead of many others still waiting in line. The *maestro* and two waiters, in a mad flurry of dishes, glasses, flatware, table linens, menus, water and wine bottles, had us seated in a matter of moments.

"Salute!" toasted Lillo, with his glass of *prosecco* held high. We all raised our glasses, thrilled and more than a little shocked. Alessandra could not understand what just happened. She looked at Lillo and said, *"Ehh."* He explained that he went inside and told the *maestro* (whom they know because they eat here often) that he had *una persona molto importante dall'America* with him. Lillo told the *maestro* that I was a very important American director and I was in the area scouting locations for my next film. That was all it took to have the best service all night. Alessandra could not get over the fact that the *maestro* and two additional waiters served us all night long. Quite frankly, it was nice to be treated as *una persona molto importante dall'America*. A person could get used to such a thing.

We started off by ordering a huge seafood *antipasti* serving for four. Fifteen different types of seafood dishes were brought out to us. Each dish served four people. We had shrimp four different ways and five types of clams and mussels, all prepared differently. We had raw oysters, two different seafood *bruschette* and three types of fried fish fresh from the lake. It was amazing to see and even better to eat. We skipped the *primo* and went right for the *secondo*. I had *sogliola*—sole—prepared *mugnaia*—mill worker—style.

(*Mugnaia* is pronounced "moon-YEI-ya.") The sole was grilled and served in a butter, lemon and parsley sauce. Lillo had the *misto*—mixed—fried fish platter. It was a combination of several varieties of prawns and fish all lightly battered and fried. Of course, Lillo insisted I try some. Alessandra had only a salad. She said she had plenty to eat with the *antipasti*. Francesca had *gnocchi*—small potato dumplings—served in a spicy seafood red sauce. Marianna and Marco stopped by about halfway through dinner to say hello. They were meeting some friends for dinner at the same *ristorante*. We found out later that their level of table service paled in comparison to ours.

After our entrees we all had *caffè*. I thanked the maestro for the incredible food and the absolutely brilliant service, *"Signore, grazie tanto! Buonissimo! Davvero, buonissimo!"* Alessandra filled in the gaps for me. The *maestro* and our waiters smiled widely and thanked us for allowing them the opportunity to serve us. For a brief moment I felt a little guilty at having taken advantage of my position as *una persona molto importante dall'America*, but as I looked at the overjoyed faces of my dining companions and servers, I abandoned all shame. *"Eh."* What could I do?

"Ciao, ciao."

"Grazie, ciao, ciao, ciao."

"Ciao e buonasera."

"Buonasera, ciao, ciao, ciao."

"Ciao, ciao."

"Buonasera. Arrivederci, ciao!" The *maestro*, still smiling, wished me well as I left.

We weren't finished eating quite yet. I think you can guess where we were headed next. Otello's did serve gelato, but few Italians ever order gelato at a *ristorante*. The best gelato can be found at only one place: *la gelateria*. There are as many *gelaterie* in every town, regardless of size, as there are Starbucks in Seattle. We passed three *gelaterie* before Lillo rounded the corner and stepped into the small but bustling fourth one—everyone has his favorite. While we were waiting to get our gelato I told Lillo that I was going to get *grasso*—fat—from eating so much gelato. Lillo looked at me and with a completely straight face said, *"Marco, non c'è problema. Il gelato è liquido!"* We all laughed when we heard Lillo's theory. His reasoning seemed scientific: why worry about getting fat from gelato? Gelato was just frozen liquid. Water is liquid. Water isn't fattening. So, liquid isn't fattening. Therefore, gelato isn't fattening. Right? Perfect! With our now newly reasoned fat-free gelatos in hand we were out on the street to take our after-dinner *passeggiata*.

Marta is a quaint and beautiful town. Each church had its opened doors draped with white and gold banners in celebration of the town festival. We poked our heads in several as we worked our way up through the ancient village to the large hilltop clock tower. It was now evening and the tower was well lit but surrounded by a construction fence and a sign warning not to trespass. It was slated to undergo renovation in the near future. The clock was no longer working and several stones from the top had fallen off. It was a simple circular stone tower crowned with parapets. Looking up at the tower instantly took me back in time. At any moment I expected archers to peer over the parapets and scare these strangely dressed intruders away. Or maybe a beautiful princess locked high in the tower by her jealous father would look down and beg us to rescue her. Everything in Italy seems romantic. My moment of imagined time travel passed, and we walked back down through the narrow streets toward the spacious boardwalk.

The evening *passeggiata* in Italy is truly an art form. I have no doubt that it has been perfected over hundreds of years. Regardless of where you go in the country you will see the same sight: women walking arm in arm and men walking with their hands clasped behind their backs. Tonight's *passeggiata* on Marta's lakefront boardwalk was no different. Lillo walked beside me, his hands clasped behind his back and a sweater tied around his neck. Strolling behind us, Alessandra and Francesca were arm in arm, whispering, giggling and occasionally stopping to look at a vendor's wares. Lillo stopped to point out the *fuochi artificiali*—fireworks—on the other side of the lake over the town of Bolsena. Tonight was their town celebration in honor of Saint

Stefano. I looked around and soaked in the sights, sounds and smells of the night. Amongst all of the chaos of a town festival there is a peace and grace about the evening *passeggiata*.

Before getting into the car, we stopped to listen to the band, still playing songs from the 1930s, '40s and '50s, hours after we first passed them. There were many couples dancing—most were *nonne e nonni*. We all piled into the car and drove back to the house chatting and laughing. It was now 12:30 a.m., and Francesca had to call her sister—technically, it was now Marianna's birthday. When she answered, Francesca cued our international chorus into a rousing, bilingual version of "Happy Birthday."

It was another perfect evening in Italy. Perfect weather, dinner, gelato, *passeggiata*, fireworks, music and companionship, all found in a beautiful lakefront village where time, like the old clock tower, had stopped. What could be better? Nothing.

Tonight I experienced *la dolce vita*.

Pollo al Pomodoro e Olive

Chicken with Tomato and Olives

I could eat this dish once a week for the rest of my life and never tire of it. Sadly, Nonna only made this once while I was in Viterbo. This is a simple, country dish and reminds me of Tuscany. Nonna cuts her chicken into small pieces—it is only 10 but in her pan it looks more like 14 since they are so small. You may cut yours to any size you desire.

1 (4 pound) chicken, cut into 8 or 10 pieces (cut into 10 by dividing the
  breast into quarters)
Salt and freshly ground black pepper to season the chicken.
2 tablespoons extra virgin olive oil

1 cup dry white wine

2 large cloves garlic, minced

¾ cup strained tomatoes, such as Pomi brand ★

1½ cups (5 ounces) whole green olives, pitted

¼ teaspoon salt, or more to taste

¼ teaspoon freshly ground black pepper, or more to taste

Dry the chicken pieces with paper towels to remove any excess moisture and liberally season with salt and pepper on both sides. Heat the oil in a large skillet on medium heat, and when the oil is hot, add the chicken pieces, skin side down and fry until nicely browned, turning to brown both sides, 3 to 5 minutes on each side.

When the chicken has browned, transfer to a plate and set aside. Add the white wine and garlic to the pan, scraping the brown bits off the bottom of the pan. After the wine has reduced by half, about 3 minutes, add the strained tomatoes, olives, salt and pepper. Stir until combined. Return the chicken to the skillet with its juices. Cover, turn the heat down to low and simmer for 20 minutes. Remove the cover and cook another 10 minutes, until the chicken is done and the sauce has thickened slightly.

Remove the chicken to a warmed platter. Adjust the seasoning of the sauce with salt and pepper, and pour the sauce and olives over the chicken. Serve hot.

Serves 6.

★Note: Strained tomatoes can be readily found in most supermarkets in either the canned tomato or pasta aisles. Sometimes the product may be referred to by its Italian name "passato" and can be found either bottled or cartoned, as is the case with the Pomi brand.

DAY EIGHT (Il Giorno Otto)

Today is Marianna's birthday.

When I woke up this morning I wasn't quite sure what we were going to make for the party. From what I understood there were going to be about ten people over for Marianna's birthday lunch. It seemed that we should be cooking all morning to feed a party of ten. As it turned out, Nonna and I prepared only three things for Marianna's birthday lunch: a rice and vegetable salad with tuna, a pork roast and a savory version of the *rotolo*.

First up was *l'insalata di riso*—rice salad. It was white rice and canned tuna in olive oil mixed with *giardinera*—pickled vegetables. In the pickle section of the grocery here, and in America, there are jars of pickled mixed vegetables. This pickled vegetable medley can be a varied combination, although usually it consists of cauliflower, banana peppers, red peppers, carrots, celery and green olives. Some other combinations include cucumbers, zucchini, green beans, eggplant and pearl onions. Until today I had never known what *giardinera* was used for. We drained the tuna and *giardinera* before adding them to the rice. Nonna also added extra virgin olive oil, salt and pepper. I mixed it up and into the *frigo* it went. (One of the few prepared dishes that went into the *frigo*, but this time it was more about chilling the salad than preventing it from spoiling.)

Next Nonna set to work on the pork roast. Yesterday at the store, Nonna had purchased thinly sliced pieces of lard that had been cured with crushed black pepper around the outside. It looked like thinly sliced strips of bacon, but with no meat—it was just the fat. It was sliced so thin that you could almost see through it. We put a couple pieces of the peppered lard in a pan with the pork roast, rosemary, sage and sliced onion. Nonna added water a little more than halfway up the roast. After bringing it to a boil she covered it and lowered the heat to let it braise. An hour into the braising she added white wine, butter, mixed in some flour, covered the pot and cooked it on low for about another hour.

The savory *rotolo* was made with chicory. We started by making a savory *pasta*—dough. It was similar to the strudel *pasta* except there was no *grappa* added this time. Nonna sautéed onions, garlic and chicory (a bitter leafy green) in some sunflower oil and lard. She sprinkled in some pepper sauce. Italians like their bitter greens *piccante*. By now the *pasta* had rested enough to be rolled out. I hauled out the pasta board and pins from the pantry. Nonna said I looked like a giant emerging through the doorway. I felt like one, too. She made me roll out the *pasta*, giving me guidance and tips on how best to do it. We spread the cooled chicory mixture across the sheet of *pasta*, then she sprinkled a layer of grated Parmigiano-Reggiano cheese on top of the chicory. Once rolled like the strudel, it baked in the oven.

The first guests to arrive for the party were Marco's parents, Anna and Giulio. They are a rather short and round couple. He was olive-skinned, bald with a black strip of hair running from ear to ear across the back of his head, and a rounded stomach that pushed his beltline out. Anna had already declared *nonna* status. Her hair was cut short and, although she did not have eyeglasses, she was wearing a simple housedress covered by a tasteful cardigan sweater and the standard issue comfortable shoes. She could have been on a pasta sauce label. They were not any older than Alessandra and Lillo but they were much more working class in dress. They are very nice people and speak no English.

Nonna and I greeted Anna and Giulio. Alessandra was upstairs getting dressed and everyone else was out of the house. Nonna did the obligatory introductions. I put my five-day-old Italian to the test and successfully greeted them both.

Nonna offered them a seat at the kitchen table and we all sat. There was a brief pause as we all silently stared and smiled at each other. I knew that our guests did not speak any English, and they seemed quite terrified of this fact. Anna had such a perplexed look on her face. It was a mixture of fear and complete lack of knowing what to do or say next. I thought to myself, "If I were to say one word to her right now she would burst into tears." I think I am the first American she had ever encountered, so I tried my best to ease the tension.

"*Allora, fa bel tempo oggi,*" I said, figuring that it is always good to start with the weather.

"*Si, si, si. È bello,*" said Giulio.

"*Si, si. Fa fresco,*" said Nonna, chiming in.

Anna just smiled and shifted her eyes to each of us as we spoke.

Silenzio.

"*Giulio, che cosa fa?*" With the weather out of the way, the only thing I could think to do was ask about his job.

"*Lavoro all'uffico postale.*"

"*Bene. Le piace il suo lavoro?*" I found myself asking him questions from the situations presented in my language book. I had started with polite greetings at the door. I mentioned the weather. I asked him what his job was. Now I was asking if he liked his job at the post office. Soon, I would run out of things to say.

"*Si, si. È cosi, cosi,*" he said.

Nonna just politely smiled. I glared at her—"Hey, Nonna. Help me out here!" She grinned a bit more at my glare.

Silenzio.

"*Allora....*" I could only think to say, "So...." My table companions smiled.

Silenzio.

"*Allora, Anna....*" She jumped a little when I mentioned her name. I had startled her. I unknowingly placed her in the glaring conversational spotlight. "*Che cosa fa?*"

"*A CASA,*" she replied, loudly and more quickly than needed.

"*Buono,*" I said.

Silenzio.

Nonna thought she would help by encouraging me to explain to Anna and Giulio what my job was and where I was from in America. I tried to explain all of this in Italian and they looked at me like confused dogs. Nonna tried to help me at one point but that only made matters worse. Now we all looked like confused dogs—our heads were cocked to the side trying to figure out what in the world anyone was talking about.

I wanted to say that I felt like a dog (confused, with my head cocked) but I couldn't remember the verb "to feel." And, in trying so hard to think of the verb "to feel," I blurted out, "*Sono un carne.*" —"I am a meat."

Ugh!

I misspoke and used the word *carne*—meat—instead of the word for dog—*cane*. Even Nonna couldn't figure out what I meant. Meat. I can't believe I actually said, "I am **a meat**." I am the village idiot.

Silenzio.

Luckily, the heavens opened and Alessandra came downstairs. Almost simultaneously, Marianna and Marco walked in. In a flash we were all standing and the Italians were off in conversation. Anna finally relaxed and truly smiled. Lillo, Francesca and Stefano all arrived in the next five minutes. We all went into the living room and watched Marianna open her presents. Mine was the last gift. She was a little dismayed that I had bought her something. I had only been here a week, and it took her by surprise that I would give her a gift. I tried to explain that it was just a little something for her birthday and housewarming. Alessandra translated for me. I am sure in trying to explain "housewarming" I would have said that we were all on fire or something equally moronic. Marianna opened her gift and loved the platter. She ran over and hugged me. I scored some points. In fact, I really think I scored more points with Anna at that moment. She looked at me and nodded her head in complete approval. For being a self-proclaimed "meat," sometimes the village idiot gets it right.

Nonna announced that lunch was ready, and we all moved into the dining room. This is the first time we had eaten at the dining room table since my arrival. This is where Alessandra and I have language class. Usually we have all of our language materials spread out over the table. This afternoon the table was draped in a pleasant tablecloth and set with nicer dishes and glasses—it was a party. We all took our seats around the table. I had Anna on my left and Alessandra on my right. Alessandra is always great about sitting next to me. This allows her to discreetly lean in to me and translate what is being said without overpowering the actual table conversation. She is always asking me questions about the topic at hand and translating my response back into the conversation. Of course, being my teacher, she expects me to speak in Italian as much as possible. If I answer a question in English when she thinks I should be able to say it in Italian she will look at me and say, *"In Italiano, per favore."* I tried to ease Anna's anxiety about being seated next to the American. I tried to charm and downright flirt with her all the way through dinner. I made sure in this "male first society" around the table that I always held the serving platter so she could serve herself before I took my portion. Her water and wine glasses never went half empty before I was refilling and asking, *"Ancore, Anna?"* For Anna, thanks to me, only the service at Otello could have better. I tried my best to make her the center of my attention. Anna was seated next to her own personal American ambassador.

I really enjoyed *l'insalata di riso*. I have never had anything like it before. The pork roast was thinly sliced and drizzled with the cooking liquid and was served as the second course. In America we would have placed both of these dishes on the same plate. I am enjoying the Italian way of separating things into individual courses. The fruit course included *ananas, melone* and *melone giallo*—an oblong shaped melon with a very textured, yellow-orange colored rind. Inside, the white/light green flesh has a similar, but milder, flavor to that of a cantaloupe. Plates were cleared and it was time for the *torta*.

Secretly, during the course of lunch, Nonna had plated and prepped the *torta*, so when she entered the dining room carrying it ablaze with 25 candles the table burst into song—*"Tanti auguri a te. Tanti auguri a te...."* Here at this very Italian table in Viterbo, "Happy Birthday" was the same as in America—the exact melody and words, except in Italian. Marianna closed her eyes, made a wish and blew out the candles, followed by rousing applause, *"Brava! Brava!"* and *"Salute!"*

The *torta* was light, lemony and slightly sweet. The room grew quiet as we ate. With every bite I savored the special tradition of this *torta*. Anna commented on how wonderful it was and asked Nonna what was in it. Nonna caught my eye and grinned before she answered Anna. I listened closely to hear what Nonna would say.

"Un po' di questo e un po' di quello." —"A little of this and a little of that."

Nonna politely did not divulge one thing about the *torta*. She would answer all of Anna's questions in a roundabout way; "Yes, the lemon is a refreshing flavor in this torte," or "I enjoy the texture of the crust, too." She never said, "Oh, I couldn't possibly tell you what is in this." When Anna asked if she could have the recipe Nonna politely said, *"Certamente,"* all the while knowing full well that she would consciously forget and never get around to giving it out. The recipe was still safe. Nonna was good under pressure.

After being served *caffè*, *arancello* and *grappa*, there was the usual *"Ciao, ciao, ciao"* contest at the door with many hugs and kisses. Anna and Giulio actually hugged me and kissed both cheeks as they made their exit. I may not have achieved world peace but I certainly felt proud about putting them at ease. Marco, Marianna, Francesca and Stefano loaded Marianna's birthday presents into the car and went off to the apartment to get ready for the housewarming party. Nonna, Tequila and Brighitta headed upstairs for an afternoon siesta. I was about to head upstairs myself when Alessandra announced that she and Lillo wanted to take me to see a "most special villa." She said that they had gotten the idea to take me to this villa earlier in the week when I was showing them photos of my house and rose parterre.

"Marco, I know you will enjoy this," Alessandra said. I have yet to be disappointed by anything here in Viterbo.

The "most special villa" was the Villa Lante located in Bagnaia, the same small town where we had experienced the karaoke and photo exhibit. When we arrived in Bagnaia's main *piazza* we made a sharp right and headed up a narrow cobblestone street toward the top of the hill that overlooked Bagnaia. The Villa Lante is located at the end of the street about halfway up the hill; an ancient stucco property wall protects the view of the villa. We walked around the wall to a side entrance where we purchased our tickets and entered through an iron gate. What I saw took my breath away—ascending, terraced formal gardens of manicured boxwoods forming geometric-patterned hedges, water features with fountains ranging from a single spout to long cascading streams, falls and pools, and statuary in animal, human and mythic forms. There is not a "villa" here per se, but two *casini*—small houses. A different cardinal built each *casino*. In 1566, Cardinal Gambara commissioned the construction of Villa Lante. The first *casino* and the upper garden were completed before his death in 1587. Later, seventeen-year-old Cardinal Alessandro Peretti di Montalto added the second *casino* and had the other gardens and water features completed. The water features are as impressive as those of the Villa d'Este in Tivoli, but on a smaller scale.

The first section of the villa complex contains the *casini* and the lowest parterre of formal hedges, urns, statuary and the grand *Fontana dei Mori*—Fountain of the Moors. This fountain's centerpiece is two pairs of classically muscled and nude bronze Moors. Two bronze lions sit between the back-to-back standing Moors, whose arms reach toward the center to hold high the Montalto family crest of five hills, which itself is topped by a multi-pointed star spouting water from each tip. In the center of each water-filled quadrant around the centerpiece, a lone water-spouting figure stands in a ship. These pools are surrounded by the large carved urns, acorns and balustrades, which are bordered by the neatly trimmed and shaped boxwood hedges.

The gardens and two additional large water features climb up the hillside to culminate at the upper garden. This garden contains a large grotto fountain flanked by a set of open-air, stone-columned *casini*. These *casini*, more like loggias, would be a romantic place to have an outside dinner party. I have no doubt that the cardinals did.

Walking with Alessandra and Lillo through the grounds, I could not stop exclaiming, *"Stupefacente!"* —"Amazing!"— It truly was. Every step up the hillside through each new garden, past fountains of river gods and sea monsters, brought a new and more glorious view. Standing in the main *piazza* of Bagnaia earlier in the week listening to karaoke I would never have imagined that this hidden gem of a villa was just a cobblestone street away. We spent several hours at the villa before driving back down to the main *piazza*. Alessandra announced that she had to have a gelato. How could I argue? It was another chance to put Lillo's *"Il gelato è liquido!"* theory to the test. *Mi piace gelato, molto!*

The *piazza* and *gelateria* were calm this late Sunday afternoon; only a couple of tables had customers. It was nice to sit outside and actually see the *piazza* with its surrounding buildings; among them were two churches and a large clock tower. Bagnaia's clock tower was very similar to Marta's. When I mentioned this to Alessandra, she told me the brief history of the Bagnaia tower. At some point during the 14th century the small town of Bagnaia was under attack by an invading army. Bagnaia's citizens were inside the tower fighting back the invaders. Legend has it that from the top of this tower a fourteen-year-old girl dropped a rock on the head of the invading army's commander—killing him and thus saving the town. I looked at Alessandra and said, *"Ehhhh,"* echoing her scolding of Lillo's exaggerations. Lillo nudged me and winked. She said I could disbelieve her, but there was a plaque mounted on a stone at the base of the tower marking this event. I took her word for it and did not walk across the *piazza* to investigate, thinking, "Why worry about the validity of a legend?" It was far more enjoyable to sit there imagining whom I might like to drop a rock on. We sat there eating our gelatos in blissful silence as the setting sun behind the clock tower gave it an angelic glow.

On the way home we stopped by Marco and Marianna's new apartment. Lillo had not seen it yet and Marianna wanted me to drop in as well. They live in a very new apartment complex located on the northern side of Viterbo. Marianna buzzed us in and we rode the elevator up to the seventh floor. We walked in to discover that, besides Francesca and Stefano, Jimmy and Nicola were also there. Since Nonna wasn't with us I looked at Alessandra and under my breath whispered, *"Francia, Francia, Francia,"* to which she replied, *"Povero Jimmy."* Lillo heard us and grinned.

I spoke with Jimmy because, as usual, he wanted to practice his English. He cornered me on the balcony while I was enjoying the views of Viterbo and the distant mountains. The apartment was very contemporary and Marianna was proud of her decorating. She rescued me from Jimmy to make sure I saw the prominent placement of my gift on their dining table. It actually fit their décor—I was pleased. I thought the entire family had been invited to the housewarming party tonight, but it was for friends only—we stayed long enough to give our approval without overstaying our welcome.

We got back to the house to find that Nonna had put together a buffet of prosciutto, salami, four kinds of cheese (asiago, provolone, gorgonzola, pecorino) and the chicory *rotolo* sliced into rounds. Today was so busy I forgot that we made, but hadn't eaten, the *rotolo*. When I asked Nonna if we forgot to serve it at lunch she said, *"No, Marco, il rotolo era per la cena."* The last remaining portions of the birthday *torta* followed the usual *l'insalata* and *melone*. We finished the evening with *caffè* and *arancello d'Alessandra*.

This has been a memorable day full of delicious wine and food, beautiful gardens and fountains, *torta* and gelato, and much attempted conversation, laughter and cocked heads.

～⊸〰⊸～

Rotolo di Verdura

Chicory Roll

*Whether it is sautéed spicy greens rolled in dough, as in this dish, meat rolled around vegetables—*involtini, *crepes filled with savory or sweet foods—*crespelle, *or a large turkey cutlet spread with a meatball mixture and lined with hardboiled eggs down the center, Italians love to roll up their food! Once sliced, these rolled dishes become pieces of culinary mosaic tile on the plate. One only has to look at the swirling greens within the slices of this* rotolo *and then look at a tiny tile mosaic of greenery on an altar in Saint Peter's to see the resemblance.*

Dough (*Pasta*):

3 cups all-purpose flour, plus additional flour for kneading and rolling out the dough

1 packet active dry yeast (instant rise)

1 teaspoon salt

3 tablespoons extra virgin olive oil

1 cup lukewarm water (follow temperature guidelines on yeast packet)

In a large bowl, mix flour, yeast and salt until combined. Add oil and water, mixing with a fork until well combined and a soft *pasta* is formed. Turn the *pasta* out onto a lightly floured surface and knead (adding a little flour if the dough is too wet or sticky) for 5 to 8 minutes, until it is smooth and elastic. Form the *pasta* into a ball, place on a floured surface and invert a medium-size bowl over the *pasta* ball. Let it rest and rise while the filling is prepared.

Chicory Filling:

1 tablespoon sunflower oil (extra virgin olive oil may be substituted)

1 small-medium onion, finely minced

2 large cloves garlic, finely minced

1 tablespoon pork lard (extra virgin olive oil may be substituted)

1¼ - 1½ pounds chicory or other bitter leafy green (escarole, chard, arugula), washed and cut into 1-inch pieces

1 teaspoon salt, or more to taste

½ teaspoon freshly ground black pepper, or more to taste

1 teaspoon pepper sauce (tabasco peppers in vinegar), or more to taste

1 cup grated Parmigiano-Reggiano cheese

Additional extra virgin olive oil to drizzle, 1 to 2 tablespoons (Nonna used extra virgin olive oil, not sunflower oil, for this.)

Preheat oven to 350 degrees.

Heat the sunflower oil in a medium pan over medium heat. When the oil is hot, add the onion and sauté until it is soft and starts to turn golden, 2 to 3 minutes. Add the lard and garlic, stirring until the lard dissolves and the garlic starts to turn golden, 1 to 2 minutes. Add the chicory (in batches, if necessary), salt and pepper, sautéing until the chicory is wilted, the stems are tender and, most importantly, the excess water is cooked off, 8 to 10 minutes. Stir in the pepper sauce and cook for one minute. Remove pan from the heat, adjust the seasoning with salt, pepper, and additional pepper sauce to taste, set aside to cool.

Uncover the *pasta* and place on a lightly floured surface, rolling it out into an 18-inch by 14-inch rectangle. Spread the chicory mixture across the *pasta* to within an inch of the edges. Evenly distribute the Parmigiano-Reggiano on top of the chicory, and drizzle the extra virgin olive oil over the cheese. Starting at a long side, roll toward the opposite long side. Brush the seam edge with a little water before the final roll. Pinch the ends closed and tuck under. Place the roll, seam-side down, on a parchment-lined cookie sheet, curving the roll into a half moon to make it fit on the sheet; brush the surface of the roll with the remaining 1 teaspoon olive oil. Loosely cover with plastic wrap and set in a warm place to rest and rise for 30 minutes.

Remove the plastic wrap and bake for 34 to 38 minutes, until golden and the surface is hard when tapped on. When done, remove from the baking sheet and place on a wire rack to cool. After it has cooled completely, slice into 1-inch rounds and serve at room temperature.

Makes 18 rounds.

This is dish is perfect for a Sunday lunch buffet, and I have even served this as an appetizer at an Easter luncheon. It makes a beautiful presentation and is a welcome change of pace when placed amongst the usual family-function buffet suspects of dips and spreads.

IL GIORNO NOVE (Day Nine)

Today begins my second week in Viterbo. Last week held such a wide variety of experiences that I cannot imagine what this week will hold.

Every morning when I'd first come downstairs, Alessandra would ask, *"Hai dormito bene, Marco?"* —"Did you sleep well, Mark?" The first couple of days my answer was always, "What?" and she would slowly repeat the question. Slowly it would dawn on me what she was asking and I would answer, *"Si, si."* This morning was a momentous occasion—I was able to answer with a complete sentence...

"Si, si, Alessandra. Ho dormito bene, grazie. E tu?"

"Bene, grazie," Alessandra said.

"Bravo, Marco. Bravo!" Nonna piped in, as she put water on to boil for my tea.

Tequila and Brighitta greeted me as usual and I took their wagging tails as proud approval.

I have only talked about two of the Stefanis' four dogs: Tequila and Brighitta—they rule the roost and are always underfoot. I don't have much contact with the other two dogs; they are a pair of white, two-year-old male West Highland Terrier littermates born to Brighitta. Their names are Crazy and Cochise, and they are wild! No longer allowed the run of the house—due to their horrible habit of marking their territory on every piece of furniture—they have been relegated to spending their days in a large backyard pen and their evenings in the spacious first floor bathroom. Twice daily they are herded between the bathroom and the outside pen. If the journey is not a direct line, the brothers will hike their legs on anything and anyone in the house—the instant Crazy marks something Cochise is right behind him re-marking it, then Crazy re-marks it, then Cochise, then Crazy, and so on. If not carefully supervised, it can instantly turn into a pee-fest with Nonna chasing the pair around the living room and kitchen yelling their names. I was even peed on while standing at the kitchen counter. I never call them by name because I cannot tell them apart, and quite frankly, after being marked in the kitchen, well ... *"Mamma mia!"*

Some people would be concerned to be in a house with four dogs, especially after being urinated on, but it is the lack of cats that concerns me most.

Nonna is always making *zuppa di gatti*—cat soup. Let me clarify by saying that Nonna has not been serving anything made from cat. I may eat a pig's foot from a gold-foiled bag, but so far nothing feline has appeared on my plate. There are no cats at the house, just the four dogs, so what is cat soup? *Zuppa di gatti* has been confusing me since day one.

A little saucepan sits on the back right-hand burner of the stovetop, and during the course of the day, Nonna tosses in odd scraps of food and liquid. Sometimes it is a small piece of leftover cheese or fat she has trimmed from meat—into the pan it goes. She will add water, broth, the last sip from a wine bottle or olive oil poured off of canned tuna. I have seen her throw in a piece of *frittata* that someone did not finish eating. One morning, in went half a handful of uncooked pasta from the bottom of a package; it is always a strange and odd collection of food remnants. When the saucepan becomes full she pours this concoction into a glass jar that sits next to the stovetop. She then starts the entire process over again as more random food scraps become available. The first day I thought that maybe she was making something for Lillo to take to work for lunch, but Lillo comes home for lunch. On the third day, when I watched her throw in large scraps of chicken fat and skin—and things I knew not even Lillo would eat—my curiosity got the better of me.

"Nonna, che cosa fai?" —"Nonna, what are you making?"

"Zuppa di gatti."

Her answer satisfied my curiosity that first time. The next morning I watched her again add stuff to the simmering pan, fill the jar with the cooked contents and cap the jar.

"Nonna, che cosa fai?"

"Zuppa di gatti, Marco."

"Nonna, dove sono i gatti?" —"Nonna, where are the cats?"

"Marco," Nonna said, laughing, and shrugged her shoulders.

Well … what kind of answer is that?

"Marco, what is the matter?" Alessandra said, walking by and noticing that I was staring dumbfounded at the jar on the counter.

"Nonna is always making *zuppa di gatti* but I haven't seen a cat anywhere around here."

"Oh," she said and laughed. Nonna joined in laughing, too.

Honestly… "Oh." Is that an answer?

I am bound and determined to figure out who eats this *zuppa di gatti*. I never see anyone take the jar away or bring it back. One minute it is there, and mysteriously, the next it is gone. Also, it is never the same jar—sometimes a quart-sized glass jar gets filled; at other times, it is only a pint jar. Whatever the size, it is always a lidded glass jar filled with the most unappetizing combination of food scraps.

I caught Nonna filling a jar this morning, so I pressed the point even farther.

"*Nonna, che cosa fai?*"

"*Zuppa di gatti, Marco.*"

"*Dunque, dove sono i gatti?*"

Nonna and Alessandra laughed.

"*No, sul serio, dove sono i gatti? DOVE? Avete quattro cani ma dove sono i gatti?*" —"No, seriously, where are the cats? WHERE? You have four dogs but where are the cats?"

Again, they laughed at me, shrugged their shoulders and went about their business.

Nonna and I made *ciambelline*, small ring-shaped cookies made with red wine; she said you could also make them with white wine, *grappa* or *limoncello*. Much like an Oreo cookie with a glass of milk in America, *ciambelline* are dipped into a glass of wine or cup of espresso. They are dry cookies similar to biscotti, but technically they are not biscotti because they are only baked once. The word *biscotti* means twice (*bis*) cooked (*cotti*). I enjoyed the *ciambelline* because, like most Italian desserts, they were not very sweet. I dipped mine into a glass of red wine after lunch.

Anna stopped by while we were cooking and was very talkative—even speaking directly to me. She brought a huge basket of fresh tomatoes from her garden as a thank-you for being invited to Marianna's birthday party. They weren't the most attractive looking tomatoes—oblong and twisted, with rough, splotchy green/red colored skin, they were very different from any variety of tomato I had ever seen. At first glance I thought Anna had brought us a basket of ripening peppers. It was only after I picked one up and smelled it that I realized it was a tomato. Now I understand why tomatoes were considered poisonous in the mid-1500s when first brought to Italy from South America. Eventually, tomatoes were referred to as "love apples," forever casting aside their previously poisonous status. I cannot imagine Italian cuisine without the tomato nor believe that the tomato was not indigenous to Italy. Anna's tomatoes certainly looked more sinister than the jolly, smooth-skinned round variety stacked in Alabama supermarkets. Sinister or not, there was a mysterious beauty about their rustic, ancient appearance.

The three ladies spoke quickly back and forth—I understood nothing. Their conversation was too fast and full of unrecognizable words for me to decipher this early in the day.

"Ciao, ciao, ciao."

"Ciao, ciao, ciao, ciao."

"Ciao, ciao, ciao, ciao, ciao…" and Anna was out the door.

"Marco, you made quite an impression on Anna. She told me that you were very nice and that she really enjoyed sitting next to you at lunch yesterday. She has invited us over to their house for pizza while you are here in Viterbo," Alessandra said. When Nonna heard the word "pizza" she added that Anna and Guilio have a wood-burning oven in their garage and Anna makes really good pizza. With Nonna's stamp of approval, how could I refuse?

Nonna decided that we would use Anna's tomatoes for lunch today. She pulled out a food mill and we started turning the sinister beauties into a sauce. When cut open, the tomatoes had almost no liquid and very few seeds; they were all flesh. I was concerned that they wouldn't make a very juicy *sugo*. Nonna cut each tomato into quarters, put them in the food mill and I turned the crank to crush them—to my surprise, the sauce was thick and juicy. (In case you didn't know, a food mill presses the tomato flesh through a sieve, keeping the seeds and skin from getting into the *sugo*.) This was my first time using a food mill, and I really liked that we were not using an electric machine to process these tomatoes. It reminded me of how my great-grandmother cooked. She never used an electric appliance, not even an electric can opener. Being in her kitchen as a child and watching her prepare everything by hand—knowing that it was her way of expressing her love for me—made a lasting impression on me and was most responsible for creating my love of cooking now. Nonna's cooking makes me feel the same way because she embraces her family with every dish she prepares—even with the *zuppa di gatti*, if I can ever figure out whom she is embracing with that!

Nonna came in from the backyard with a handful of fresh basil, and instantly the kitchen was scented with a mixture of freshly milled tomatoes and basil—a heavenly perfume! She did not cook this *sugo*; she left it raw and added salt, pepper, the basil leaves torn into pieces and some extra virgin olive oil. *"Finito!"* she said. The hot cooked pasta (bow tie) was stirred into the bowl of *sugo crudo* and it went immediately to the table. We topped our individual servings with freshly grated Parmigiano-Reggiano and local pecorino cheeses.

Breaded and pan-fried pork cutlets, drizzled with freshly squeezed lemon juice followed the pasta course. The cutlets—*le cotolette*—were not prepared until after we had finished eating the pasta. This is important because the cutlets come to the table hot, crispy and lemony. If they had been prepared before the pasta they would have been soggy by the time they were served. It only took Nonna and Alessandra ten minutes to prepare the cutlets. I am learning the importance of this type of preparation. First, the food always comes to the table hot and perfectly prepared. Second, it gives you some time between courses to digest your food, drink some wine and feel as if you have eaten a lot when actually, because the portions are smaller, you have eaten less than you would sitting at an American table. It ended up being a very simple lunch.

Dinner was simple, too. We made *crespelle*—crêpes—filled with a spinach and ricotta cheese mixture. When Nonna asked me how the *crespelle* tasted, I could not answer—words were not enough to express how good they were. I jumped up from my seat, kissed her on both cheeks and said, *"Brava, Nonna. Buonissimi!"* Nonna blushed. We all laughed and applauded. Lillo got a big kick out of seeing Nonna blush. I sat back down and unleashed my American appetite on the *crespelle*. I ate too many—an embarrassing amount by Italian standards, I am sure, but they were just too good to stop at a polite amount. This was the first time I sat at the table and really ate until I could eat no more—and then more was served. The meal was rounded out by more of the pork cutlets (prepared as at lunch), the usual salad, melon and another red wine. We have yet to repeat the same wine. I really should have been writing down each and every wine we have had, but I forgot to start a list on day one and I have given up on trying to reconstruct it at this point. *Mi dispiace molto!*

For dessert, we had tiramisù that was leftover from Marianna's housewarming party. Marianna's friend, Silvia, made a huge pan of this famous Italian dessert. It was good, but Nonna said hers was better and Alessandra agreed. Last week, my mother e-mailed me a tiramisù recipe she found in her local newspaper. Tiramisù is her favorite dessert and she could not get enough of it when we were in Italy in 2001. She wanted me to ask Nonna and Alessandra if the newspaper recipe was similar to how they make it. Tonight, while we were having the Nonna vs. Silvia's tiramisù debate, I read the recipe to them. Their faces started to scrunch up as if they smelled something bad. The more I read—the worse the stench.

"Va bene?" —"Is it good?"— I asked.

"No!" was their singular and unison reply.

With that, tiramisù was added to the ever-growing list of things to make before I leave. I am not sure if it was added to teach me how to make it or to give Nonna the opportunity to prove that hers was better than Silvia's. Either way, hooray for me!

Biscotti "Ciambelline"

Ring Cookies

In America, we have a tradition of dunking round pastries into our drinks—there is the cliché of policemen dunking donuts into coffee instead of patrolling the streets. And what could be more American than dunking chocolate chip cookies into a large glass of cold milk? But we don't have a tradition of dunking round cookies into our after-dinner drinks or into a glass of wine as a mid-day snack. Pity. The Italians do and here is a classic.

¾ cup sugar

¾ cup white or red wine

½ cup sunflower oil (vegetable oil may be substituted)

¼ cup extra virgin olive oil

⅛ teaspoon salt

4 cups all-purpose flour, plus more for kneading

Preheat oven to 350 degrees. Line a baking sheet with parchment paper.

In a medium bowl, mix together sugar, wine, oils and salt, stirring until well combined. Stir in one cup of flour at a time, mixing well between each addition, until a soft *pasta* (dough) is formed.

Turn the *pasta* out onto a lightly floured surface and knead for 5 minutes (adding a little additional flour if the *pasta* is too sticky) until smooth. Break off a golf ball-size piece of the *pasta* and cover the remaining with plastic wrap to keep moist.

Place the piece of *pasta* on the board and, using both hands, gently roll the dough into a cigar-shape. Continue rolling your hands back and forth, and while rolling from the center out to the ends, spread you fingers apart to lightly stretch the dough into a longer and thinner piece. (This is the same process used to shape *gnocchi*.)

Continue rolling until the dough is between the diameter of a pencil and the thickness of your little finger. Cut into 3 ½-inch to 4-inch long pieces. Take each piece and make a small ring by overlapping the two ends and pushing the top end into the bottom end to seal. Place on the parchment lined baking sheet. Continue the process by breaking off another golf ball-size piece of *pasta*, rolling into a cigar-shape, etc.

Bake for 12 to 14 minutes until the bottoms are golden brown and the tops are firm. Remove *ciambelline* to a wire rack to cool.

Makes about 96.

While I was in Viterbo, we didn't always dunk these into wine or after-dinner drinks. Lillo liked to dip his into an espresso. I enjoyed them just as regular cookies; not as sweet as an American cookie, but still an enjoyable mid-afternoon nibble before language class.

IL GIORNO DIECI (Day Ten)

The temperature outside has been dropping over the past several days—
fantastico! Last night, I finally turned off my bedroom fan and slept in
silence. I do get fresh air—even if it is hot air—up in my room because
the five skylights are always kept open, unless it is raining. Sometimes I do miss
being able to see out of a window, but honestly, I am never up there during the
day except for my afternoon siesta, and, trust me, my eyes are shut then.

Today's lunch menu focused on dishes native to Palermo, Sicily, where
Nonna's husband was raised. She grew up on the opposite end of Italy in
the Veneto region of northern Italy. Because of this, she has a wide range of
recipes reflecting these two completely different regions and cooking styles.

Our Sicilian cooking class started with *caponata di melanzane*. A *caponata*
is similar to a relish or chutney and is usually eaten as a side dish. I have seen it
served as a topping for meat or on bread as a *bruschetta*, but today it was served
as the second course. Nonna's *caponata* is a combination of eggplant, olives,

celery, onions, tomatoes and vinegar—the key ingredient. Nonna makes her own vinegar and insists that it has to be *forte*—strong. When it was time to add the vinegar to the simmering vegetables she pulled from the cupboard a bottle containing a murky looking substance—a witch's potion. It was cloudy and had things floating in it. Perhaps "eye of newt" or "lizard's tongue." I had never heard of anyone making her own vinegar. I asked Nonna how it was done but got lost in her explanation, and Alessandra was not around to translate. *"Capito, Marco?"* Nonna said. I said, *"Si, si."* I really didn't understand, but I figured it might be for the best if I didn't know the intricacies of conjuring up a bottle of vinegar. Hers was definitely *forte* and had a bite—no doubt the lizard's tongue.

Next, we started preparing saffron infused *risotto* and a *ragù* with green peas to use as components in making *arancini*—fried rice balls stuffed with meat and cheese. The word for "orange" in Italian is *arancia*—therefore, *arancini* are little oranges. Their fried, golden color makes them reminiscent of oranges.

To assemble the *arancini* you take a small handful of the cooled, sticky risotto and shape it into a cup—a small bird's nest—in the palm of your hand. Next, cubes of mozzarella and a little of the *ragù* are placed into the cup, and the sides of the nest are carefully formed up around the filling so the *ragù* and cheese are enclosed in the newly formed ball. Once the *arancini* are rolled in bread crumbs, they are deep fat fried in sunflower oil until golden brown, removed, drained on paper towels and sprinkled with sea salt. It may sound like a lot of work, and maybe it is, but the results are well worth the effort. I have a feeling that this dish was created by a clever *nonna* who needed a tasty way to empty the fridge of leftover risotto, meat sauce and cheese—nothing can ever be wasted.

Nonna assembled the first one and I did the rest. She was impressed because I did not ruin any of them. She said a lot of students destroy the *arancini* during the closing process.

"Bravo, Marco. Bravo!" Apparently, I did it perfectly.

These *arancini* were large, about the size of a billiard ball. They needed to be more substantial than a little appetizer because the *caponata di melanzane* was a simple second course. Nonna said the *arancini* could be made smaller by reducing the amount of filling and could be made with only cheese in the center if you wanted something bite-sized.

It must seem that all I do here is eat, sleep and go out for gelato. Trust me, the language class is my workout for the day. It is hard, but I am learning a lot and enjoying it. There are definite stumbling blocks. Besides my confused and embarrassing use of the words *carne* and *cane*, there are other words that are jumbled in my head. In the hope of gaining your sympathy, I have grouped, by letter, the words that I am struggling with at the moment:

<u>The "M" group:</u>

"*miei*" (mee-ay-ee) is the masculine plural form of "my."

"*male*" (mah-lay) means "ill" or "evil" or "trouble."

"*mela*" (may-lah) means "apple."

"*mele*" (may-lay) means "apples."

"*miele*" (mee-ay-lay) means "honey."

"*maiale*" (mah-ee-ah-lay) means "pork."

<u>The "P" group:</u>

"*può*" (poo-OH) is "She/He/It can," or the formal "You can."

"*più*" (pee-you) means "more."

"*po'*" (poh) means "little."

"*puoi*" (poo-oh-yee) is the familiar "You can."

<u>The "V" group:</u>

"*venire*" (vay-neer-ay) is the verb for "to come or to arrive."

"*vedere*" (vay-dare-ay) is the verb for "to see or to look at."

"*vendere*" (ven-dare-ay) is the verb for "to sell."

<u>The "C" group:</u>

"*cavolo*" (cahv-o-low) means "cabbage."

"*cavallo*" (cah-VAHL-low) means "horse."

Imagine how easy it would be to say, *"Mi piace mangiare cavallo con miele"* —"I like to eat horse with honey,"— when you meant to say, *"Mi piace mangiare cavolo con maiale."* —"I like to eat cabbage with pork." Or instead of saying, *"Più mele, per favore"* —"More apples, please,"— you actually said, *"Più male, per favore."* —"More evil, please." That's a rough idea of what I face four hours a day, five days a week. *Mio Dio!*

While sitting around the table at dinner last night, talking about food, Nonna and Alessandra agreed that there wasn't enough time to teach me all the recipes on our ever-increasing list. I started thinking about canceling my previously planned trip to *Firenze*—Florence—the weekend after this one. Everyone was thrilled when I told them of my change of plans at lunch today. It sparked a new excitement in planning what to cook and which village festival to go to next. Lillo seems to be in the know about nearby festivals, and he said he would start researching as soon as he got back to work. Francesca said I was not allowed to go back home to Alabama until after Christmas, even suggesting that the next student coming here should go to Alabama instead. She decided that on the kitchen calendar she would scratch out *"agosto"*—August—and write in "Marco" to insure that I returned next year. Isn't it fun to be loved?!

Lillo asked if there were particular foods associated with where I grew up north of Chicago and with where I live now in Alabama. For Alabama, I told him that Coca-Cola and barbecue were a very popular classic combination. It took me a while to explain to Alessandra what barbecue was so she could accurately translate to Lillo. Lillo's eyes lit up. He said that there was something very similar to that here in Italy called *porchetta,* and in his nearby hometown of Blera there was a place that made his favorite. He told Nonna he'd bring some home for dinner tonight.

For as much as Lillo loves food and gets excited about every dish that Nonna puts in front of him, I never see him take an interest in the actual cooking of a meal. He never walks through the kitchen to lift a lid and see what is cooking and filling the house with such a wonderful *profumo—*

smell—and he never picks up a spoon to stir the pot. The girls have not bragged about a special dish that only their father makes, so he must not do that either. In my family, all the various male relatives have at least one dish that they alone cook and reign supreme. At Easter, after my brother and sisters and I had found all of the hidden hard-boiled eggs, my father would use them to make "creamed eggs on toast." It certainly wasn't a fancy dish, as the name implies, but there was something very special about it—the fact that it was the only dish my father cooked and we only ate it on Easter morning. The same holds true for my grandfather, who was the king of the Christmas turkey and stuffing. Long ago my grandmother had been banned from even lifting the foil on the cooking bird; he alone seasoned the stuffing with the precise amount of sage and was in charge of the bird from assembly to the last knife stroke when carving. His Christmas turkey was so prized in my family, becoming legend in the recent years since he passed away, that in order to avoid failing by harsh comparison, one of my uncles, early on, became the master of our family's Thanksgiving turkey by taking it in a completely different direction—he prepares his birds on the grill. For all of Lillo's interest in and love of food, I have yet to see him take the extra step to get personally involved with its preparation.

Nonna asked me what food was particular to Chicago. Besides pizza, I told her that sausages were very popular in my hometown, Johnsburg, north of Chicago. In the mid-1800s, German Catholic immigrants settled Johnsburg, so naturally sausages and bratwurst are very popular there. Nonna knows a butcher in Viterbo that makes wonderful sausages—those were added to the list of foods to taste before I leave. I cannot emphasize enough how much I enjoy that it is conversation that inspires the menu here. Talking about food turns into a wonderful food frenzy—one person's comments will inspire another's, and that sparks another and another. This creates anticipation and excitement about the dishes that are going to be prepared and eaten. Meals instantly have an importance and history particular to this moment in time. Joyous!

Dinner ended up being a little of this and that. Nonna made a *torta di formaggi*—egg and cheese pie— similar to a quiche. Lillo brought home some *porchetta*—slow-roasted pork shoulder—that was something like Southern barbecue, except it wasn't smoked and there was no sauce. The outside of the *porchetta* had a nice black pepper crust, but it certainly wasn't a secret fourteen-spice Southern BBQ rub. Still, it was very moist, tender and flavorful. Leftovers completed the meal: *arancini*, the extra *ragù* filling and the ricotta and spinach *crespelle*.

Francesca got a big thrill when Lillo walked in with a two-liter bottle of Coke. I have yet to see anyone drink soda here. I was a little dismayed when Francesca poured us all a glass of room temperature Coke and served it—with no ice. NO ICE! I quickly told them that in America it would be very odd, and almost criminal, to serve Coke this way. Coke had to be kept chilled in the *frigo*—refrigerator—and it must be served over *ghiaccio*—ice. Nonna hunched over and headed toward the pantry freezer and came out with ten ice cubes to use between the five of us. Italians don't use ice cubes. Ice cubes are not in drinks at restaurants or in bins in home freezers. With only a meager amount of ice in our glasses, everyone said the Coke did taste better cold, though it was more cool than cold. The bottle went into the *frigo*. We'll see what they think of it tomorrow after it has chilled.

For dessert tonight we finished off the *ciambelline* with *caffè* and *arancello*. I enjoyed dipping mine in the orange flavored liqueur, and I will certainly enjoy falling asleep the minute my head hits the pillow.

Arancini Siciliani

Sicilian Rice Balls

This is an easy dish, but it is an involved one—I will be right up front about it. The origin of this dish no doubt came from a frugal nonna's desire to use up leftover risotto and sauce to avoid any waste. If you find yourself with leftover sauce or risotto, then you will cut the prep time by half. You can also make the components of this dish on two separate days—in a sense, creating unused leftovers, which will help spread out the prep time. Or you can be daring and just go for it all at once!

For the rice:

6 cups canned, low-sodium chicken broth

¼ teaspoon saffron threads

4 tablespoons unsalted butter, divided

2 cups imported Arborio rice, or other rice specifically for risotto

½ cup grated Parmigiano-Reggiano cheese

Heat the broth in a medium saucepan over low heat. Once the chicken broth is warm, add the saffron threads, stirring to combine. Keep the broth warm over low heat while preparing the rice.

Melt 2 tablespoons butter in a medium skillet over medium heat. When the butter starts to foam, stir in the rice until it is coated with the butter, 1 to 2 minutes. Add a ½ cup of the simmering broth, stirring until the broth is almost completely absorbed. Add another ½ cup broth and continue cooking, stirring continuously, repeating the process of adding broth when it is almost absorbed. It should take 15 to 18 minutes to cook the risotto.

When the last addition of broth is almost absorbed, remove the risotto pan from the heat and stir in 2 tablespoons butter and the Parmigiano-Reggiano until well combined. Set pan aside to let the risotto cool while the filling is prepared.

For the ragù filling:

2 tablespoons extra virgin olive oil, divided

1 pound top round steak, cut into ½-inch cubes

1 teaspoon salt

½ teaspoon fresh ground black pepper

1 medium onion, finely minced

1 large clove garlic, finely minced

½ cup red or white wine (Nonna used leftover Spumanti)

1 (28-ounce) can whole peeled Italian tomatoes (preferably San Marzano
tomatoes), placed in a bowl and crushed by hand, reserving all of the
liquid

1 cup strained tomatoes, such as Pomi brand

1 cup frozen green peas

1 (8-ounce) ball of fresh mozzarella, cut into ¼-inch cubes

Heat oil in a medium skillet over medium heat. When the oil is hot, stir
in the cubed beef, salt and pepper. Cook until the beef is browned on all
sides, 3 to 5 minutes. With a slotted spoon, transfer the browned beef to a
plate and set aside.

Add 1 tablespoon oil to the hot skillet and stir in the onion and garlic,
cooking for 2 to 3 minutes until the onions are soft and golden. Stir in the
wine and reduce by half. Return the browned beef to the skillet, stirring
until well combined with the onion and wine mixture. Add the crushed
tomatoes with all their juices, strained tomatoes, salt and pepper, and stir
until the mixture starts to come to a boil. Reduce heat to low and simmer
for 25 to 30 minutes, stirring occasionally. Add the frozen peas at the end,
stirring until well combined. Remove skillet from heat and set aside to cool.

To assemble:

Place ⅓ cup of the cooled risotto into the palm of your hand. Form into a
cup or nest shape. In the center of the cup, place two cubes of mozzarella

and a teaspoon of the filling, making sure that there is a piece of meat and some peas in the teaspoon. Add one more mozzarella cube to the filling. Slowly form the cup over the filling into a ball, enclosing the filling inside the ball. Set aside while you prepare the rest of the rice into balls.

To fry:
1 cup water
½ cup all-purpose flour
1 cup plain dried bread crumbs, placed in a shallow dish
Oil to fry in (Nonna used sunflower oil. Vegetable or canola oil can be
   substituted.)
Salt to taste

In a small bowl, whisk together the water and flour until a thin batter is formed. Roll the *arancini* (rice balls) in the batter mixture to coat, then roll in the bread crumbs, covering completely and shaking off any excess bread crumbs. Set on a plate while the rest of the *arancini* are breaded.

Heat oil in a deep fat fryer. Once the oil is hot, fry the *arancini*, a couple at a time, until they are golden brown, 5 to 8 minutes. Remove from the oil, drain on paper towels and salt the *arancini* while still hot.

Makes 12-14 large *arancini*.

* Note: to make smaller arancini, *omit the tomato/beef filling, and take a heaping tablespoon of the risotto mixture, form into a cup, place 1 or two cubes of mozzarella into the cup, and close around the cheese. Bread the* arancini *as indicated in the recipe. They can be fried either in a pan like meatballs (see Meatball recipe, page 31) or in a deep fat fryer until golden brown.*

About the leftover filling and cheese: Arancini *were originally made from leftover risotto and ragù. When making this recipe there will be extra filling and mozzarella left over. Use the filling as the sauce for a baked pasta dish with mozzarella. Cook 1 pound* *of pasta (*ziti, penne *or* rigatoni*) and drain. Add it to the filling and mix until well combined. Butter and bread crumb a medium baking dish. Place a layer of the pasta mixture into the bottom of the dish. Top with half of the left over cubed mozzarella. Layer in the rest of the pasta mixture and top with the rest of the mozzarella and ½ cup of grated Parmigiano-Reggiano. Sprinkle the top with bread crumbs and dot with butter. Bake in a 350-degree oven for 30 minutes, until the top is golden and the pasta is bubbling.*

IL GIORNO UNDICI (Day Eleven)

T oday's cooking lesson was handmade pasta, *orecchiette*—little ears. Finally, on Day 11, we are making "pasta." Is Pavarotti singing in the background? Absolutely not! There was nothing cliché about today's lesson.

Pasta is named after the shape it resembles: *linguine* is named for its thin tongue—*lingua*—shape; *fettuccine* because it is a wider slice—*fetta*; *penne* resembles the point of a fountain pen; *farfalle* (known as bow tie pasta in America) is shaped like a butterfly—*farfalla*; *gemelli*—twins—is two pieces of identical pasta twisted around each other.

The pasta board and bag of rolling pins were both slung over *Babbo Natale*'s back as she emerged from behind the pantry curtain. The ear shape is achieved by rolling a piece of dough into a ½-inch thick rope about 18 inches long. The rope is cut into individual ½-inch pieces. Taking a knife with a serrated edge, Nonna dragged the knife-edge across the piece of dough with a fair amount of pressure, pulling the pasta into a flat disk shape leaving striations on the face of the disk. It doesn't resemble a human ear shape; the striations make it resemble the veining in a pig's ear. The striations are important because they help hold the sauce to the pasta. Nonna made the first four or five before I muscled my way in to try my knife dragging skills. It was not as easy as it looked. The first couple of times I pressed way too hard with the serrated edge and tore each piece into shreds. The next several ended up long and without striations because I did not use enough pressure. Nonna took the knife and said, *"Marco, guarda. Attento!"* I watched and paid attention. Again, I tried. Again, she showed me. Again, I watched.

Nonna refers to our hands as *"arnesi del Signore."*—"the tools of God." I just might need some divine intervention when it comes to *orecchiette*. Slowly, I learned the technique. The best way to learn how to cook is by rolling up your sleeves and getting your hands in it. That is particularly true with pasta making. You must sense the texture of the pasta as you mix, knead, roll out and shape it all by hand. That is why a *nonna* is a master pasta maker. She has been making it for decades. She feels if the dough needs more moisture or if it is too wet. The smooth texture of the dough lets her know that it has been kneaded enough. Her rolling pin and knife skills are unmatched when shaping the pasta. She has been using God's tools a long time.

In no time the kitchen table was strewn with hundreds of little ears drying on top of the tablecloth. Nonna's were much more uniform in shape than mine, but she said that I was improving with every pull of the knife. It definitely gave me a sense of accomplishment, even if, between compliments, her continual note to me about the size of my ears was, *"Troppo grande, Marco. Troppo grande!"* —"Too big, Mark. Too big!"

The *orecchiette* were to be served with a *sugo* that included sausages from Nonna's favorite butcher, but this morning she discovered *la macelleria*—the butcher shop—was closed for August vacation. Nonna said that those were the only sausages that would work; none were as good as this particular butcher's, and just like the eggplant last week, if it isn't perfect it isn't worth eating. In

America, we would just go for the next best sausage, but that doesn't work here, and it definitely doesn't work with Nonna. Only the freshest and best of everything is used, so out with the idea of sausages and in with cubed pork.

Usually in Italy when a sauce is prepared with meat in it, the meat is removed from the *sugo* and served all by itself after the pasta course. Even when a sausage or meatball is part of a sauce it is removed and served as the second course. There are no heaping plates of spaghetti topped by meatballs or sausages. The exception, of course, is when the meat is ground or cubed, as with the pork today. The *orecchiette con maiale* were topped with freshly grated pecorino cheese. Lillo and I added some drops of spicy pepper sauce for a little heat.

I learned my first idiomatic phrase this afternoon in my language lesson. An idiomatic phrase is an expression that does not make literal sense. For example, a common idiomatic phrase is "It rained like cats and dogs." The phrase I learned is a good luck phrase. It is similar in spirit to the American theatrical "Break a leg" used before a show when wishing someone a good performance. In Italy, before taking a big test or when faced with a daunting task, the well-wishing phrase is *"In bocca al lupo!"* —"Into the wolf's mouth!" The response to this phrase is, *"Crepi!"* —"Kill it!" I love the fact that there is a response. In the theatre when someone says, "break a leg" the usual response is just "thanks," but in Italy there is a forceful declaration of action towards the task—"Kill it!" Nothing like being inspired not only to overcome an obstacle, but also to obliterate it.

La cena—dinner—started with a tomato and basil *frittata*. It was a simple way to begin dinner. A *frittata* differs from an omelet because it is finished in the oven. Nonna roasted potatoes to go with some of the leftover cubed pork. The potatoes were sliced into thick spears and roasted with fennel seed and rosemary. The fennel seed was a new flavor for me to experience on potatoes. Nonna enjoys using fennel; since I have been here it has flavored trout, pork and now, potatoes.

While we were eating *ananas*—pineapple—at the end of dinner, Alessandra announced we were going to Capodimonte for gelato. I was stuffed. I made a fat face and Lillo said, *"Ricordati, il gelato è liquido."* —"Remember, gelato is liquid." I do enjoy his gelato theory. I believe that

Lillo will soon declare that gelato is the cure for many ailments and diseases and that it could bring about world peace. I might just agree with him.

Capodimonte is a small boating village on the banks of Lago di Bolsena just north of Marta. The sailboats in its small harbor offer excursions to the two islands. From this mast-filled harbor the town climbs the hillside toward its crowning glory, *La Rocca*—the fortress. *La Rocca*, much like the village, is stoic and unadorned. It derives its beauty from its age and position overlooking the lake. To me, any castle, fortress or ancient stone structure seems romantic and beautiful because we don't see those things in America. Maybe Italians feel the same way, even though the sight of a castle or fortress is an everyday occurrence for them. Alessandra and Lillo were certainly proud to show off Capodimonte, though it paled in comparison to the architecture of Viterbo.

We parked near *La Rocca* and walked around its tall, well-lit walls, but for Lillo there didn't seem to be the anticipated nightlife near the fortress, and before we walked too far down the hillside streets, he decided we should drive down into town and park closer to the harbor. This turned out to be a great idea because the harbor area was bustling. The same boardwalk that runs along the shore of Marta continues here along the shoreline of Capodimonte. The village was having its town celebration, so the activity lining the boardwalk was identical to Marta's—vendors selling their various wares. Lillo said the *gelateria* was farther down, away from the harbor.

We paused to watch a performance in a park. The local dance school was having a recital and ballroom dance exhibition. A grandstand filled with spectators bordered the far side of the paved court that served as tonight's dance floor. The performers ranged in age from eight years old through their early twenties. Every routine was set to American music. When we first arrived the elementary students were performing a routine to the theme song from the *Addams Family* TV show. Their costumes reminded me of Michael Jackson's *Thriller* video—lots of scary Halloween zombies. I was surprised that the whole audience knew the song.

"Duh, duh, duh, duh." Snap. Snap.

"Duh, duh, duh, duh." Snap. Snap.

"Duh, duh, duh, duh. Duh, duh, duh, duh. Duh, duh, duh, duh." Snap. Snap.

They all snapped their fingers at the correct places. No one sang the words—I don't think anyone knew the words—but they certainly had the snaps down. Again, it amazes me to be in Italy and hear only American music. I know American pop culture impacts the world, but I found it incredible that even the *Addams Family* theme song was a part of this little town's culture. When have we ever known a theme song from an Italian TV show? Now that I think about it, maybe the mid-1970s commercial for the Plymouth Volarè burned its theme song into the American consciousness.

The *Addams Family* routine was followed by a ballroom dance exhibition of the tango, set to another American song, and, surprisingly, it was not Bon Jovi. The audience enthusiastically welcomed the college-aged performers to the stage. Ballroom dance is very popular in Italy, and the performance was really beautiful. We joined in the raucous applause at the end of the number, then headed on our *passeggiata* toward the gelato pavilion.

Lillo is downright scientific when it comes to ordering gelato. It is meant to be experienced with two scoops or *gusti*—tastes. The *gusti* should always be complementary flavors, never a double scoop of the same flavor. Lillo believes one taste should always be a fruit flavor. He seems to pair cantaloupe, lemon or fig with vanilla, yogurt or cinnamon. I enjoy combining a flavor from Lillo's second group with a nut flavor, but my favorite is *un gusto* of chocolate chip paired with *un gusto* of chocolate hazelnut. For Lillo, this combination is not good because there is too much chocolate—*"Troppo cioccolato, Marco!"* Too much chocolate? Who has ever heard of such a thing? He is always trying to persuade me to trust the science behind his gelato *gusti* perfection. Tonight was no different; he really put the pressure on until I finally gave in and went with *un gusto* of raspberry paired with *un gusto* of mint. *"Bravo, Marco. Bravo."* He had cantaloupe and yogurt.

Alessandra always has a single *gusto*, never two. She is more concerned about calories and fat than Lillo and I. Honestly, I don't think I have seen a low-fat or no-fat gelato. She is probably smart for having only one taste considering how often we eat gelato, but we always walk while eating it, and for me, that cancels out the fat. I know that isn't true, but right now it is what I am going to believe with every gelato-filled fiber of my being.

Lillo's gelato theory proved to be *delizioso*. The flavor of the mint cut the tang of the raspberry and I could see why Lillo enjoyed this type of combination. The contrast of complementary flavors allowed my taste buds to experience two flavors whose tastes enhanced and played off of each other, while my instinct is to go straight for a single flavor onslaught of overindulgence. I think of his theory as promoting the subtle harmonies of apple pie à la mode, while he thinks my preference for double chocolate fudge with chocolate chips and a swirl of chocolate syrup to be a one-note symphony. There is no doubt that his theory is good and sound, and I will be using it to guide me again, but my primal desire for chocolate will not be tamed or denied.

On the walk back toward the car, we stopped to watch some distant fireworks over the lake.

"*Lillo, dove sono i fuochi artificiali?*" —"Lillo, where are the fireworks?" I asked.

"*Sono a San Lorenzo, Marco.*"

San Lorenzo, a town on the north side of Lake Bolsena, was celebrating its patron saint's day. On Monday, Lillo wants to come back for Capodimonte's fireworks over the harbor. I am all for that.

Gelato and a lakeside view of fireworks over a distant, ancient town— once again, life is good.

"*VO-LARE... OH... OH.*"

"*CAN-TARE... OH, OH, OH, OH.*"

Patate con Semi di Finocchio

Potatoes with Fennel Seed

In Italy, vegetable side dishes are known as contorni *and, at a* ristorante, *must be ordered individually in addition to your main meat course. Roasted potatoes are a standard and here is Nonna's version.*

1 teaspoon whole fennel seed

6 medium potatoes (2 to 2½ pounds)

2 tablespoons extra virgin olive oil

2 cloves garlic, finely minced

1 teaspoon salt

½ teaspoon freshly ground black pepper

1 teaspoon chopped fresh rosemary

Preheat oven to 400 degrees.

Place the fennel seed in a spice grinder, or using a mortar and pestle, crush to a medium-fine grind. Set aside.

Peel the potatoes and cut lengthwise in half. Cut each half lengthwise in half again, and cut the quarters on angle into halves again (you are creating spears by cutting each potato into eighths). Place the spears into a large bowl and add the oil, garlic, salt, pepper, rosemary and ground fennel seed. Stir until well combined and the potatoes are well coated.

Place the potatoes on a baking sheet and roast for 35 to 40 minutes, until well browned. Halfway through the cooking process use a spatula to turn the potatoes so they roast evenly.

Makes 6 servings.

Variations on a theme: This is a recipe that can be switched up to suit your mood and tastes. If you really enjoy the flavor of garlic, add a clove or two more. Want your potatoes spicy? Then add a ¼ teaspoon red pepper flakes and a couple of grinds of freshly ground black pepper. Not too hip on the taste of fennel? Omit it, slice a medium onion into ¼-inch half-rounds and add to the bowl with the potatoes and rosemary. Think rosemary is too strong? Leave it out and substitute a ¼ cup finely chopped fresh Italian flat-leaf parsley, tossing it with the potatoes after they come out of the oven.

IL GIORNO DODICI (Day Twelve)

"**N**onna, dove sono i gatti?"

I caught her placing the last bit of cereal from my Italian Cheerios box into the cat soup jar.

"*Marco, ai gatti piacciono i cereali.*" —"Mark, cats like cereal."

"*Davvero, Nonna?*" —"Really, Nonna?"

"*Si, si.*"

"*Allora ... DOVE SONO I GATTI?*"

She laughed and changed the subject to *mortadella*. The mystery of cat soup continues.

"*Marco, ti piace la mortadella?*"

"*Si, si, Nonna.*"

I do like *mortadella*, an Italian-style bologna. It is a large 12-inch diameter log studded with white chunks of fat, black pepper and pistachios. At the butcher's counter *mortadella* looks like the neighborhood fat kid sitting next to his slight, lean salami friends. Thinly sliced, it is a wonderful addition to an *antipasto* platter of *salumi*, or it makes a wonderful *panino*—sandwich.

Quick Italian lesson: *Panino* is the masculine singular for "sandwich." *Panini*, now a common word in American restaurants, is the masculine plural for "sandwiches." You might look at a list of *panini,* but you order a *panino.*

Sliced thicker, *mortadella* can be cubed for use in a pasta sauce or a potato casserole. Nonna winked when she caught my eye at the meat counter as she asked the butcher for several slices of this flavorful bologna. I am becoming her spoiled grandchild while at the grocery store, and why shouldn't she spoil me? I have mastered the return of the shopping cart, the sorting of the recyclables and the answer to the checkout clerk's eternal question, *"Busta?"* *"No, grazie."*

After the recyclable stop, Nonna made a sharp right and, instead of heading home as we always did, she started driving toward *il centro*—the center—of Viterbo.

"Nonna, dove andiamo?" —"Where are we going?"

"Marco, vedrai." —"You'll see."

She pulled the car into the parking lot of what looked like an auto repair shop. It was a long narrow building and she parked about halfway down on the right side. *"Vieni,"* she said, and we got out of the car and went into a side storefront.

It was a bakery. The exterior was simple but cute—a couple of potted plants, a simple striped awning, a red scooter parked next to the door; however, the interior was plain—nothing romantic or charming and cute about it; white walls, florescent lighting and plain display cases that did not help the breads and desserts they held look at all appetizing. While we were standing in line I noticed that Nonna wasn't checking out any of the things in the cases; she was focused on the counter at the far side of the shop by the cash register.

"*Prego?*" —"May I help you?"— asked the girl behind the counter when it was our turn to order.

"*Due pezzi di pizza bianca croccante, per favore.*" Nonna pointed over the counter at a large, thin, bread-like cracker with dark brown edges. The girl grabbed a large knife and sliced two big square pieces off an almost four-foot long sheet of this *pizza bianca*. While the girl was ringing us up, I looked behind her through the beaded curtain that separated the baking room from the front counter. There were large, wheeled, six-foot long wooden racks that held the freshly baked *pizze bianche* to cool after coming out of the oven. Each individual pizza was seven to eight feet long and a foot wide, and longer than the rack that held it. Bakers slid these long *pizze* onto individual wooden-slatted shelves on the rack to cool. When a double-sided rack was full, six *pizze* to a side, it was wheeled across the baking room and out of my sight to cool.

"Wow!" I said, seeing the racks. The girl looked up from the cash register and gave me a funny look.

"*Lui è nuovo a Viterbo,*" —"He is new to Viterbo,"— Nonna said to the girl and grabbed my arm to leave.

"*Buona giornata e grazie … Ciao, ciao, ciao!*" I called back over my shoulder as we left.

In the car Nonna opened the bag and broke off a piece of the crunchy pizza and gave it to me. This *pizza bianca* was incredible—thin, crunchy, salty and heavily brushed with olive oil. This was the shop with the *pizza bianca* that Nonna said was better than the one we tried last Saturday at Le Clerc. Nonna is never wrong—this was so much better. I am not sure if it was the crunchy texture of the dough, the sea salt, or the fruity flavor of the olive oil, but this *pizza bianca* was *buonissima!* Light-years beyond Le Clerc's.

Nonna broke off a second piece for me and a large piece for herself, started the car and drove us back to the house. When we came in the front door carrying the groceries, Alessandra immediately came over and grabbed the *pizza bianca* bag, reaching in to break off a piece.

"Marco, questa è buona, yes?" she asked.

"Si, si, si! È buonissima!" I said, reaching for the last of the first *pezzo*—piece. Alessandra said we would save the second *pezzo* for Lillo and Francesca to share later.

Nonna's morning cooking lesson started with *tavalli*—the Italian version of a pretzel—flavored with fennel seed, boiled, and then baked, producing a soft pretzel. The *tavalli* were shaped like the lapel ribbons that have become synonymous with breast cancer, HIV and support for our troops. It didn't take us long to mix, roll, cut, twist, boil, bake and fill a bowl with these savory "charity ribbons" that were to be our afternoon *spuntino*—snack. We always have a little *spuntino* and a glass of water after our siesta before heading into my afternoon language class.

Lunch's *antipasto:* stuffed tomatoes. Nonna's style of preparation is what surprised me about her stuffed tomatoes. Holding the tomato in her hand, she made a cut just under the stem, slicing across the top of the tomato, stopping short of cutting the top completely off. This created a hinged lid for the tomato. Using a spoon she removed the seeds and fleshy chamber walls, placing the "innards" in a mesh strainer over a bowl to collect the juice. The hollowed cavity was filled with a mixture of uncooked rice, freshly torn basil leaves, the strained and reserved tomato juices, minced garlic and salt and pepper. The lid was closed and topped with a pinch of salt, bread crumbs and drizzled with olive oil. This was different than a pepper stuffed with meat and precooked rice. With Nonna's tomatoes, the rice cooked in the liquid-filled tomato cavity. As always, Nonna prepared the first tomato.

"Guarda, Marco. Attento." She handed me the second and supervised my work. I was pretty skeptical that the tomatoes would turn out—there

was so much liquid and so little rice inside each cavity, but by now I should have learned never to doubt Nonna's recipes. The tomatoes were baked until the breaded lids browned and slightly popped open, hinting at the swollen, flavor-absorbed rice inside. Perfection.

Per il secundo piatto—veal and turkey cutlets grilled Palermo-style. The cutlets were rubbed with olive oil, patted with a mixture of bread crumbs and Parmigiano-Reggiano and grilled. The bread crumbs brown and the cheese melts to help hold the coating to the cutlets. Grilling, and not using egg to bread the cutlets, gives them a lighter texture and taste.

It was only my two *professoresse* with me at the table for lunch today. Francesca was off with Stefano, and Lillo had a meeting at the university. I enjoyed my alone time with Nonna and Alessandra since lunch can be such a flurry of activity some days. It was nice to sit at the table and attempt to chat with just the two of them. Tomorrow I am going to Rome for the weekend, so we figured out tomorrow's schedule of lessons and from which train station I should leave. Viterbo has two stations, but Alessandra thought that it might be better for me to leave from the nearby town of Orte, where there are more frequent and direct trains to Rome. Nonna said that Orte is only twenty minutes away and she didn't mind taking me there. I felt bad for imposing myself on them, but they would not hear of me leaving from Viterbo.

"Marco, you will waste so much time changing trains if you leave from Viterbo. You will want the extra time in *Roma*. We are taking you to Orte," Alessandra said. Trying to change the mind of a determined Italian woman— let alone, two Italian women—is an impossible feat. I have learned to be gracious and just say, *"Grazie."*

The *tavalli* were a savory change from the usually sweet after-siesta snack—yet another way Nonna has used fennel seed. I was hoping that they would provide me with some fortification going into my afternoon language lesson. I was struggling with the daunting and near impossible task of learning *l'articoli e le preposizioni*—articles ("the," "a," "an") and prepositions ("from," "at," "to," "of," "on," "for"). There are seven ways to say "the"—because words are masculine and feminine, singular and plural—therefore, there are sixty-four different articles and prepositions. There seems no rhyme or reason for their usage. Alessandra says this is even hard for Italians to learn. For example, to go "to" a country is said one way, to go "to" a town is said another. I think I need more than Italian pretzels to get me through this. Where is the wine?

Alessandra is so supportive and focused on the task of teaching me Italian. I am the type of student who learns best by writing, writing, writing and writing. The physical action of my hand writing down the answer or copying sentence structure helps to lock the solution into my brain. The workbook that I use has a limited number of examples, so Alessandra goes out of her way to provide extra exercises—pages and pages of extra exercises from other workbooks. She has gone to the local copy shop many times since my arrival, and because she doesn't drive it is truly a commitment on her part to figure out how to get there without interrupting my lesson time with her or Nonna. Marianna, Lillo and even Stefano with Francesca have helped Alessandra get the copies made. She really wants me to succeed and her support is heartfelt. I never want to disappoint her by not making progress. Who needs *tavalli* when you have Alessandra? She is my fortification.

I emerged blurry-eyed from the den and met Nonna in the kitchen.

"Marco, come stai." —"Mark, how are you?"

"Nonna, la mia testa … è stanca." —"Nonna, my head … it is tired."

"Povero, Marco. I preposizioni sono molto difficile." —"Poor, Mark. Prepositions are very hard."

"Si, si. È vero, Nonna."

She patted me on the back, half consoling me and half sarcastically hinting that I should get over myself. I looked at her as pitifully as I could before we broke out into laughter. I might be spoiled but I certainly cannot get away with anything. While I was trying to wrap my brain around *preposizioni* in the den, Nonna was in the kitchen making dough for *panzerotti*. Shaped like tiny calzone, they are filled with either *prosciutto cotto* and mozzarella enriched with an egg or with mozzarella and *acciughe*, then deep fat fried.

I have noticed a pattern to our meals. Tonight we started dinner with the *panzerotti*—something new—followed by cutlets and stuffed tomatoes—lunch leftovers. Growing up, when my mother was getting rid of leftovers our entire dinner would be only that—leftovers—nothing new. BOOORRING! Nonna was serving leftovers, but she always included one new thing. Unless you really pay attention, you don't notice that you are eating leftovers. This keeps the *zuppa di gatti* ingredients down to a minimum and the interest in dinner at a maximum. Nonna is a clever one.

During dinner I tried to speak in Italian more than I usually do. I really pushed myself not to be so concerned about perfection, but to embrace the idea that the attempt was far more important than the execution. Well, "execution" is the perfect description of my attempt. I left a lot of linguistic carnage strewn about that kitchen table. I got the gender wrong for each and every word I spoke. (Dr. Freud might have had something to say about that.) I was lovingly corrected at every misstep but my sense of failure and idiocy was mounting. When I start to critique myself, I get less talkative and eventually silent. There are days when the Italian coming out of my mouth is in great form and other days when even saying *ciao* is completely wrong. Tonight was the latter. Sensing that the collapse of my confidence was at hand, Alessandra said, *"Bravo, Marco!* You are trying. *Quello è l'importante."*

I will just have to trust her on that.

Panzerotti

Fried Dough Pockets

Panzerotti are popular throughout Italy, and the choice of fillings is only limited to one's imagination. Popular versions include fillings such as tomato, basil and mozzarella, and spinach with mushrooms. I have often thought of trying the ragù and mozzarella filling from Nonna's Arancini Siciliani recipe (see page 114). Here are Nonna's favorites.

Dough (*pasta*):
Use the Rotolo di Verdura dough recipe on page 94.

Filling:
8 ounces mozzarella cheese, cut into ½-inch cubes

1 egg, separated

4 ounces cooked ham, cut into ½-inch cubes

1 anchovy filet, minced (If anchovies truly aren't your thing, you may leave them out and double the amount of ham.)

Oil for frying (Nonna used sunflower oil, but you can use your favorite frying oil.)

To prepare the dough, follow the same dough recipe on page 94 through the kneading process and place it under a bowl to rise.

While the dough is resting, place the cubed mozzarella and the yolk of one egg (reserving the egg white in a small bowl) in a medium bowl, and using a wooden spoon, gently mix together until well combined. Place half of the egg and mozzarella mixture into a second bowl and to it, stir in the cubed ham until well combined. To the first bowl, add the anchovy, stirring until well combined. Set both mixtures aside.

Unwrap the dough, and on a lightly floured surface, roll it out to ⅛-inch thick. Cut dough in 4-inch rounds using a cookie cutter, or the mouth of a large plastic container or mouth of a glass. The scrap dough can be kneaded, re-rolled and cut into additional rounds.

Slightly beat the reserved egg white in its bowl. Taking one of the cut rounds, brush the egg white about a ¼-inch all the way around the outside edge. Place a tablespoon of the filling mixture in the center, staying a ¼-inch from the edge of the dough. Bring each side of the dough up over the filling and pinch the outside edges together, creating a half-round. Make sure that the edges of the *panzerotti* are well sealed or the filling will leak out while frying. Set the prepared *panzerotti* aside to rest and repeat the filling process: fill 12 of the cut rounds with the ham mixture and 12 with the anchovy mixture.

Using a deep fat fryer, or heavy saucepan with tall sides, heat oil to 350 degrees. When the oil has come to temperature, cook the *panzerotti* in batches (3 or 4 at a time), until they are golden brown, 2 to 3 minutes. (Note: Turn the *panzerotti* often as they cook, especially when they are first placed in the oil. This will prevent them from developing an air pocket on one side making it harder to brown both sides evenly as they cook.) Remove from the oil and place on paper towels to drain and slightly cool. Serve warm, but may also be enjoyed at room temperature.

This recipe makes 24 *Panzerotti*: 12 Ham and Cheese; 12 Cheese and Anchovy.

IL GIORNO TREDICI (Day Thirteen)

*C*iao, ciao da Roma!

Earlier today for lunch in Viterbo, Nonna made *l'insalata di polipi*—baby octopus salad. I like octopus and, as you know, around here if I say I like something, it is served. The octopus salad consisted of small octopuses cut up into pieces, quickly sautéed and dressed with olive oil and freshly squeezed lemon juice. This salad was then placed into the *frigo* and served chilled. Finally, a prepared dish that I thought should go into the fridge actually went into it and not into the toaster oven to sit until served. I am slowly learning the foods that have the privilege of being stored in the refrigerator: seafood, cheeses, milk, butter, raw eggs, *salumi*, sliced fruit, lettuce, water, white wine and now, thanks to me, Coca-Cola.

In addition to the *polipi*, she made spaghetti with a *sugo* of anchovies, minced garlic and bread crumbs, all sautéed in olive oil—quick, simple and *molto delizioso*.

After lunch, Nonna drove Alessandra and me the twenty minutes east to Orte. It gave me a chance to see more of the surrounding countryside and mountains. The region of Viterbo is so picturesque. I saw fields of grazing sheep but contained myself from shouting *"Ciao, ciao, ciao!"* out the window. Just outside of Viterbo, off in the distance to our right, we passed Mount Cimino. Nonna told Alessandra that we should go to the nature reserve there for a picnic next weekend. Alessandra thought it was a great idea. She said, "Marco, we have not been on a picnic for a long time and it would be great to take you there." I agreed. I am really glad I canceled my trip to *Firenze*.

The train was packed and I had to stand on the connecting platform between cars for the hour-long, hot, and sweaty ride to Rome. I was relieved to spill out of the train at the Stazione Termini and take *La Metro* (Rome's subway system is called *La Metropoliana*—*La Metro* for short) towards the apartment I had rented for the weekend. The apartment exceeded my expectations. It is in Prati, a neighborhood that is only a quick ten-minute walk north of the Vatican and Saint Peter's. Rome's neighborhoods, or districts—*rione*—are numbered much in the same way as the districts of Paris. *Rione I* is the oldest neighborhood of Rome, dating back to the early first century, and Prati (*rione XXII*) is the newest—if one can classify something from 1900 as new. Staying in the working class Prati surrounded by Romans is more interesting to me than being next to the Spanish Steps in a row of hotels filled with tourists. I imagined myself a Roman citizen for the weekend and challenged myself to speak only Italian—a self-imposed mid-term exam. *"In bocca al lupo! ...CREPI!"*

Arriving at my apartment was the first part of the exam. Stefano, the landlord, speaks very little English and was embarrassed to try. I may have sounded like a two-year-old but I held on and spoke only in Italian. Stefano seemed impressed with my attempt. I really pushed myself to strike up a conversation even if it was basically about the weather, the neighborhood and the apartment. Fortunately, I managed to keep myself from declaring that I was "a meat." I understood his "Do's and Don't's" of the apartment and also answered some of his basic questions about where I was from, if I had ever been to Rome before and what I planned on seeing while I was here. I successfully asked him where the nearest *gelateria* was—I do have priorities—and understood his directions. Luckily, it is close to the apartment—gelato was in my near future.

This weekend in the Eternal City is about exploring the neighborhoods and seeing the sights that I didn't have time for on previous trips. I headed out of the apartment walking east along the wide and tree-lined Viale delle Milizie, crossing over the Tiber River, through the Campo Marzio neighborhood (*rione* IV), toward the Piazza del Popolo. The architecture of Campo Marzio's old villas told of the rich and noble Romans that developed this area some 300 years ago. I passed fashionable shops and *caffè* filled with today's Romans enjoying an afternoon espresso or *spuntino*. Small wine shops—*enoteca*—were also busy with locals enjoying a glass of wine during their afternoon siesta, instead of taking a nap. There were no flag-holding guides leading packs of tourists through this neighborhood. It was easy to convince myself that I truly was a Roman citizen here, so … "When in Rome…." I stepped into my first *gelateria* of the weekend. *"Buonasera, vorrei un medio gelato. Un gusto di fico ed un gusto di crema, per favore."* In honor of Lillo I asked for fig and cream. I walked several more blocks before arriving at the grand Piazza del Popolo. I came to this *piazza* to check out the church, Santa Maria del Popolo, containing two Caravaggio paintings: the "Conversion of Saint Paul" and the "Crucifixion of Saint Peter." I am fascinated by Italian churches, which is why I go into every one I happen upon. Churches here portray both good and evil, Heaven and Hell, forgiveness and judgment, life and death, salvation and eternal damnation. Images inside American churches focus only on what is good, but in Italy evil is also portrayed to remind you of what makes good so … well … good. Maybe we think that having images of skulls and death inside a baptistry is morbid, but here it reminds me of how fragile life is, which in turn makes me feel joyous for the life I have been given. It is the Christian idea that in death eternal life is achieved. On a more secular note, it is the idea that without sorrow you cannot appreciate joy—there must be a yin and a yang.

The two Caravaggio paintings hang on opposing walls of the Cerasi Chapel. On the left wall is the large painting of Saint Peter being crucified. His intense look is one of dismay mixed with pain as he gazes over at the nail in his left hand, while three men are assisting each other in raising the foot of his cross into the air. Opposite is the painting of Saint Paul being converted to Christianity. He is lying on his back, arms outstretched toward heaven, his eyes closed in ecstasy as he faces upward into the harsh light streaming down from above. Another man, who seems oblivious to Paul's calling, is trying to control Paul's horse. Painful crucifixion and soul-saving passion, death and life, are portrayed in opposition in this chapel—emotional, thought provoking and beautiful.

On my way out of the church I noticed a tomb to the right of the door. The carved marble figure of a skeleton draped in a white cloak with its hands crossed over its chest shares a cage with a butterfly. The symbol of death (the skeleton) and the symbol of rebirth (the butterfly) carved together in marble was a more subtle way of showing life and death than Caravaggio's paintings. I don't know that I have ever seen a skeleton used to help illustrate the power of life over death. Truly, a beautiful tomb—it filled me with joy and a peaceful sense of hope. I found myself smiling. As I walked away I thought, "Was the skeleton grinning, too?" I looked back over my shoulder, and it certainly looked as if he knew something about joy as well.

My early evening *passeggiata* continued along the enormous grounds of the Villa Borghese park, where I stopped at a park vendor selling commercially produced gelato bars on a stick. It was not as good as the gelato from a *gelateria*, but it was gelato nonetheless. I tried to remember how to get to the Trevi Fountain, but somehow I got turned around and couldn't find it. I have seen it twice before—maybe the coins I threw in the fountain on those visits are the reason I am here now. Tradition says you should throw three coins over your shoulder into the fountain. The first coin is to guarantee a return visit to Rome; the second, to find your true love; the third, to find your true love in Rome. I should have tried harder to find the fountain and throw in another set of coins to insure a next trip to Rome.

After wandering around for a while, I did find the Pantheon, which is one of my favorite buildings in Rome. Someday I will take a winter trip here in the hope of seeing it snow through the large oculus (eye) in the center of the domed ceiling. I think it would be a tremendous sight. There are holes in the floor directly under the opening in the dome to drain away any water. As with many ancient pagan sites in Rome, the Pantheon has been consecrated as a church. Even the Colosseum, famous as the venue for many Christian deaths, was consecrated, and the chapel from the 6th century still exists below one of its arches.

It was a quick walk from the Pantheon to the Piazza Navona, another of Rome's large *piazzas*, full of the vendors and street performers that cater to the touring throngs—definitely too many tourists for my taste. I know it seems odd to have a distaste for tourists, considering that I am one myself, but it is more about a distaste for the idea of being herded around, interested only in a street performing Sphinx that stands on a box and bows when a coin is deposited into a pail at its feet. I have no interest in that kind of performance—I work in the theatre, after all.

In the oval Piazza Navona there are three beautiful fountains that outshine any tourist trap. The large central fountain is the most famous of the three and was created by Bernini in 1651. The Fountain of the Four Rivers has a figure representing a river from each of the four corners of the world. The figure representing the Plata River has his hand held up in front of his face as if shunning the view of the building he faces in the *piazza*. It is said that Bernini did not like this particular building or its architect, so he purposefully designed the Plata figure's public display of disgust. I will take that type of humor and attitude in a fountain over a Sphinx bowing on a box for tips any time.

I thinned myself from the herd and headed back to my apartment to shower and regroup before heading out to dinner. There was a quaint *ristorante* two blocks from my apartment, off the beaten path that I'd noticed before. Besides ordering the *gelati* earlier in the day, I hadn't really spoken to anyone—so much for putting my Italian to the test. I asked the hostess for a table for one and she put me at a little table in the corner of the outside dining area, which gave me a chance to people watch. I asked for water and a glass of red wine and was given an Italian menu. Most *ristorante* menus in Rome are in Italian and English, but my hostess must have thought I was Italian since I was given an Italian-only menu. Or maybe they only had menus written in Italian at this *ristorante*, but I am telling myself that she gave me the menu because my Italian was just that good—it helps to convince myself of that.

"Vorrei polipi per il primo e per il secundo vorrei il gnocchi con scampi." I ordered meatballs to start and for my pasta course I ordered *gnocchi* in a light red sauce served with two large scampi. After the hostess walked away I realized that I did not order the *gnocchi* correctly. I forgot that, in Italian, pasta is not a single item but a plural item (because there is more than one piece of pasta on your plate), so I should have used the masculine plural form of "the" because *gnocchi* is a masculine plural word, and, to complicate it further, the word starts with a "gn." So, I should have asked for *"gli gnocchi"* not *"il gnocchi."* It might not seem like a big deal, but it definitely blew my cover as a Roman citizen.

She brought my bottled water and a glass of the house red wine while I waited for my first course. I was really looking forward to starting off dinner with some good ole Italian meatballs and then having the *gnocchi* with shrimp—a little Italian style surf-n-turf, if you will. I have not had meatballs on this trip to Italy. Nonna made eggplant meatballs, which were vegetarian, and *arancini*, which only had a small piece of meat, but so far, no <u>meat</u>balls.

I usually don't enjoy eating dinner alone at a restaurant, but I sipped my wine and watched people on the street pass by. Luckily, it wasn't long before the hostess brought out my first course. *"I suoi polipi. Buon appetito,"* she said, and walked away. I was in the middle of taking a drink of wine and choked on it when I looked down at my plate—no meatballs—there were a half dozen baby octopuses in a red sauce. I tried to catch the hostess' eye, but she was gone. I looked at my plate, looked for her again, and then looked back at the menu. I realized my mistake: I ordered *"i polipi"*—baby octopuses—when I thought I was ordering *"le polpette"*—meatballs. Ugh! I couldn't even read it, let alone say it correctly. I am failing my Italian exam and now my entire meal was going to be seafood. I stuck myself with my second serving of octopus for the day. Don't misunderstand me, *i polipi erano buonissimi*—the baby octopuses were very good—but a plate of meatballs is what I really wanted. *Povero Marco!*

An Italian family and three college-aged German girls were seated at the table behind me. I couldn't figure out how they knew each other, but it was interesting to listen to the Germans attempt Italian and slaughter English—the common language between the six of them. I shouldn't be too judgmental. The girls spoke three languages, regardless of how poor their English and Italian were. My attempt at Italian is nothing to be proud of—didn't I just order octopus instead of meatballs?

The multi-lingual table behind me caught my attention because I could hear a difference in the family's Italian accent. Alessandra has been pointing out regional accents to me in our lessons, and tonight I was able to discern two of them: Roman (my hostess tonight) and Tuscan (the family seated behind me). Alessandra, whose accent is Roman, is always making fun of the Tuscan accent in the same way that northerners in America make fun of a Southern accent. When she plays a language cassette in our lessons and the speaker is Tuscan she just laughs and laughs. At first, I could not hear the difference between Roman, Tuscan, Sicilian and Venetian accents, but as she continues to point them out I am slowly getting the idea.

"Marco, people from Tuscany say *'Hoca-Hola'* when pronouncing Coca-Cola." She says it with a thick, Spanish sounding accent—*"Hhok-ka Hhola"*—as if trying to clear her throat. It doesn't sound very funny to me but Alessandra might as well be a New Yorker watching an episode of *Hee-Haw*—she can't help breaking into a fit of laughter at the absurdity of the accent. The Italian family's rough Tuscan accent makes me chuckle, knowing that Alessandra would be bent over in gut-wrenching hysterics had she heard them. I can't wait to get home and tell her that I could pick out the Tuscan accent. (Hmm, I guess that is a true statement—Viterbo is home and I can't wait to get back to the family—my family, now—and tell them my new discoveries. I love Italy!)

I finished dinner without really understanding the connection between the Italians and Germans. I got the impression that the girls had met the family during the course of the day and had been invited out to dinner. If nothing else, they provided me with great dinner entertainment as I eavesdropped on their conversation, trying to create a fascinating story explaining their relationship.

After dinner, I went to the *gelateria* that Stefano, the apartment landlord, had recommended earlier in the day. This time I did not use Lillo's theory of flavor selection, but instead went for my favorites: *stracciatella*—vanilla with chocolate shavings (an Italian version of chocolate chip) and *cioccolato*—chocolate. Lillo would have been disappointed, but I was so happy walking toward my apartment, while eating my third gelato of the day.

Spaghetti con Aglio e Acciugge

Spaghetti with Garlic and Anchovies

This is one of those great, quick pasta dishes—you prepare the sauce as the pasta cooks. And remember, in Italy, the pasta waits for nothing. It would be culinary high treason to have the pasta not used and served immediately after being cooked, which is why when Nonna announces the pasta has been dropped into the water, you have to get cleaned up and be seated at the table before it comes out—"Punto!" ("Period!") as Nonna would say. No excuses—end of discussion.

1 pound spaghetti

½ cup extra virgin olive oil, or more if needed

3 large cloves garlic, sliced

3 anchovy filets, finely chopped

1 teaspoon freshly ground black pepper, or more to taste

3 tablespoons plain dried bread crumbs

3 tablespoons chopped fresh Italian flat-leaf parsley

½ teaspoon salt

½ cup grated pecorino or Parmigiano-Reggiano cheese, or more to taste
   (optional)*

Bring a large pot of water to a boil. Once boiling, add 2 tablespoons salt and the spaghetti, stirring occasionally to keep the pasta from sticking together. Cook until *al dente*—tender, but firm to the bite, about 10-12 minutes. Once you add the pasta to the boiling water, start preparing the *sugo*.

In a large skillet over medium heat, add the oil, garlic and anchovies, and bring up to temperature, stirring to dissolve the anchovies. Cook until the garlic starts to turn golden, about a minute once it starts to simmer. Add the pepper and bread crumbs, stirring until the bread crumbs are lightly golden—be aware, this happens really fast. Turn off the heat.

Drain the pasta well and add to the garlic and anchovy skillet. Add the parsley and ½ teaspoon salt (start with a little less, since the anchovies are salty), and toss the pasta with the garlic and anchovy *sugo* over low heat, until well combined. Remove the skillet from the heat.

If the pasta seems a little dry after being mixed with the *sugo*, drizzle it with an additional tablespoon or two of extra virgin olive oil. Taste and adjust the seasoning. This is where you can add more salt, if you wish. Serve immediately.

This makes 6 to 8 servings.

*Nonna prefers this dish without cheese, but Lillo and I like cheese with it. If you would like to use cheese, Nonna said to add it at the very end, once the pasta is off the heat.

IL GIORNO QUATTORDICI (Day Fourteen)

I have to admit that even though *colazione* in Viterbo is simple, I did miss it this morning as I was having a cup of tea and a rather plain, almost tasteless, pre-packaged croissant in my apartment. And I miss the smell of the mysterious *zuppa di gatti* simmering on the back burner.

This morning I went to the top of the *cupola* (the dome) of Saint Peter's. While I was climbing the hundreds of steps up to the top, I had no sense of how high I was until I emerged onto the viewing gallery encircling the top of the *cupola*. The views of Rome, and even of the roof of Saint Peter's below, are amazing. From here you have a 360-degree view of Rome, its seven hills, and even a view of the Vatican gardens behind Saint Peter's. It was worth every step up.

I stopped at a pizzeria near the Vatican museum for lunch. I have eaten here before and their zucchini blossom and anchovy pizza is wonderful. At this pizzeria you order by telling them how big of a piece to cut from the large rectangular-shaped pizza. The pieces are cut into squares, and you are charged by the weight of the square. I also had a piece of porcini mushroom pizza and ate as I walked toward the Castel Sant'Angelo (originally Hadrian's Mausoleum). I did stop for gelato on the way—I thought I was showing tremendous restraint by waiting this long to have *il mio primo gelato del giorno*.

Walking along the bank of the Tiber, I headed into Trastevere, the original Jewish ghetto of ancient Rome. Trastevere means "to traverse or to cross over" and it is still very much a working class neighborhood. The streets are very narrow and the well-worn and aged buildings are very close to each other, providing a time-forgotten atmosphere. This is not the prettiest part of Rome, but it feels the most authentic and that makes it beautiful. I went into every church that was open to see if they differed from churches in wealthier neighborhoods. Although simpler in nature, I was surprised by the number of famous works (paintings, mosaics and statues) by very famous people—Michelangelo, Bernini and Leonardo da Vinci—that existed in these working class churches.

From Trastevere, I walked up the hill (a half mile up the hill) to the *Passeggiata del Gianicolo*—the Gianicolo Promenade—that snakes along the Janiculum Hill. It is a lovely walk along a tree-lined avenue, dotted with monuments and memorials, providing yet another great view of Rome. I stopped and had gelato *(menta e cioccolato)* by the Monument of Giuseppe Garibaldi. There is a large viewing terrace there, and it was a perfect place to sit and take a break in the almost three-mile walk through this large park on the crest of the Janiculum. The second gelato of the day certainly helped me to regain my fortitude to finish this afternoon *passeggiata*—it was a steep half-mile up and it was a steep half-mile down. Usually down is easier, but this down was just as tiring as the up. I was now at the opposite end of Trastevere, on the southwest side of Rome.

It was siesta time, so I headed out of Trastevere, crossing over the island in the Tiber, and continued my walk north through the Piazza Campo dei Fiori and into the Piazza Navona—I was starving and needed *uno spuntino con un bicchiere di vino.* The *piazza* was not as crowded as it was last night, so the atmosphere was much more calm and gracious. I stopped at a *ristorante* to read the menu posted in front of the outdoor seating area, when the maitre d' came rushing out to greet me, "Please, come and sit at a table." Before I could say anything, I was hurriedly, but politely, whisked to a table under one of the many large umbrellas, with a perfect view of the Fountain of the Four Rivers. He put an English menu in front of me and asked, "What may I get for you?"

"*Vorrei una bottiglia d'aqua … frizzante … per favore,*" I said.

"*Mi dispiace, Signore,*" he said, looking panicked as he immediately removed my menu, replaced it with an Italian-only menu, and raced inside to get my bottle of water. I guess my Italian was good enough to embarrass him for assuming that I did not speak his language.

"*È il melone fresco?*" I asked, when he brought my water.

"*Si, signore, il melone è molto fresco.*"

"*Buono. Vorrei il prosciutto con melone e un bicchiere di vino bianco a casa.*"

"*Perfetto. Grazie, signore.*"

Moments later he returned with a plate of cantaloupe slices wrapped in prosciutto served with some sliced bread and a glass of the house white wine. The cantaloupe was sweet and the prosciutto was salty, which made this classic Italian *antipasto* a perfect afternoon snack. It was relaxing to sit in the shade, leisurely eating my *spuntino*, sipping my wine and listening to the water spewing forth from the open mouths of the fountain's water creatures. Pairs of tourists passed by, Romans walking their dogs strolled through the *piazza*, and at this moment I was truly a Roman citizen enjoying an afternoon siesta.

"*Scusi, signore. Va tutto bene?*" —"Excuse me, sir. Is it okay?"— the maitre d' asked.

"*Si, si. Tutti sono buonissimi.*" —"Yes, everything is very good."

"*Bene. Di dove sei?*" —"Good. Where are you from?"— he asked.

"*Sono d'America. Sono qui in l'Italia per università, ma sono a Roma per il weekend.*" —"I am from America. I am here in Italy for school, but I am in Rome for the weekend."

"Il suo italiano è molto buono," —"Your Italian is very good,"— he said.
"Grazie, provo." —"Thanks, I try."

"Prego," he said and was off to greet the next customers looking at the posted menu—an American couple wearing matching shirts, Bermuda shorts, white tennis shoes and fanny packs. He looked back at me, winked, and then said to them, "Please, come and sit at a table."

The apartment was a welcome sight after all of my walking today. I took a nap and woke up at 8:00 p.m., hungry and ready to head back out for my second night in Rome. I wasn't sure what I wanted to eat. I passed by the *ristorante* from last night and the hostess waved *ciao* to me. I smiled and waved back. Hmm, maybe I am a resident of Rome now. I love walking around Rome at night: *Ristoranti* crowd small neighborhood streets with rows of tightly packed dining tables and chairs; street performers work for tips in the larger *piazzas*; ancient buildings are flooded in vibrant colored light—pink, green, blue and red.

Strolling down the Via dei Fori Imperiali, with the Roman Forum to my right and the Colosseum looming directly in front of me at the end of the street, images of chariots, gladiators and toga-wearing senators filled my imagination. This is the part of Rome where the ancient world is most apparent. In this antique place, however, I am quickly reminded of the time I live in by the honking cabs and passing buses. The avenue curves to the left around the Colosseum, but I decided to walk to the right through the Piazza del Colosseo.

The *piazza* side of the Colosseum was splashed with hot pink light. To my right, the Arco di Constantino, built in AD 315 in honor of the Emperor Constantine's tenth year in power, was now a glowing tribute in vivid aquamarine light. Some people may find it distasteful to see these old structures so garishly lit, but in a city where vast neon billboards and flashing signs do not exist, this is a great way to put a modern twist on these ancient sites. Trust me, I would rather see a fuchsia-lit Colosseum than a silvered, forty-foot, shimmering Niketown billboard any night.

I read in one of my guidebooks that there was a gay bar near the Colosseum, appropriately called "Coming Out." I always like checking out the local gay culture outside of the United States. I like to see how people are different and that usually ends up showing me how much we are all the same. I didn't realize that the bar was literally across the street from the hot pink Colosseum and aquamarine arch—maybe that should have tipped me off! The street outside the bar was crowded with men standing around, sitting on the curb and on the railing that enclosed an archeological site across the street. The inside of the bar was tiny, which explains why the street outside was crowded. I bought a bottle of water, headed out across the street through the throng of men and found an empty spot along the railing to lean. This was definitely a great place to people watch.

Watching heterosexual tourists unknowingly work their way through this internationally diverse collection of gay men was my entertainment for the evening. I would watch a straight couple coming from the Colosseum, holding hands to cross the street, start to make their way through the crowd. Entering the crowded street of men, the couple would be totally oblivious to their surroundings, still wrapped in their own personal conversation, until a look of puzzlement came across their faces as they noticed that this crowd was made up entirely of men. They slowed down and took in their surroundings. The moment of realization became apparent—they were engulfed by gay men. Some couples would smile, silently acknowledging to each other that they had figured out where they were. Others acted a little panicked and picked up their pace, almost pushing through the crowd to be clear of us as quickly as possible. Two older American couples had found their way into the crowd. Their puzzlement stopped them dead in their tracks, and as they looked around, the light bulb of realization first turned on above the wives' heads. Simultaneously, they tightly grabbed their husbands' arms and exclaimed, "OH!" I wasn't sure if they grabbed their husbands for protection or if they held tight to them because they were concerned that this group of men would seize their husbands, instantly turning them into fabulous hairdressers and interior designers. The latter seemed to be more the case.

I broke out laughing the moment the panicked ladies blurted out, "OH!"—and so did the two German guys standing to my left. We looked at each other and then pointed at the ladies, who were now pulling their oblivious husbands through the crowd as if running from a fire. The Germans and I laughed louder when we realized that we had been watching the same thing. They didn't speak Italian and I don't speak German, so English became our common language. Pity, because I really wanted to practice my Italian in a social setting. They were on vacation in Rome for the weekend before heading south to Naples. It was their first time in Rome and we compared stories about what sights we had seen, each trying to encourage the other to go experience our favorite things. I told them that they had to go to the *cupola* of Saint Peter's and they encouraged me to wander the Aventine Hill and see the pyramid.

As they were telling me about the pyramid, the Italian guy to my right, overhearing our conversation, joined in. He was from Palermo, Sicily, and spoke very little English, so when our English was beyond his comprehension I tried to translate into Italian. It was harder than I expected because, as Nonna and Alessandra explained to me one night, a Sicilian would have a very hard time understanding a Venetian—the accents and use of the Italian language are that different. Identical words had different syllables emphasized. Consider how different sounding the word "emphasis" would be if it were pronounced "em-PHA-sis." Also, regional slang comes into play. In America, someone from California might say "excellent," while a person from Boston would say "wicked good." I had to speak very slowly in Italian to our newfound Sicilian friend and he had to do the same for me, but at least I was getting a chance to speak directly to an Italian in his almost native tongue.

It was an evening of international conversation between the Germans, the Sicilian and me. We chatted about Rome, our homelands, the people that passed through the crowd and the crowd of guys itself. Seeing this wide variety of gay men proved to us how homosexuality could not be attributed to anything other than genetics. We doubted that all of these men from around the world had overbearing mothers and weak fathers or that being gay was due to their environment. Sorry, Sigmund.

I wished my new friends *un buon viaggio*—a good vacation—and walked back toward my apartment, stopping at a pizzeria near the Pantheon to eat a couple pieces of mushroom pizza. Of course, I went to the same *gelateria* as last night, and I just finished my third gelato of the day—*cioccolato e bacio*—chocolate and chocolate with hazelnuts. *Mi piace gelato molto!*

★ Even though I did not cook anything today, here is a recipe for one of the simplest and most famous Italian antipasti—prosciutto e melone. *Served with a glass of white wine while seated in a* piazza *enjoying a break from the afternoon rush, well*—perfetto!

Prosciutto e Melone

Prosciutto and Cantaloupe

2-inch cubes of peeled and seeded cantaloupe
Sliced prosciutto, 1 slice per 4 cubes of cantaloupe

Cut each slice of prosciutto in half length-wise and then cut those halves in half cross-wise, creating 4 pieces of prosciutto per original slice.

Wrap a piece of the quartered prosciutto around each piece of cantaloupe, overlapping the ends and securing with a toothpick.

Arrange on a platter and serve.

Makes as many as you wish to prepare.

It couldn't be easier or more refreshing. "Molto semplice, no?"

IL GIORNO QUINDICI (Day Fifteen)

I didn't want to waste a minute of my last day *a Roma*, so I was out the door early to mail postcards from the Vatican post office and take the Germans' advice from last night—I took the metro across Rome to explore the Aventine Hill, the *Piramide* and the *Cimitero Acattolico*—non-Catholic, Protestant Cemetery.

There are many famous people buried in this cemetery, the English poets Keats and Shelley are two. Sadly, the cemetery was closed, but it didn't matter because one section of the cemetery wall had openings in it, just above head height. Some stray stones had been stacked below several of these openings. Obviously, other tourists, as desperate as I, had figured out a way to see into the closed cemetery. I'm sure I looked comical balancing on a stack of uneven stones with my arms stretched above my head trying to take pictures of the cemetery. I wasn't able to see any famous tombstones, but my camera showed me the lush setting inside the walls.

According to the sign posted outside the Protestant Cemetery of Rome, the earliest graves were from 1738. Viterbo has a large cemetery within walking distance of the house that I now want to visit, since this Roman cemetery has again sparked my unexplainable fascination with old graves.

The more I walk around Rome, the more it intrigues me. There is such a collection of ancient and modern, past and present, everyday and out-of-the-ordinary. I passed the *Piramide*, which is the tomb of Caius Cestius, a Roman magistrate, who died in 12 BC. The large, white marble pyramid was such an odd sight—I always think of pyramids being surrounded by sand and camels, not being in the middle of a busy thoroughfare, next to a lush cemetery and adjacent to a large park. I remember how intrigued I was by the King Tut exhibit I saw on a field trip to Chicago when I was a freshman in high school. Wasn't everyone in America intrigued by that exhibit, and everything Egyptian, as it toured the country in 1979? It seems the same was true for Roman citizens after conquering Egypt in 30 BC. The mysteries of Egypt captured Caius Cestius's imagination in 12 BC as much as they did mine almost 2000 years later in Chicago and here, again, on a Roman street corner in 2005.

In the adjacent park, on my way up to the top of the Aventine Hill, there was another fascinating sight—on the park benches, local women had set up shop as beauticians. I guess today was haircut Sunday in this park. About twenty women had each claimed a bench by placing their plastic carrier/bag of supplies at one end of the bench, and stood behind the back cutting or styling their seated and caped clients' hair. The clients were of all ages—little kids, young women, fashionable middle-aged men and women and retirees. Some of the beauticians had three or four people waiting in line. It was a sight from a time long past, from a post-WWII Italy or earlier. As odd as it appeared, it was a gorgeous day to sit outside in a park, so why not get a haircut, too?

I took a rather roundabout way from the park to the top of the Aventine Hill. A back alley—more of a path—wound its way up behind some houses heading toward the walled Parco Savello. The path was so steep that as it climbed higher and higher, I was even with the terra-cotta rooftops of the houses lining the path below to my right. Almost at the top, the alley took a hard left and, had I continued walking straight, I would have walked up an ancient set of stone steps that led to a large wrought iron gate in the corner of the *parco's* wall. I stopped at the bottom of these steps, because a fat black cat was picturesquely sitting against the gate where it hinged to the wall. We noticed each other at the same time—his ears perked up when he caught sight of me, just as I felt my head react in the same way.

Rome is famous for its abundance of feral cats that live amongst its ruins. At every souvenir stand throughout the city, photos of these cats are placed on everything from mugs and t-shirts to postcards and calendars. This Roman cat was perfectly staged at this gate for my own souvenir photo. We faced each other off for a moment before I slowly reached into my bag and ever so discreetly took out my camera. I did not want to scare him off, and just as I was about to take the picture, a child came running around the corner and spooked my fat Roman under the gate and out of sight.

I was not happy—I wanted to ring his neck. Honestly, I couldn't be mad at him; after all, he was just doing what children do, but I thought long and hard about what kind of flavor he would add to Nonna's *zuppa di gatti*—maybe that would attract my fat cat back. Seconds later his parents rounded the corner and followed him up the steps to peer through the gate. There was going to be no chance of a souvenir photo now.

As I put my camera back into my bag, a nearby church bell started striking noon. I immediately took out my cell phone and called Richard. He has a passion for hearing church bells ring, and regardless of whether we are at the Episcopal cathedral in Birmingham, a Catholic church in Chicago, an abbey in England, in front of Notre Dame in Paris or outside Saint Peter's in Rome, life for Richard comes to a dead stop as he stands and listens to the bells peal. Italian bells have a very distinctive and particular tone—rather flat and tinny, as if Time had tarnished and cracked their once deep and resonate notes like those of their French, English and American cousins.

He answered the phone at the stroke of four and I held the phone high over my head so he could listen.

Clang...

Clang... "Hello? ...Hello?" I could hear Richard's voice faintly come from over my head.

"Shhh, quiet...." *Clang...* "Just listen," I said, putting the phone back up into the air.

Clang...

Clang... "Who is this?" he asked.

"It's me. I'm in Rome. Be quiet and listen to the bells."

Clang...

Clang...

Clang... "Mark, what are you doing?"

"Did you hear the bells? It's noon in Rome, I'm in an alley, and church bells started ringing so I called you. Did you hear them?"

"Faintly."

"Faintly? Damn. I thought you'd love hearing the bells live from Rome."

"Mark, it's 5 o'clock in the morning here."

In my excitement to call him I completely forgot about the time change.

"Oops! Sorry, Richard, I forgot."

"I'm going back to bed. Bye."

"Okay. *Ciao, ciao, ciao!!*"

He had hung up.

Oh well. Sometimes good intentions are poorly timed—no pun intended. Cell phones are great, but there are times when the immediacy of a long distance call is only exactly that—a long distance.

I walked up the rest of the alley, made a right along the front of the park with its small orchard of orange trees and down a wide walkway that led to a viewing terrace on the edge of the hill. High above the Tiber, the view is of Trastevere and beyond to the dome of Saint Peter's. To the right, the view overlooks the tree-lined Palatine Hill with the Vittorio Emanuele II

Monument rising above the treetops exposing its two large bronze sculptures of horse drawn chariots carrying winged victories. Romans have enjoyed the view from this terrace for over a thousand years. Today, a rainbow colored hot air balloon aimlessly floated high above the chariots. What a peaceful view. I sat on the edge of the terrace feeling homesick and wished that Richard could have been here. I realized that previously shared experiences of stopping to listen to church bells were magical only because we were experiencing them together—this time there was only magic in the moment of dialing a phone. I needed the serenity of this view to get over the awkwardness of my well intentioned, but clunky, call to Richard. I sat there staring out over Rome for a long time. Long enough to hear the tarnished tones toll again.

Down the street from the park is the *Piazza dei Cavalieri di Malta*—the Square of the Knights of Malta. The *piazza* is bordered on three sides by the walls of two different properties: the grounds of the Benedictine Monastery of Sant'Anselmo and the Grand Priory of the Sovereign Order of Malta. The walls are high and studded with obelisks, plaques, monuments and urns celebrating the achievements of the knights. The *piazza* was empty except for a parked police car with two policemen inside. I felt a little odd standing in the cobblestone *piazza* alone, while being watched by the police—why were they there? The only time I have noticed police officers just sitting around is when they were guarding a government building or an historic site. What was special about this *piazza*?

I took several pictures and tried to decipher the information on the plaques—all in the shadow of *la polizia*. Suddenly, a taxi pulled into the *piazza* and parked. Two passengers climbed out, walked over to the large, green-painted wooden doors of the Grand Priory entrance and bent down to peer through the keyhole. I could hear "oohs" and "ahs" as they each took a turn at the keyhole.

The police certainly didn't care about these Peeping Toms, but why were they peeping? They jumped back into the waiting taxi and off they sped. My curiosity was piqued but not to the point of doing anything about it. I went through the large gates leading to Sant'Anselmo. The grounds were littered with mature palm trees and beds of roses in full bloom, but the cloister was under renovation so I couldn't go into the church or walk the entire complex.

When I came back out through the gates, four new tourists were peering through the keyhole. My curiosity was starting to get the better of me. I sat on a marble bench against one of the *piazza* walls and waited until the four climbed back into their waiting taxi and left. I walked over to the *polizia* and tried my minimal Italian.

"*Scusi, signori. Le persone guardando alla toppa, perchè?*" —"Excuse me, sirs. Why are people looking at the keyhole?"

"*Guarda,*" one of the cops said.

I smiled and headed to the keyhole, bent over, and just before looking through, I glanced over at the cops, who waved me on, as if saying, "Go on, look!" I felt a little like Alice in Wonderland. Through the keyhole was a wondrous sight: down a long hedge-lined walk was the distant dome of Saint Peter's, perfectly centered in the gothic window-shape trimmed hedges. This keyhole provided a magical view of the dome of Saint Peter's. How Piranesi, the architect of this priory in 1765, perfectly centered the dome, which must be two kilometers away, in a walkway that could be spied from a keyhole, is beyond me. Alice may have stepped through the looking glass, but I wanted one of her shrinking pills so I could jump through the keyhole and tour the magical garden on the other side.

"WOW!" I said, pointing at the keyhole and looking at the cops, as if they should come over and see the view.

"*Si,*" said the cops, laughing at my stunned reaction.

"*Questa vista è stupificente,*" —"This view is amazing,"— I said.

"*Ha ragione,*" —"You are right,"— one said.

Another taxi pulled up, and a young couple got out and headed my way. I walked away from the keyhole with a Cheshire cat grin on my face and passed by the officers.

"*Grazie. Grazie, signori!*" I said.

"*Certo.*"

"*Buona giornata,*" I said.

"*Anche a Lei.*" —"You, too."

I headed back toward the alley that lead up to this magical hill. I don't remember much history about the Knights of Malta other than at one point they were a military order that protected pilgrims during the Crusades. I get them confused with the Knights Templar and the Priory of Sion—the religious sect that added all of the intrigue and drama to the book "The Da Vinci Code." The truth and fiction of these three organizations are intertwined in my head and peering through the keyhole of a silent, secretive, guarded priory added to the mystery and confusion. From the *Piramide*, the *Cimitero Acattolico* and the park full of hairdressers to the back alley hike up to the orange orchard and view from Parco Savello, the Piazza dei Cavalieri di Malta and the keyhole view of Saint Peter's, the Aventine Hill, with all of these things, is a most spectacular place.

The metro ride back to the apartment gave me a little extra time to stop and have my last gelato in Rome. I savored the *pistacchio e cioccolato gusti*—pistachio and chocolate tastes—while enjoying my last walk through the Prati. Stefano and Anna Maria, his wife, were such kind hosts, and I must have made a good impression, because they were nice enough to let me keep my things in the apartment until 3:00 p.m. (checkout is supposed to be 10:30 a.m.). My simple Italian is keeping me in good stead. I was hugged and kissed on each cheek by them both as I left the apartment.

"*Ciao, Marco. Ciao. Ciao.*"

"*Ciao, ciao, ciao. Grazie per tutti. Il vostro appartamento è bellissimo.*"

"*Ciao, ciao, ciao. Ciao, ciao.*"

"*Ciao, ciao, ciao,*" I said, as the gate closed behind me and I waved back at my hosts—my new friends.

"*Ciao, ciao, ciao, ciao,*" they said, arms poking through the gate, still waving at me, but out of sight. Even in Rome they play the "*Ciao, Ciao*" game—and win!

The train ride north was much more pleasant than the ride down to Rome. I actually got to sit, put my feet up and take a little nap. Lillo and Alessandra picked me up at the Orte station and we were off on a new adventure. I thought we were heading back to the house, but we drove through Viterbo and out into *la campagnia*—the countryside—to Blera, Lillo's hometown. It was a quaint little village that we passed through in a blink of an eye. He did point out his favorite *gelateria*, bread shop and the butcher where he got the *porchetta*. Just outside of Blera we crossed over a bridge that spanned a deep and densely forested ravine. Lillo pulled over to the side of the road the moment we crossed the bridge.

"Marco, Lillo wants to show you this bridge and the view of Blera from it," Alessandra said.

"Certo, Lillo. Ho il piacere," —"Sure, Lillo. I'd like that,"— I said.

"Marco, vieni," Lillo said, and we were all out of the car, walking back across the narrow two-lane bridge. Lillo stopped in the middle and pointed to Blera. From there, looking across the lush green ravine, the stucco buildings glowed warm and bright in the setting sun. Buildings with modern conveniences (satellite dishes and TV antennas) and cars were visible between the narrow and crowded streets, but this tiny village clinging to the side of a ravine was still timeless. Church steeples with their crosses silhouetted the sky, long reaching vines climbed brick walls connecting the buildings to the forest below—the 20th century melted away.

"Lillo, la tua città è bellissima!" —"Lillo, your city is beautiful!"

"Grazie, Marco. Sono d'accordo con te." —"Thanks, Mark. I agree."

The three of us stood silently on the bridge enjoying the moment, but it wasn't long before a car came speeding over the bridge and broke the mood. *"Marco, guarda,"* Lillo said, pointing down toward the bottom of the ravine. There, tucked into the trees, was a small stone bridge that looked as if it had been there for hundreds of years.

"Lillo, quel ponte è molto vecchio?" —"Lillo, is that bridge very old?"

"Si, si, Marco. Gli Etruschi hanno costruito quel ponte." —"Yes. The Etruscans built that bridge."

"*Stupefacente!*"

I wanted to figure out the way down to that bridge, to walk across the past, to stand on it and look up at the future, but it was at the bottom of the ravine and I could tell that Lillo wanted to get back to the car.

We drove on a bit further before Lillo pulled over on the left-hand shoulder and parked. I thought there might have been car trouble, but Alessandra told me to get out and follow Lillo. He was heading down a little driveway that was behind the parked car. I quickly caught up with him and saw a thatched roof lean-to with five large white cows feeding from a wooden trough. It was a very rustic shelter, and beyond it was another one with two beautiful horses under it. I turned around and asked Alessandra if this was their farm. "*Si, si, Marco.*"

Marianna's SUV pulled up and out she jumped followed by Marco, Anna and Giulio. What a great surprise! We all hugged and kissed. I was chatting with Anna and Giulio as best I could when Marianna brought her horse around to greet me. He was a beautiful dark chocolate brown and was so friendly that he leaned his head immediately into my chest when I reached up to pet him.

"*Marco, gli piaci,*" —"Mark, he likes you,"— Marianna said.

"*Naturalmente, sono una persona molto importante dall'America.*"

"*Naturalmente,*" Marianna said, smirking at me—even Anna and Giulio laughed at that.

Marianna was eager to show me a trick she had trained her horse to perform. She got a white feed bucket, stood in front of him, and holding the bucket up said, "*Hai fame?*" —"Are you hungry?" The horse nodded his head several times. "*Buono. Dici per favore.*" —"Good. Say please." He bent his right front leg and, leaning back, tucked his head low and bowed to her. When he stood back up, she asked, "*Sei sicuro?*" —"Are you sure?" Enthusiastically, he nodded, throwing his long mane around, leaving his bangs over his eyes like a teenage boy in need of a haircut. I applauded, "*Brava e bravo!*" Marianna opened the bucket, took out an apple and gave it to him. I swear he laughed, if that is even possible, when he took the apple from her hand. Marianna and her horse have a very special bond, and the connection between them, above and beyond the trick, was apparent. Her horse not only liked her, he loved her and she loved him right back.

Marianna, Lillo and Marco went to feed the cows and horses while Alessandra and I chatted with Anna and Giulio. Actually, they chatted and I tried to stay afloat in the conversation. I felt something brush up against my leg and looked down to see a cat rubbing itself on me. When I reached down to pet it, three more cats came running over to me.

"Marco ... DOVE I GATTI?"

I looked up; Alessandra was looking right into my eyes, as she nodded her head to the right. Cats. There they were—at least ten more cats romping around the stables. Pointing wildly, I said, *"Alessandra, qui. I gatti sono qui! E qua! Qua! Qua! LA ZUPPA DI GATTI È PER QUESTI GATTI!"*

"Marco, sei geniale!" Alessandra said and applauded my discovery. Anna and Giulio looked at us as if we were crazy. The mystery of *zuppa di gatti* was solved! Nonna was making the soup for Lillo to bring to the farm and feed the cats. What a great way to feed the cats without spending any money on cat food. Nonna is the clever one, not me.

We left the farm and a little farther up the road we arrived at the tiny town of Civitella Cesi for their annual summer festival. Francesca and Stefano pulled up behind Marianna's SUV just as we parked our cars a distance outside the town's ancient wall. Nonna was now the only one missing. I wished she had climbed out of Stefano's car, too. That would have been such a great treat, but she stayed at home, as usual, and no doubt enjoyed the peace and quiet. I couldn't believe the number of people heading toward the narrow *porta* entrance. We got in line and slowly worked our way toward the opening in the ancient wall. At one time, this *porta* was the only way in or out of the town. It was only ten feet wide and the old wooden gate, which would have been lowered at night to keep the town safe, had long since vanished. On the wall just outside the *porta*, a handmade, decorative, shield-shaped cardboard menu was posted:

Fettuccine al Tartufo	€7.00
Fettuccine al Ragù	€5.00
Bistecca	€6.00
Rollè al Tartufo	€5.00
Bocconcini Vitella Tartufo	€5.00
Fagioli con Cotiche	€4.00
Patate al Tartufo	€2.50
Pancetta	€1.50
Salsiccia	€1.00
Bruschetta	€.50
Acqua Lt 1.5	€1.00
Vino Lt 1	€2.50

There was a lot of debate about what we should get and how we should divide it among us. At times I felt as if we were at a Chinese restaurant trying to figure out the perfect combination of dishes to share in order to satisfy everyone's particular tastes.

"*Marco, che cosa mangi?*" —"Mark, what do you want to eat?"— Alessandra asked.

"*Tutti! Tutti! Tutti!*" —"Everything!"

I knew that wasn't possible, of course, but it all sounded so good. *Tartufo*—truffles—seemed to be a popular ingredient and it is one of my favorite things.

"*Alessandra, mi piace tartufi. Allora, vorrei mangiare qualcosa con tartufi.*"

"*Certamente, Marco.*"

When I told Lillo that I had decided on the *fettuccine al tartufo,* he insisted that I also had to have the *rollè al tartufo*—a thin piece of beef rolled around black truffles, sautéed and braised in red wine—and the *fagioli con cotiche*—beans cooked with pork rind (an Italian version of pork & beans). Lillo and Giulio took everyone's order as we walked through the *porta* and purchased the appropriate food tickets at the table just inside. Giulio also bought three one-liter bottles of red wine—you can't enjoy Italian food without a little *vino*.

Once inside the city wall, we continued walking through the food line exchanging our tickets for the various items from the individual food stations. One of the stations was all about grilled bread; there was a guy whose only task was to grill bread. On the huge rectangular grill of glowing red coals, he had dozens of slices of bread toasting to a dark brown, almost blackened color, with beautiful dark grill marks running diagonally across both sides of each slice. He was a young guy, and although you might think the job of grilling bread to be unglamorous, here in Italy, a perfectly grilled slice of bread is as important to a meal as the entrée itself. Smiling wide, he took great pride in each and every piece he handed out. In Italy, each dish is a simple combination of perfect ingredients, and without perfectly grilled bread, a bruschetta would never be perfect, and that would be criminal, especially in a small town where everyone takes tremendous honor in providing gracious hospitality to their visitors. If he failed with the bread, his family and the family name would be shamed forever, not to mention his poor *nonna* having to try to hold her head up in church, all the time knowing her grandson had failed her—just try to grill bread with that kind of pressure.

When we arrived at the *fettuccine* station, I handed my ticket over the table and the guy went to get my pasta from the curtain behind him; he left it partially opened as he disappeared. There was no wizard behind this curtain pulling levers to create the pasta; instead there were a dozen townswomen making the *fettuccine* by hand. I turned to Lillo and said, *"Guardi, Lillo. Guardi."* He explained to me that this was the third day of the festival and that over the past two days the women had served over 4,000 plates of *fettuccine*—4,000 plates of <u>handmade</u> *fettuccine*. These women were not using machines to make the pasta. They were mixing it by hand on pasta boards, kneading it, rolling it out with long rolling pins, cutting it and, finally, cooking it. I couldn't believe what a Herculean effort that must have been—many of the women were *nonne* who looked as if they had been making pasta for decades ... many, many decades.

"Wow!" I said.

"*Si, Marco.* Wa-ow!" Lillo said. It was the first English word Lillo has ever used in front of me. It shouldn't really surprise me—the look on my face and the amazement in my voice were more than enough for Lillo to understand the meaning.

We were all carrying multiple plates, glasses, wine and water bottles, looking as if we hadn't eaten in weeks, as we made our way through the town's little *piazza* toward the seating area. The *piazza* was cute, quaint and kind of what I expected it to be—a stereotypical movie version of a town festival—it was authentic but did seem predictable: strings of large multi-colored lights were strung between buildings across the *piazza*, and a little stage had been set up for a DJ to play music. American music—a Bon Jovi song was playing as we walked through.

"*Ricordi l'uomo canta il karaoke a Bagnaia? Dov'è adesso?*" —"Remember the man singing karaoke in Bagnaia? Where is he now?"—I said to Alessandra.

"*A casa che canta con i suoi cani,*" —"At home singing with his dogs,"—she said.

"*Si, si, lo credo. Poveri cani!*" —"Yes, I believe it. Poor dogs!"— Lillo said.

The seating arrangement, however, was definitely unexpected. We turned the corner to sit down and in front of me was a single, unending row of folding tables placed end-to-end, centered in the middle of the street. The row stretched for blocks down the slightly twisting and turning cobblestone street until it turned out of sight—it was one long, single table seating for 2,000 or more. We found an empty section of table between some other families and sat down on the benches. In a heartbeat, everyone was passing plates of food and glasses of wine and making sure that I had a taste of everything—Lillo had even purchased extra sausages. Giulio made sure that our wine glasses never went more than half empty. Many of the passing townspeople stopped to speak to Lillo and Alessandra. Since Lillo had grown up in nearby Blera, he knew many people here, too. It was fun to see them socialize with friends and acquaintances.

It may have been the setting and my dining companions, or that I had seen the pasta crew behind the curtain, or maybe it was the five glasses of wine Giulio poured me, but I have never had better tasting food in my life. The $10 plate of *fettuccine al tartufo* would have cost twice that in a fine Italian restaurant in a larger city and could not have tasted nearly as delicious. The sausages were spicy without being volcanic, the *fagioli con cotiche* was salty and flavorful with just a hint of tomato and pepper and the *rollè al tartufo* was earthy, rustic and tender.

American music played on—mercifully, no one sang—and dusk turned to dark as we sat under the stars and street lights, eating, laughing, drinking and enjoying every moment of being together—new family, childhood friends, old acquaintances and one very full and slightly tipsy *persona molto importante dall'America.*

Tortino di Formaggio

Cheese Tart

This is the recipe for the cheese tart Nonna and I made on Tuesday, since I didn't cook anything while in Rome today. Serve this with a side salad of mixed greens lightly dressed with a balsamic vinaigrette and have a simple and perfect summer lunch.

2 tablespoons plus 1 teaspoon unsalted butter

3 tablespoons plain dried bread crumbs

8 sheets phyllo dough

2 eggs

1 cup milk

1 teaspoon salt

½ teaspoon freshly ground black pepper, or more to taste (Nonna used 1 teaspoon of pepper)

1 cup mixture (½ cup each) of 2 grated cheeses (such as fontina, provolone, gruyère or asiago. Do not use mozzarella because it is too wet; also do not use Parmigiano-Reggiano, Grana Padano or a pecorino cheese because they are too dry.)

Preheat oven to 350 degrees.

Melt 2 tablespoons butter in a small pan over low heat. Remove from heat and set aside to cool.

Using the remaining 1 teaspoon butter, coat the inside of a 10-inch springform nonstick pan. Place the bread crumbs in the pan and shake the pan until the bread crumbs entirely coat the butter, discarding any excess bread crumbs. Set aside.

Place a sheet of phyllo dough on a flat surface and brush with melted butter. Place a second sheet on top and butter it. Looking down on the springform pan as if at a clock, place the dough in the pan, running lengthwise from 12 to 6. Form the dough to the shape of the pan. Take the next two sheets of phyllo dough and butter as the first set. Place in pan running from 9 to 3, forming to fit the pan. Keep the long ends against the sides if they start to fall down. Repeat the process with the remaining 4 sheets running them in pairs from 10 to 4 and 8 to 2.

In a medium bowl, combine the eggs, milk, salt and pepper and whisk until well combined and frothy. Whisk in the cheese until combined. Pour the cheese mixture into the pan, making sure the cheese is evenly distributed. Bake for 35 to 40 minutes, or until the phyllo dough is golden and the center is set.*

Cool in pan on a wire rack. When cooled (or just slightly warm), remove from pan and serve at, or just above, room temperature. Slice into pie-shaped wedges.

This makes 4 to 8 servings.

* *Note: As the tortino bakes, the phyllo dough going up the sides of the pan will collapse over the top of the cheese mixture forming a partial top crust. Pretty ingenious.*

Il Giorno Sedici (Day Sixteen)

I woke up this morning still thinking about how much fun we had at the festival last night in Civitella Cesi. That long continuous table packed with people and running block after block down the main street, disappearing out of sight, was a priceless communal experience.

Today is *Ferragosto* (Assumption Day)—a national holiday celebrating the Virgin Mary's ascension into heaven. Major holidays here are celebrated as holidays in America were celebrated forty years ago: the vast majority of Italians have the day off and almost all businesses are closed. Banks, gas stations, grocery stores and shopping malls aren't open today, so a national holiday is just that—a holiday for the nation. Alessandra says that businesses here are slowly adopting the practice of staying open for holidays or an afternoon siesta, that more American fast food restaurants are opening and that there seems to be a movement toward people beginning to work round the clock. That saddens Alessandra and me because it would remove the very fabric of *la dolce vita*. Italians could become as rushed as we are and no longer take moments to enjoy *una passeggiata, un gelato* or *una siesta. La dolce vita* celebrates the fact that life is not only about a paycheck, or being able to get a hamburger and fries at 2:00 a.m., or having to work throughout the night restocking grocery store shelves or going to the all-night gym. Life is about savoring the sunset, taking a rejuvenating nap in the middle of the day, pausing to appreciate the beauty of a rose on the side of the road, having your children's laughter fill your soul—letting those moments inspire your life. That might be more of a romantic perception than the exact truth of the situation, but it is certainly the truth I have come to witness, embrace and appreciate while living in Viterbo. *"Eh,"*—who needs the exact truth when in Italy? Life is all about the metaphor.

There was no rushing on this *Ferragosto* morning; we all slept in later than usual. When I came downstairs, Lillo was heading out to the farm to check on the horses and cows—and to dole out the *zuppa di gatti*.

"Nonna, ti ho preso! So la storia della zuppa di gatti!" —"Nonna, I caught you! I know the story of cat soup!"— I said, seeing Nonna cap the jar and hand it to Lillo. Without blinking an eye, Nonna said, *"Hai dormito bene, Marco?"* Cutting me off before I could answer, she stuck her tongue out at me—and laughed.

"Nonna, ricordati che Marco è geniale," —"Nonna, remember that Mark is clever,"— Lillo said.

"Si, si, Nonna. È vero. Io sono geniale! Dunque ... e perchè, ieri sera ho visto i gatti," —"Yes, Nonna. It's true. I am clever! Well ... and because last night I saw the cats,"— I said.

"Marco è Sherlock Holmes," Nonna said. We all got a big kick out of that. Lillo laughed all the way through the backyard and out the back gate.

Alessandra asked me if I have dreamed in Italian yet. I wasn't sure if she was asking if I had dreamt of Italian things or if there was Italian dialogue in my dreams. She explained that students who spend more than a week usually have Italian-only conversations in their dreams. I have dreamed of

Italian things since my arrival, but Italian dialogue has not yet invaded my subconscious. She assured me that it is only a matter of time until it does.

Even though it was a holiday, I still had my lessons, which is fine, because I never think of them as a chore. In the kitchen we started making *una crostata di marmellata*—a sweet-crusted tart covered with Nonna's homemade plum jam. Everyday we make a dessert or something to snack on and it is not always something sweet. We make as many, if not more, savory desserts and snacks. It is refreshing to eat *uno spuntino* and not feel my teeth ache from the high sugar content.

Several days ago we were talking about *gnocchi*—small dumplings. The classic version is made from either potatoes or ricotta cheese, but Nonna said that she had a recipe for roasted pumpkin *gnocchi*. She was concerned that it might be impossible to find fresh pumpkin this early in the season, but she added it to the list of things we had to make. So today I was surprised and thrilled when Nonna pulled sliced pumpkin out of the refrigerator—Lillo found fresh pumpkin yesterday morning while I was still in Rome. *Bravo, Lillo!*

"*Nonna, oggi facciamo gli gnocchi di zucca?*" —"Nonna, we are making pumpkin *gnocchi* today?"

"*Certamente, per te faremo tutta la lista.*" —"Of course, we are going to make the whole list for you."

"*Grazie, Nonna. Grazie tanto,*" I said, and leaned over and hugged her.

"*Marco,*" she said, blushing, "*Lavoriamo.*" —"Let's work."

We brushed the pumpkin slices with olive oil, sea salt and black pepper and placed them on a tray to roast in the toaster oven. Even though the daily temperature has dropped since I first arrived, Nonna said it was still *troppo caldo*—too hot—to use the kitchen oven.

We served *gli gnocchi* two ways: in a red *sugo* with basil, and with melted butter, fresh sage leaves and Parmigiano. *Buonissimi!* Nonna also made veal roast cooked in wine, garlic, butter, water, rosemary, sage and thyme.

Lillo called to say that he was going to be a few minutes late for lunch, and while we waited for him, Francesca came downstairs to the kitchen table looking glum. She plopped herself down in her chair at the table and let out a huge sigh. I thought, "Once again, the Scorpion is having a bad moment."

"*Cosa c'è?*"—"What's the matter?"— asked Alessandra. The Scorpion let out another big sigh and a single tear ran down her face. Nonna patted her on the back, and Francesca started her way through a sad story that was punctuated by wild hand gestures, big sighs and tears that flooded her large, chestnut eyes. Alessandra explained to me that Francesca had broken up with her old boyfriend four months ago to the day, and although she was thrilled to be dating Stefano now, today she could not get the happy moments with Luca out of her mind. The three women talked back and forth as mother and grandmother tried to comfort their melancholy Scorpion. Alessandra surprised me when she asked, "Marco, what would you say to Francesca?" "Wow, I really am part of the family now," I thought to myself. It took a moment to think what I would say to my daughter, if I had one, in this situation. All the beautiful images of Rome came to mind— the images inside Santa Maria del Popolo, which provoked me to embrace all of life and not just the happy moments. It is life's juxtapositions that make it worth living.

"Um, well ... I can completely understand that missing the happy moments with Luca is making her sad, but ... and this may sound odd ... she should be happy about being sad. Life is about joy and sorrow, the good times and the bad. Her sadness shows that she felt love for Luca, and even though that relationship didn't last, without that love and its loss she would not be able to appreciate the happiness she now feels with Stefano." Alessandra translated and Francesca agreed. Even Nonna nodded approvingly. I was now the fourth family member around the kitchen table—coming together to lift up the one in pain.

When I woke up from my afternoon siesta, I decided to give Richard a quick call. We hadn't spoken since the church bells in Rome, and Francesca's melancholy over Luca put me in the mood to call home.

"Hey! Are you all right?" he asked.

"Yeah, why?"

"Well, you never call at this time. Usually you call me in the afternoon at work."

"Oh, I know, but I was feeling weird about how our last conversation ended and I wanted to call to make sure that you weren't mad."

He laughed. *"Sweetie dahlin', everythin's fine."* (Every now and then he exaggerates his southern accent for comic effect.) "I enjoyed *hearin'* the bells … from what I can remember."

I laughed. "Okay, well, I am glad to hear that."

"I'm off to work. Talk to you later. Gotta go…."

"Okay, love you."

"Love you, too."

Tonight for dinner we breaded and fried sliced eggplant. Nonna showed me how to make a Sicilian frittata (simply eggs, pecorino cheese, parsley, salt and pepper), which was rolled up like a scroll as it cooked, instead of being folded in half like an omelet. We finished off the leftover veal roast from lunch.

Dessert was "American" watermelon. It is considered American because its shape is elongated—Italian watermelons are round. I had some more of the plum jam *crostata*, too.

Even though I was very happy while I was gorging myself at dinner tonight, I am now a little sad about feeling so stuffed. It's time to waddle off to bed.

Crostata di Marmellata

Jam Tart

I like this tart because the filling is so simple—just open a jar of your favorite homemade preserves. If you are not a jam-making person, no worries, use your favorite store-bought brand. Semplice, semplice, semplice!

To prepare the pan:
Unsalted butter
All-purpose flour

For the crust:
2 cups plus 1 tablespoon all-purpose flour
½ cup plus 1 tablespoon sugar
⅛ teaspoon salt
9 tablespoons unsalted butter, room temperature
1 tablespoon fresh lemon juice
1 tablespoon *grappa* (water may be substituted)
1 large egg, slightly beaten

For the filling:
¾ cup plum, apricot, peach or mixed berry preserves (homemade fruit
   preserves are preferred—use your favorite one)

Preheat oven to 350 degrees.

Butter and flour a 9 ½-inch non-stick tart pan with removable bottom. Set aside.

In a large bowl combine the flour, sugar and salt, using a fork to mix. Add the butter in small pieces, lemon juice, *grappa* and egg to the dry mixture.

Using a fork, stir the ingredients together, incorporating the butter until the dough just starts to come together as a whole. Using your hands, form the dough into a ball, and knead it slightly in the bowl until all the flour has been worked into the dough. Do not overwork the dough.

Put two-thirds of the dough into the prepared tart pan, and using your fingers, evenly distribute and form the dough to fit the pan, going up the fluted sides to form the crust. Place the tart pan into the refrigerator for 30 minutes to firm and chill the crust. Take the remaining ⅓ dough, form it into a ball, wrap in plastic wrap and place in the refrigerator to chill for 30 minutes, too. This dough will be used to form a lattice-patterned top crust.

After chilling, remove the tart pan from the refrigerator and spread the preserves evenly across the bottom of the crust. Set aside.

To form the lattice crust, remove the reserved ⅓ dough from the refrigerator and unwrap onto a rolling surface. Break off ¼ of the dough and form it into a cigar-shape between the palms of your hands. Place the cigar-shaped dough on the surface and, using your fingers, gently, but quickly, roll the dough back and forth, stretching it out from the middle, to create a "rope" that is roughly the size of your little finger. (Note: Because of the amount of butter, the heat of your hands will soften the dough. Do not become discouraged if the rope breaks or if it gets too sticky. Simply pinch the broken ends together and continue gently rolling. This is a rustic tart, so the ropes do not have to be perfect. They are supposed to look handmade.)

Evenly space 4 "ropes" along the top of the jam, pressing the ends to connect to the dough at the sides of the pan. Give the pan a quarter turn and repeat by placing another 4 "ropes" across the top of the first "ropes," creating a lattice pattern. Secure the ends by pressing into the dough at the edge of the pan.

Bake for 37 to 40 minutes, until the edges and top crust are golden brown.* Place the tart pan on a wire rack to cool. When cooled, remove the outer ring and gently slide the tart off the bottom pan onto a serving plate. Cut into wedges and serve warm or at room temperature.

This makes 8 standard servings.

★Note: The bottom crust will have a tendency to get an air "bubble" around 20 minutes into the baking process. Using a fork, puncture the bubble down through the bottom crust to release the trapped air. Repeat if any additional "bubbles" occur.

IL GIORNO DICIASETTE (Day Seventeen)

Nonna and I started preparing tonight's dinner by roasting red peppers, which in Italian are called *peperoni*—yes, red bell peppers, and not a pizza sausage, are called *peperoni*. When Nonna and her husband went to America in the early 1970s, they were very surprised when the waiter brought them a pizza covered in a spicy sliced sausage—they thought they were going to get peppers when they ordered *una pizza con peperoni*.

We also made *una torta dolce*—a sweet cake. It is a very simple recipe that uses a single serving container of flavored yogurt (we used mixed berry), and the rest of the ingredients are measured with that same yogurt container. She added freshly sliced apple and pear from Stefano's almost daily fruit delivery from his parents' estate south of Rome. Nonna calls the recipe *"Cuppa, Cuppa, Cuppa,"* because it was a cup of this and a cup of that, and all the ingredients were measured with the same *"cuppa."*

Next were Italian-style deviled eggs, which means the filling was a mixture of canned tuna, capers, olive oil, anchovy paste, bread and the yolks of the hard boiled eggs. It is all pureed with a stick blender and then placed into the halved hard-boiled eggs and topped with a slice of plum tomato. This needs to be tried before saying "Yuck" to these different flavor combinations.

With tonight's dinner done, we moved on to the lunch menu: *risotto con funghi*—rice with mushrooms and *cotolette di tacchino*—turkey cutlets dusted with flour, lightly fried and dressed with some white wine and lemon juice. While we all sat around the table savoring the last flavors of lunch, I remembered that my mother had e-mailed a menu from an Italian-American neighbors' wedding reception that my parents had recently attended. My mother is getting very interested in how Italian and Italian-American things compare and contrast. I brought down the menu and read it aloud. They knew what almost everything was and were amazed that Italian-Americans put on such an authentic Italian feast. Nonna wondered how many *nonne* it took to cook all that food and, as with my mother, the Stefanis enjoyed hearing how the Italian culture has adapted in transferring to America.

After my afternoon language class, Alessandra went upstairs to rest before dinner, but instead of heading upstairs myself, I sat with Nonna in the den and watched TV. Today was *Il Palio di Siena*—a bareback horse race around Siena's central Piazza del Campo. This version of *Il Palio* dates back to 1656 (earlier contests in Siena date back to the 1400s), and is a race between the seventeen *contrade*—neighborhoods—of Siena. Each neighborhood has a different name, symbol and colored flag: *Aquila*, the eagle; *Bruco*, the caterpillar; *Chiocciola*, the snail; *Civetta*, the little owl; *Drago*, the dragon; *Giraffa*, the giraffe; *Istrice*, the porcupine; *Leocorno*, the unicorn; *Lupa*, the female wolf; *Nicchio*, the seashell; *Oca*, the goose; *Onda*, the wave; *Pantera*, the black panther; *Selva*, the forest; *Tartuca*, the tortoise; *Torre*, the tower; and *Montone*, the ram. Here are a few examples of symbols and colors: *Selva*, Forest, is represented by a rhinoceros holding a huge tree hung with hunting items, and its colors are green and orange-yellow with white bands; *Onda*, Wave, is represented by a swimming, crown-wearing dolphin, and its colors are blue and white; and *Torre*, Tower, is presented by an elephant carrying a brick tower on its back, and its colors are dark purple-red with blue and white bands.

When walking through Siena, individual neighborhoods can be identified by the streetlight sconces that line both sides of every street. The streetlights are design- and color-specific to each *contrada*—the *Torre* sconces are a quadrafoil design and have a purple-red shield bearing the image of the elephant with its tower.

The rivalries between *le contrade* are ancient (some dating as far back as the 15th century) and violent (during the 16th century some contest events turned into battles with weapons). Today, in this modern *Il Palio*—yes, the 1656 version is still considered the modern version—ten of the seventeen *contrade* are chosen (seven by right and three by lottery) to compete in the race, so it is a great honor and a blessing to be running in *Il Palio*.

Il Palio festivities start days before the race. There are the *contrade* dinners that, much like the city festival at Civitella Cesi, occur at an endless long table running through the neighborhood streets, and there is the neighborhood church service to bless the *contrada* and its rider—even the horse is brought into the church and given communion at the altar.

The live broadcast started with the pre-race parade of *le contrade* and important town dignitaries—all wearing medieval costumes and wigs, some styles dating back to the mid-1400s. The TV announcers gave background details about the people, riders, costumes and horses much like American TV announcers do during the Macy's Thanksgiving Day or Rose Bowl parades. Nonna was very excited about this year's race because her son (Alessandra's brother Luca) is a member of the *Contrada di Torre*, and they are one of the ten horses running today. As we watched, Nonna tried to explain the roles of the people in the parade; sometimes I understood that it was a town official and his family, or a rival of the *Torre*, but more often than not I was clueless.

She was describing something about the flag throwers in the parade—I smiled and acted like I understood. I don't think I fooled Nonna, but I don't think that either of us was concerned about it. For the most part, we were on the same wavelength.

Unlike the Macy's parade, the end of this parade was not marked by the arrival of Santa, but by a cart pulled by huge oxen. This brought great cheers from the audience that packed the center of the *piazza* and from those seated around the outer edge in VIP bleachers which had been put up for this special event—well over 60,000 people get packed into *il Campo*. The TV cameras panned from the officials and trumpeters inside the ox cart to the buildings around the *piazza,* showing the residents and guests hanging out of windows and crowding the balconies, proudly cheering and chanting, waving the flags and colors of their favorite *contrada.* It was as if the very *piazza* itself, from the cobblestone and brick paving to the brick and stucco buildings, was alive and celebrating in the fervor of the moment.

As the ox cart made its way around *il Campo,* I marveled at the amount of work that had gone into turning this very pedestrian-friendly *piazza* into a racetrack. It is not a race-friendly elliptical *piazza* either, but a slightly askew square that has three corners rounded off and a less than 90-degree angle for the most treacherous corner—San Martino. The center of *il Campo* is paved entirely in red brick and slopes up from the Palazzo Pubblico with its famous bell tower toward the sunken Fountain of Joy at the opposite side. The street that rings the *piazza* is grey cobblestone, and the only way to tell if you are on the street or in the center of this ancient amphitheatre-shaped *piazza* is to look down and see what type of paver you are walking on—brick or cobblestone. For the race, dirt is hauled in to cover the street's cobblestones, providing a surface for the horses to run on. Lining both sides of the street, fencing, hay bales and mattresses are placed to protect the spectators (who are crammed tight inside the brick center of the *piazza*) and the buildings and spectator-filled bleachers that ring the outer edge of the street from getting hurt by falling horses and riders who might get hurled off or crash during the race. No insurance company or city attorney in America would EVER let this race take place, but here, everyone knows the risks involved by attending. Horses, riders and spectators have all been injured or killed at this race by a horse falling and careening off the track. Nonna said that last year three horses died during the race—that is the reason Alessandra is not watching with us; she hates to see crashes. *"Disastro, Marco. Un disastro, veramente!"*

The dignitaries and trumpeters climbed out of the ox cart at the grandstand in front of the Palazzo Pubblico, and as they took their places the starting rope was raised and the horses started the process of lining up— instead of a starting gate, a heavy braided rope is held up across the track to indicate the start. Trying to get the horses into position at the rope is not an easy task. The riders try to jockey their horses into the side-by-side starting position. Horses bump into each other and knock each other out of position. It is a free-for-all at the rope. I couldn't figure out what determined when the race would start. Several times there was a brief moment of calm with the horses at the rope, which seemed to me to be the moment to start, but it was only a fleeting moment, and as quickly as the calm appeared, it would erupt into a great commotion of shuffling and pushing, causing some of the horses to rear up, almost losing their riders—remember, this is a bareback horse race. The horses wear the colors of their *contrada* between their ears, attached to a bridle with reins, and that is all the rider has to hold onto on the horse—the reins and, of course, his sheer strength. In America, jockeys wear tight-fitting outfits, but here, each rider is dressed in what looks to be silk pajamas and white sneakers. Well, they looked like silk pajamas to me ... shiny over-sized shirt and pants in the specific *contrada* colors with the *contrada* symbol on the shirt back. They do get to wear helmets, but it cannot be safe or easy to wear loose-fitting silk pajamas and sneakers for a bareback horse race.

I wanted Nonna to explain how the start was determined—they had been trying to line up for the past 15 minutes—but I couldn't think of how to ask such a difficult question in my infantile Italian, so I just sat there and tried to figure it out for myself. I did manage to ask why one of the ten horses was not allowed to line up at the rope. The tenth horse is kept off to the far side of the track and a couple of body-lengths behind the others positioning themselves at the rope. Nonna explained that he was the wild card in the race. Wild cards, even with this seeming disadvantage, have won the race before.

Another moment of calm appeared, and this time the men dropped the rope, a gun fired, the horses sprang forward, the crowd erupted and Nonna grabbed my left knee and yelled, *"Torre!"* We were off!

The horses headed down the first stretch with *Torre* in third place, and as they approached the first turn, the rider for *Onda*, the Wave, used his riding crop to beat the *Torre* rider on the back. I looked at Nonna, *"È possibile?"* *"Sì, Marco, al Palio tutto è possibile!"* Wow, everything is possible. A three-lap race where the only rule seems to be "anything goes"—and the first horse to cross the finish line still wearing its colors determines the winner, regardless of whether or not there is a rider on its back. Riderless horses have won the *Palio*.

Being whipped on the back through the first turn, *Torre* fell back to fourth place. They came out of the turn and Nonna squeezed my knee harder, *"Torre, Marco, Torre,"*—every *"Torre"* being punctuated with a hard squeeze of my knee. Nonna was as determined as the jockey; with the next two corners providing no change of positions, her only focus was on the lead. At each of those corners she would regrip my knee and say with fierce determination, *"Torre, Marco. Torre"*—two more hard squeezes.

San Martino, the fourth corner, is the most dangerous corner of the track because of its severe angle—the horses must make a hard cut to the right at full speed. This corner is responsible for most crashes, injuries and deaths. As the horses approached San Martino, Nonna's grip tightened. Several horses went wide, others cut to the inside, but all survived the turn, and the rider for *Torre* used it as his moment to take the lead. The broadcast changed camera angles showing that *Torre* was now the leader, and with that, Nonna's grip released from my knee, turned into a clenched fist and came back down on my thigh, *"Torre! ...Mi dispiace, Marco... Torre! Torre!"* She apologized for the first hit, but it didn't change her exuberance and commitment to strikes two and three. Nonna was in this to win, and I was hoping my thigh could take two more laps.

The second lap caused Nonna to scoot forward and perch on the edge of the sofa, almost assuming a riding position herself. With this lap, the pitch of her voice and her volume went up. *"Torre!"*—through the first corner of lap two *Torre* held the lead with *Selva*, the Forest, and *Chiocciola*, the Snail, a very close second and third. The Snail gained ground and overtook the Forest at the second corner. I was getting caught up in Nonna's excitement, and as *Torre* seemed to add distance to its lead, I started hitting my other thigh and yelling, *"Torre! Torre!"* right along with Nonna—both of our fists clenched tight as we cheered on the Tower. The Snail gained some lost ground and was closing in at the third corner, but the harder we cheered and hit my thighs, the more *Torre* held on to its lead. Nonna and I held our breath as we approached San Martino and cheered with joy when there had been no *disastro*—we still had the lead. *"Torre, Torre, Torre!"*

I thought lap three was going to be the death of Nonna. *Torre* was holding off the Snail through the first corner and Nonna had given up hitting me. She was now hitting her own thighs. *"Torre! Torre!! Torre!!!"*—each one intensifying to the point where she would start to stand and then sit back down quickly. Up. Then down. Up and down—no longer the jockey, she was now the horse for *Torre*, lunging forward with each stride to keep her lead.

The Tower and the Snail were a tight first and second through turns two and three. As San Martino approached, Nonna and I unconsciously stood and held each other, trying to protect ourselves from the impending doom of corner number four. *"TORRE!" "TORRE!"* Nonna yelled as tears starting streaming down her face. We entered San Martino, closed our eyes and turned our heads to the side briefly, hoping to miss an accident—to avoid the feeling of our feet losing traction on the dirt track, the sight of our bodies crashing into a wall and witnessing the possible end of our hopes and dreams. We shouted, *"TORRE!!!!!!"* and held our breath....

For Italians, the first horse across the line is the winner and the only loser of *Il Palio* is horse number two—the rest of the horses are only remembered as competitors—not losers. If you think about it, Americans are the same way about Miss America—"...and the first runner up is..."—and the moment her name is announced we immediately shift our focus and cheer for number one. There is no moment of glory for being number two—that is the loser.

"TORRE! MARCO! TORRE!!!!!" Nonna had opened her eyes first. We had survived San Martino and were still in the lead, but not by much. The Snail was right at our back. We immediately pounced back down on the edge of the sofa while we ran for the finish. We had to complete the first turn of the fourth lap and not become the loser. Nonna was crying and screaming, *"TORRE! TORRE!"*—as if her very life depended on it. I started crying, too; I was so caught up in her emotions. The horse turned the first corner—

At 79 years old, Nonna jumped up harder and higher than I thought humanly possible—had there not been a ceiling above us I think she would have launched herself to the moon. *"TOOOORRRRRREEEEE!!!!!!!!!!!!!!!! QUARANTRA-QUATTRO ANNI! MIO DIO! QUARANTRA-QUATTRO ANNI!"* La Contrada di Torre had won the race. It had been 44 years—*quarantra-quattro anni*—since the last *Torre* victory in 1961. Nonna jumped and cried and screamed and paced, holding her chest and head as if she had run the race herself. I wiped my tears away as we both headed out of the den into the living room to be greeted by Francesca running downstairs waving her *banderia di Torre*—flag—and singing at the top of her lungs. Tequila and Brighitta followed close on her heels, wildly barking, while Francesca and Nonna jumped around like schoolgirls, holding each other while laughing, crying and singing. Alessandra came running downstairs to make sure that there had been no injuries during the race, and after I told her that there were no crashes or deaths, she applauded, and we all headed into the den to watch the race again on instant replay.

Back in Siena, the live broadcast showed the rider, still on horseback, slowly working his way through the huge crowd that surrounded them. Both were being mauled by the joyous *Torre* crowd—people rubbed their *Torre* flags on the horse for good luck, and by now, the rider had lost his pajama top and had been stripped down to his white tank undershirt. He would wipe tears from his eyes, tug on the horse's ear, then lean over and kiss the horse and kiss members of the crowd, the men of the *Contrada di Torre*, who were congratulating him. It was a mob scene, and I don't know how the horse kept calm in all of that chaos.

They replayed the race and it was now Alessandra's turn to lose her mind while watching it. She was not as animated as Nonna, but she was just as excited. Francesca joined her mother in the excitement of the replay, but Nonna had been ruined by the first race. She sat back in the sofa as if in ecstasy and occasionally leaned her head forward to see the TV and breathlessly exclaim, *"Torre ... Torre,"* before collapsing back on the sofa to catch her breath again.

When the replay had finished, Alessandra and Nonna went to the phone and called Luca in Siena. When Luca answered, you could hear the crowd still going crazy in the background. He was on his cell in the thick of the celebration. Nonna talked very fast and would throw in a *"Torre, Luca, Torre"* every now and then. Alessandra was much calmer, but her joy was just as great as Nonna and Francesca's. The *"Ciao, Ciao"* game was played as Alessandra hung up the phone with Luca. We all took a deep sigh and went about our business—Nonna and I started to get dinner ready, Alessandra and Francesca went back upstairs and Tequila and Brighitta headed out into the backyard to wait for Lillo.

Nonna was still overcome by the victory; as we set out plates, sliced the bread, washed and prepared the lettuce for the salad, Nonna would randomly stop, placing her hands on the table, or the counter, or her waist, lower her head, and exclaim *"Torre, Torre."* She would catch her breath and start another task only to stop again, midstream, and burst out. At times, I would stop and put my hand on her back and she would, without looking up at me, shake her head and say, *"Marco, Marco..."* (pausing to catch her breath) *"...Torre, Torre, Torre,"* and resume her activity.

"SA-RAH, SA-RAH LA TOR-OR-RAY...

KAY TREE-OWN-FAIR-AH!"

Lillo entered the back gate singing the chorus of *La Contrada di Torre*'s song. All four of the dogs joined in as his resounding canine chorus. Tequila jumped around and Brighitta furiously wagged her tail, as if both were dancing, as Lillo made his way toward the kitchen door. Upstairs, Francesca heard her father singing and came running downstairs. As he entered triumphantly through the kitchen door with a proud arm high in the air, Nonna and Francesca joined Lillo and the dancing Tequila and Brighitta, to sing:

"SA-RAH, SA-RAH LA TOR-OR-RAY... [*Sarà, sarà la Torre*—It will be, it will be the Tower]

KAY TREE-OWN-FAIR-AH!" [*che trionferà*—that triumphs!]

There was much laughter, hugging and kissing. Crazy and Cochise still barked wildly from the pen outside, egged on by Tequila and Brighitta's excitement in the kitchen. All of this celebrating brought Alessandra downstairs and the three ladies recapped the race for Lillo—Nonna even showed Lillo how the *Torre* rider was getting whipped on the back by using a kitchen towel on me.

With all the excitement of the race and the victory, dinner was kept very simple: the tuna stuffed deviled eggs and roasted red peppers plus slices of cheese, bread, a salad, watermelon and for dessert—the yogurt cake.

After dinner, Francesca, Tequila and Brighitta went up to the family quarters on the second floor—a door that I have yet to go beyond—and I went up to mine on the third floor. Alessandra, Lillo and Nonna went out into the backyard to sit and have a cigarette.

As I sit here writing, I can just barely hear snippets of their backyard conversation wafting upward in the warm summer evening's air, finding its way in through my open skylights. I cannot understand what they are saying—but occasionally, I do hear Nonna....

"*Torre....*"

"*Torre....*"

"*Torre....*"

I wonder what she will dream of tonight?

⊰⊹⊱

Cuppa, Cuppa, Cuppa

Yogurt Cake

In the original play, and later the movie, Steel Magnolias, *there is a recipe called* "Cuppa, Cuppa, Cuppa", *in which Truvy declares that she "serves it with a scoop of ice cream to cut the sweetness." This is NOT that recipe. Here the recipe's Italian name refers to the use of the yogurt container as the measuring cup (*"cuppa"*) for all of the ingredients. I have included both sets of measurements— the use of a standard American measuring cup and the use of the yogurt container* "cuppa."

1 teaspoon unsalted butter

3 tablespoons plain dried bread crumbs

1 6-ounce (single serving-sized) container of yogurt, mixed berry flavor or flavor of your choice

2 large eggs

1½ yogurt containers sugar (or 1 cup sugar)

1 yogurt container sunflower oil (or ¾ cup sunflower oil—vegetable oil may be substituted)

1½ teaspoons vanilla extract

4 yogurt containers all-purpose flour (or 2¾ cups flour)

1 tablespoon baking powder

½ teaspoon salt

1 cup peeled, diced tart apple (such as a Granny Smith)

1 cup peeled, diced pear

Powdered sugar for garnish

Preheat oven to 350 degrees.

Prepare a nonstick 10-inch springform pan with the butter and plain bread crumbs. Set aside.

In a large bowl, mix together the yogurt, eggs, sugar, oil and vanilla until well combined. Set aside.

In a medium bowl, mix together the flour, baking powder and salt.

In batches, add a third of the dry mixture to the wet mixture, mixing until well combined between each addition. Next, stir in the apple and pear until mixed throughout. Pour into the prepared springform pan and bake for 15 minutes, then reduce the heat to 300 degrees and bake for an additional 40 to 45 minutes, until the top is golden brown and a toothpick inserted in the center comes out clean. Cool completely in the pan on a wire rack.

To serve, remove from the pan, dust with powdered sugar and place on a serving plate.

This serves 8 to 10.

IL GIORNO DICIOTTO (Day Eighteen)

Tonight is the pizza party at Anna and Giulio's, so that is the focus of the day. If you were wondering, "Giulio" is the masculine version of Giulia (Julia), so it is pronounced "Julio."

I have been so caught up in telling you about recent events that I have not brought you up to date on my language classes. Trust me, Alessandra and I have been working very hard. We are working on reflexive verb tenses at the moment, and I thought prepositions (which I still haven't mastered) were hard—Yikes! A reflexive verb form is used when a person or thing is doing the action to itself. For example, "I washed myself" uses the reflexive form of the verb "to wash." In Italian, the reflexive verb form is used a lot more often than in English. In Italian, when saying, "I put my head on her shoulder," you would use the reflexive form of the verb "to put" because you are the one putting your head on her shoulder. What makes it hard is that I have to think of how the action is being done—honestly, don't I already have enough things to worry about when speaking without having to concern myself with who, or what, is doing whatever to whomever?! *Mamma mia!*

For *il pranzo* we made beef tips in a red *sugo* served over polenta. We also had homemade sauerkraut, or "sour kraut" as my family spells it, and we ate the last of the roasted peppers. Nonna used her "witch's potion" vinegar to make the sauerkraut, which she started last night. Even though both sides of my family are of German descent, I had to come to Italy to learn how to make sauerkraut. I don't know why my family always buys it canned; it is such an easy thing to make, and it tastes so much better freshly prepared. The only hard thing about the process is that it has to marinate overnight, and how difficult is that?

Since we are going over to Marco's parents' house—and they are soon to be in-laws—Nonna and I are making two fancy desserts to take with us tonight. It is always good to butter up the future relations. For my afternoon cooking class I learned to make *crostoli* and *ciambelline con patate*.

Crostoli are fried, diamond-shaped cookies. The dough is made with *grappa* and white wine and rolled out into a large sheet. Using a pastry wheel, the dough is cut into large diamond shapes—the pastry wheel gives them a fancy, crinkled edge. The 4-inch diamonds are fried in sunflower oil and then coated in powdered sugar. This is not necessarily my idea of fancy, but Nonna said that these are usually made at Christmas, so it will be considered very special that we made them for this occasion.

The same is true for the *ciambelline con patate*. These *ciambelline* are very different than the biscotti-like rings we made the first week. These are like potato donuts. Fresh yeast is proofed in warmed milk and added to mashed potatoes, olive oil, *limoncello* (Nonna said you could also use marsala wine) and flour. Once the dough is kneaded, it is formed into golfball-sized balls and left to rest and rise for about 2 hours. Once risen, you use your index finger to poke a hole in the center of the ball, turning it into a ring-shaped *ciambelline*. They are fried to a golden brown, resembling a donut, and rolled in granulated sugar immediately after coming out of the oil.

Lillo came home from work a little early so he could get cleaned up before we headed over to Anna and Giulio's. Nonna and I placed the special Christmas desserts on a large platter and covered it with a fancy dishtowel. I noticed that Nonna had changed clothes, too. She was going with us. This will be the first time that Nonna has gone out with us in the evening. Alessandra, Lillo, Nonna and I headed out the back gate, but I was stopped as I turned to go to Lillo's car. *"No, Marco, camminiamo,"* —"No, Mark, we are walking,"— Lillo said. I had no idea that they lived within walking distance.

Besides being excited about finally having pizza, there was something very special about Nonna being with us tonight. I don't know how to describe what I was feeling as we walked, the four of us, through the neighborhood— maybe it was pride, or maybe it was the sense that I was walking with my family. I can't put my finger on it. Lillo, Alessandra and I have been on wonderful evening walks before but there was definitely something special about this brief *passeggiata* that included Nonna. It might be that in my third week I no longer feel like a student or a tourist—I believe I am a member of the family. I don't feel that Lillo and Alessandra are my parents; we are close enough in age that I think of them as friends, contemporaries. Nonna is definitely my grandmother. Being with her in the kitchen is like being with my great-grandmother in her kitchen when I was in my teens. Tonight I was happy to be walking down the street with my friends and my grandmother— my family.

We arrived at Anna and Giulio's house—Wow! They live only three blocks from the Stefanis, and I have seen this house before. I actually took photos of their yard the night of my solo evening *passeggiata* the Thursday of my first week. I was thrilled to be going in. Giulio buzzed us in the car gate and we walked along the path of pavers through the lush green grass, past the beds of blooming orange marigolds, pink vermillion-throated Rose of Sharon, tall purple cockscomb fronted by flowering purple verbena—all backed by a fence thickly covered with dark green ivy. There were pots of fresh herbs and two potted Sorrento lemon trees, one dripping with the huge grapefruit-size yellow lemons that are used to make the famous *limoncello*. Next to the house, on the lawn, a large canopy covered white plastic outdoor chairs and a metal table that was set for tonight's meal. The house, yard, flowers and table setting were quaint and charming, much like our hosts.

Anna came running out of the house wearing an apron over her sweater and housedress—looking even more like the stereotypical *nonna*. Giulio was hot on her heels and they met us in the yard. There were the usual hugs, kisses on both cheeks and "ohs and ahs" over the desserts we brought with us—Anna peeked under the towel and made a big deal of thanking Nonna. Marianna and Marco came out of the house next, followed by Marco's cousin, Elenora. She was on vacation visiting for a couple of days. At 15, she is beautiful beyond her years and had just won an international ballroom dance title. She is quite the celebrity in Marco's family. It was the nine of us for dinner, and I was thrilled to have Marianna there—I hadn't seen that much of her since she moved out, so I was looking forward to spending some quality time with her. Marianna took the dessert tray from me as Giulio grabbed my arm to give me a personal tour.

Our first stop was an attached utility room that held his pride and joy—a wood-burning pizza oven. I was most impressed. For some reason, I thought the wood-burning oven was going to be some rustic chimney-looking thing out in the backyard, a glorified BBQ pit, if you will. It wasn't that at all. It was a modern, wood-burning oven with a thermostat, fans and controls. He explained how it worked, and as with Nonna yesterday about the parade, some of it I understood and other parts went right over my head. I tried to sound as impressed as possible, but he could have been saying, "…and here is where I put the severed heads to shrink them," with my response being, *"Mmmmm, buono, buono!"*

Anna came into the utility room from the kitchen carrying a large, circular pizza pan, which she placed on the ovenside table among the other pizzas. Besides this round pan, there were four large, square pizza pans on the table.

Anna had made a pizza Margherita (tomato, mozzarella and basil—named for Queen Margherita in honor of her visit to Naples in 1889), a zucchini blossom and anchovy pizza, a prosciutto, porcini mushroom and artichoke heart pizza, her version of *pizza bianca*—white pizza (rosemary, olive oil and sea salt only), and in the round pan, a dessert pizza made with a potato crust and topped with butter, cinnamon and sugar. She made FIVE large pizzas for the nine of us, and Elenora looked as if she had never eaten a thing in her life. How in the world were we ever going to eat all this pizza?! Of course, as I stood there I desperately wanted to try them all, and I thought, "I can eat five pieces of pizza. That should be fine." After explaining all the pizzas, Anna told Giulio to get back to work baking the last of them, then grabbed my arm and took me into the house to finish the tour. As we walked into the house, I complimented Anna on how beautiful her pizzas looked and that, *"Mi piace molto pizza con fiori degli zucchine e acciugge."*—"I really like pizza with zucchini blossoms and anchovies."

The house was modest and comfortable, filled with a lot of photos of Marco, their only child. I have gathered from other conversations that Anna is very protective of Marco and that has been a sticking point at times between her and Marianna. Last year, Marco and Marianna were supposed to get married, but Marianna called the wedding off a month before the big day. Alessandra's family was very supportive of Marianna's decision, not because they didn't like Marco, but because there were issues that Marianna felt should be resolved, and Alessandra thought Marianna was smart for wanting to correct them before the wedding. Getting divorced in Italy is not an easy thing—it is a Catholic nation, remember, so better to call off a wedding than to live with the unresolved issues forever. Not surprisingly, Marco's family was hurt by the postponement, and Marco and Marianna have only gotten back together in the last several months. I think this contributed to both sets of parents' trepidation over Marco and Marianna moving in together. If there are any hard feelings, I certainly can't tell. Everyone seems to be getting along and I don't see any negativity between anyone. I truly must be a member of the family—look at me gossiping about them. *Mi dispiace!*

Marco came in the house to find Anna and me standing in his room looking at typical childhood photos—soccer team photos, pictures of friends in high school and vacation photos. And as expected, Anna was proud to show them to me and Marco was highly embarrassed. Proud mothers are proud mothers regardless of nationality. *"Mamma, per favore, andiamo fuori!"* —"Mom, please, let's go outside!"

We all took our places around the table. Being the *"molto importante persone dall'America"* that I am, I was seated at one end of the table. Nonna was to my left and Alessandra was to my right. Everyone else filled in around the table while Giulio filled everyone's glasses with the white wine that he had made using grapes from his small vineyard out in the country. With the last glass filled, Giulio took his place at the head of the table and lifted his glass high and toasted us, *"Salute!"* *"Salute! ...Cin-cin,"* we all toasted and clinked glasses and drank. The wine was nice, not too dry or sweet. I raised my glass again and toasted Giulio's wine, *"Bravo, Giulio! Bravo!"* Everyone agreed and clinked glasses.

Anna and Marianna jumped up and started to serve us. Of course, Anna served me first and then Lillo and Giulio, while Marianna served Marco first. The men were served before the women. Nonna and Alessandra were served next, followed by Elenora. Marianna and Anna served themselves last. I usually wait for everyone to be seated at the table before eating, but that isn't the custom here in Italy. Also, it is good manners in Italy to have both arms on the table—that way you can see what a person is doing (the custom stems from ancient times when people had been killed by dinner guests concealing weapons). Despite the fact that in America, it is usually considered good manners to eat with one hand in your lap, I let my Italian dining companions eat in safety by keeping both my arms on the table.

Since she knew it was my favorite, Anna brought me two pieces of the zucchini blossom pizza. The blossoms were sweet and tender and the anchovy was a nice salty contrast. *"Va bene, Marco?"* Anna asked me, while I was chewing. Italians have a great way to respond to this question when their mouths are full. I took my right hand and, sticking my index finger out and my thumb up (as a child would do to make a gun while playing "Cops and Robbers"), I put my index finger into my right cheek with my thumb facing my ear, and in a quick motion, turned my hand forward, raising my thumb up. This is the Italian hand gesture to exclaim that whatever you are eating is really good—the polite way to say *"Buonissimo!"* without having to talk with your mouth full. It did not take me long to eat both pieces. *"Ancora, Marco?"* —"More, Mark?"— Anna asked me, getting up and grabbing my plate as I swallowed my last bite. *"Certo. Vorrei la pizza Margherita prossimo."* —"Sure, I would like the Margherita pizza next."

"Grazie, Anna. La pizza di fiori degli zucchine era bellissima!" —"Thanks, Anna. The zucchini blossom pizza was great!"— I said, as she put my plate back in front of me—with two pieces of the pizza. I looked down at my plate and thought, "Oh my God, I am going to have to eat TEN pieces of pizza tonight—two of each one!!" I discreetly reached under the table and undid the top button of my pants to give myself some more room to eat. This was going to be a Thanksgiving Day type of meal. As I did this, it dawned on me that maybe this was the real reason why people in ancient times used to kill their dinner hosts. They weren't angry over politics or seeking some type of revenge; they were just trying to keep themselves from being overfed at the table.

True to form, I was given two pieces of the prosciutto pizza next, followed by another two pieces of the Margherita. Wait—the pattern had been broken. I was supposed to get the *pizza bianca* next, not repeat the Margherita. I was doomed. The second helping of Margherita was followed by two pieces of the white pizza. I was up to ten pieces at this point. *"Va bene, Marco?"* How was it going? Couldn't Anna see the pizza starting to come out of my ears? I really wanted to be brave and say, *"Basta!"* —"Enough!"— but that would have been rude, since I had not tasted all of the pizzas that she had made in honor of my special visit. I was polite and between bites squeaked out, *"Si, si, va bene."* I hope I sounded convincing and not miserably stuffed.

I think Anna's pride was getting the better of her, which was not helpful to me—I was next served another piece of the Margherita. Okay, that makes a total of five pieces of the Margherita, alone. *Mio Dio!* When will I be allowed to stop eating? Finally, two pieces of the sweet pizza were put in front of me. I was now socially at the end of my dining commitment—until I looked over and saw that we still had to eat the desserts that Nonna and I had made. I couldn't offend Nonna and not eat the *crostoli* or the *ciambelline*.

Dusk had given way to night. Marco turned on the party lights that were strung above our heads inside the canopy. Giulio made sure that our glasses never went more than half empty before refilling, and Elenora was in the limelight because of her recent dancing title. We drank, laughed and wanted for nothing—well, I could have used a second stomach toward the end of the meal. At 13 pieces of pizza, I was the winner, not that anyone was counting but me.

Marco, Marianna and Elenora said their goodbyes after dinner and headed out to meet Nicola and Jimmy. I wanted to warn Elenora to bring some mace with her since she was meeting Jimmy. She was beautiful, and I had no doubt that Jimmy was going to be flirting with her nonstop. *Povero Jimmy!* We all said our *"Ciao, ciao, ciao's"* and as the three of them left, the rest of us sat back down at the table to talk.

Besides making his own wine, Giulio also uses the grapes to make *grappa* and the lemons from his trees for *limoncello*. He is very proud of them and poured glasses for us all (*grappa* for the men and *limoncello* for the ladies)—even Nonna had some, which impressed Giulio. She usually stays away from strong drinks and spicy food. I am beginning to think she has an ulcer, because she has medicine that she takes when her stomach is bothering her.

Giulio's first question to me, which seems to be every Italian's first question to this American, was "What do you think of your President Bush?" Alessandra translated his question for me, even though, by now, that Italian question is very familiar to me. I kept my answer short. Beyond politics, the after-dinner conversation had turned to the retirement system—*pensione*—in Italy. Giulio, who works for the post office, can retire early in 2007. There was much conversation and disagreement between Lillo and Giulio about how the system works. Lillo works for the university in Viterbo, and I think his retirement plan differed from Giulio's government worker retirement plan. The discussion did get quite heated from time to time (as Italian conversations do), and even the wives jumped in to take their husbands' side. It always stayed friendly, but there were definite opinions on the subject. Nonna sat quietly listening, sipping her *limoncello* and only jumped in once to correct Lillo and Giulio. She was the only *in pensione* person at the table, and by default she was the expert.

In heated conversation, Giulio uses his hands a lot. Lillo talks a lot with his hands, but Giulio's hands move as fast as his mouth and you know how fast people speak in a heated discussion. At one point, Alessandra leaned over and asked if I understood what Giulio was saying. I whispered to her, "I think I would have a better chance of understanding Giulio if I were deaf and knew sign language. His hands are like a hummingbird's wings." She laughed and agreed.

At some point, after finishing her shot of *limoncello,* Nonna got comfortable and lit a cigarette. I think she was enjoying herself, too. I was actually a little shocked to see Nonna smoke. I know that Nonna, Lillo and Alessandra smoke, but they never do it in the house and never in front of me. At the end of the day, after I go upstairs to bed, the three of them usually go outside in the backyard to smoke. The only reason I know they smoke is because I have seen their cigarette cases (they were the kind my grandmother used—vinyl with a metal clasp and large enough to hold a single pack and a lighter) on the side buffet behind the kitchen table, and they grab them as they go outside and I am ascending the stairs.

It was late into the evening, almost midnight, when we made our way home. Anna and Giulio had been gracious and perfect hosts. The *pizze* were *buonissime* and just the way I like wood fired pizza—smoky, crisp and slightly burnt in spots. I can see why Nonna doesn't make pizza. Anna's are brilliant and there can be no contest. We split the remaining desserts; Anna took some of ours and we took some of the dessert pizza. Lillo had to carry home a half-full dessert tray. I had more than enough to drink and I wasn't quite sure if I would drop the tray on our brief walk home.

When we got back home and settled the dogs down, Nonna said that we had enough dessert to last through next week. I was so full and tipsy that all I could muster the energy to say—to moan, actually—as I climbed the stairs to my room was, *"Torre ... Torre ... Torre."*

"Bravo, Marco!"

Tonight, I won the race.

Spezzatino della Nonna con Polenta

Veal Tips with Polenta

This is hearty Italian comfort food at its best. Served with some crusty country bread and a full-bodied red wine, this will take the chill off of any fall evening, whether in Viterbo, Italy, or in Alabama, where I live.

Veal Tips:

3 tablespoons extra virgin olive oil

1 tablespoon unsalted butter

1 small onion, finely minced

1 large clove garlic, finely minced

1½ pounds veal top round, cut into 1-inch cubes (beef tips or stew meat may be substituted)

1 cup dry white wine

1 teaspoon salt, or more to taste

½ teaspoon freshly ground black pepper, or more to taste

6 whole peeled canned Italian plum tomatoes (if using fresh plum

    tomatoes, run them through a food mill to remove the skins and seeds)

1 tablespoon finely chopped fresh rosemary, stems removed

In a large pan over medium heat, heat the oil and butter until the butter has melted and is bubbling. Add the onion and veal tips and cook until browned, 8 to 10 minutes. Add the garlic, stirring until combined, and cook for 1 minute. Add the wine, scraping the browned pieces from the bottom of the pan, and cook until the wine has almost evaporated, 3 to 4 minutes. Add the salt and pepper. Place the tomatoes into a small bowl, and using your hand, crush them into small pieces. Add the rosemary and crushed tomatoes (and their juices) to the pan, mixing until well combined. Lower the heat, cover the pan and simmer for 35 to 40 minutes, stirring occasionally, until the meat is tender. If the sauce starts to thicken or dry out too much, stir in some hot water, one tablespoon at a time.

Polenta:

10 cups water

1 tablespoons salt

3 cups yellow polenta, medium-grind

1 cup freshly grated Parmigiano-Reggiano or Pecorino Romano cheese, or

    more to taste

In a large pot, bring the water to a boil over medium heat. Stir in the salt and as the water starts to come up to a boil again, lower the heat slightly and, using a whisk, slowly pour in the polenta in a thin stream, whisking it into the water, always whisking in the same direction to help prevent lumps. When the cornmeal is completely incorporated into the water, switch to using a wooden spoon and stir the polenta, crushing any lumps against the side of the pan to remove them. If the polenta is boiling or spitting too much, lower the heat a little at a time, until it sputters without coming out of the pot. As the polenta cooks it will thicken.

Cook the polenta, stirring frequently, for 25 to 30 minutes until it is thick and starts to pull away easily from the sides of the pan. Turn off the heat and stir in the cheese.

Spoon the hot polenta into serving dishes and top with the veal tips and some of their sauce. **Makes 6 servings.**

Wondering what to do with the leftover polenta?

Pour the extra polenta onto a 9 x 13-inch baking sheet and spread until it is level. Let the polenta cool for 10 to 15 minutes and cover with plastic wrap to keep a skin from developing. When the polenta has cooled, using a knife dipped in water, cut into 3-inch squares and place in layers, separated by parchment paper, in an airtight container in the fridge. Leftover polenta slices can be grilled, pan-fried in some olive oil or layered with sugo and mozzarella and baked in a casserole.

IL GIORNO DICIANOVE (Day Nineteen)

"*Hai dormito bene ieri sera?*"

"*Si, si. Ho dormito bene. E tu?*"

"*Si, si, naturalmente.*" Alessandra went on, "And did you dream in Italian?"

"No. Well, I don't remember dreaming at all last night. *Mi dispiace, no italiano.*"

"*Presto, molto presto*—Soon, very soon," she said.

Nonna and I ran our morning errands, and while we were at the grocery store, we bought speck, *mortadella*, several different *formaggi di pecorino, un melone,* and had the butcher fillet a turkey breast into a large cutlet. The employees of this store, our usual grocery haunt, are getting used to seeing me with Nonna. Besides saying hello to her, they are now starting to chat a little with me. The butcher is very friendly. Last week, the ladies who work the registers were talking to Nonna about me, and I heard them mention *nipote*—grandchild. They talked back and forth while we were being checked out, and I really didn't catch on to exactly what they were saying. They smiled and nodded—I smiled and nodded. It was only today that I remembered that *nipote*, besides meaning "grandson/ granddaughter" is also the word for "nephew/niece." Last week I was thrilled to have been considered Nonna's grandson; now I realize I am probably being mistaken for her nephew—a lot farther up the family tree as age goes.

Rollè di tacchino—turkey roll—was this morning's first cooking project. Hard-boiled eggs are the center of a meatloaf mixture that is rolled up inside a large turkey cutlet. The stuffed cutlet—*rollè*—is closed with toothpicks and browned in a pan. White wine, crushed garlic cloves and water are added and it simmers for quite a while. Learning how to do this type of thing is a lot of fun because it is so different from anything I am used to cooking. Sometimes a dish seems too complicated and time consuming, but I think that has something to do with our American culture of "everything must take under 5 minutes because our lives are SO busy." Occasionally, I need to remind myself that there is nothing wrong with a dish taking 30 minutes to prepare and more than an hour to cook. Are we in such a hurry to get to the next thing that we are overlooking and missing out on the moments that are intrinsically more valuable to the meaning of our lives?

While the *rollè* simmered, we prepared a cream sauce with speck—smoked prosciutto—and green peas. Green peas are not one of my favorite things, but at this point, I am not about to change one of Nonna's recipes. I can choke them down if they are in a dish, and I do understand the idea of the sweet tasting peas being combined with the salty, smoked speck. Nonna has yet to disappoint me, so I trust her palate. This *sugo* is going to be served with *penne* pasta.

I was about to head into the den for my morning language class when someone rang the bell for the back gate, which always sends the dogs into a barking frenzy. Nonna buzzed the gate open and soon Jimmy and Nicola were walking through the back door. They dropped by to see what Francesca and Stefano were doing today. Francesca came downstairs and they chatted for a while. From what I could understand, Stefano was supposed to be arriving shortly and they were going out, but I couldn't understand where or why. While everyone was standing around chatting and being offered the leftover desserts from the pizza party, I noticed that Jimmy was sporting white Nike shoes, white tennis shorts and a white polo—for being so pro-France he looked VERY American. Last week, they stopped by for a quick visit on their way back from the beach on Lake Bolsena, and Jimmy was wearing a ratty baseball cap turned backward on his head and leather flip-flops. He looked like every 19-year-old fraternity guy in America. With his very American name, his American dress, and his "I only want to speak English" attitude, how can he be so "Go France!"?

Stefano rang the gate bell, causing the dogs to get wound up again, and was buzzed in. Everyone said their hellos and goodbyes at the same time as the four of them headed out together. Tequila and Brighitta stayed out in the backyard, Nonna poked around the *rollè*, and Alessandra and I finally went into the den for the lesson.

Today's lesson did not go well. It felt as if my head was completely full and I couldn't access any information. There have been days when everything just clicks and I feel like I am making progress, but every now and then, my brain seems overloaded. I was not very pleased with myself today. Alessandra says I am doing well, but I have high expectations for myself, and today I was once again the village idiot.

It was the four of us for lunch—Lillo, Alessandra, Nonna and me. We started with the pea and speck *penne* as our *primi*. The peas were a great contrast to the speck, and I didn't have to eat around them or pick them out—a social crisis averted. The *rollè di tacchino* was very similar to the extraterrestrial stuffed chicken we had my second day here, except the colorful addition of the hard-boiled eggs in the center of each slice added richness to the dish.

I took full advantage of my siesta today. Sometimes I don't actually take a nap; instead I either read my lesson book, or get a jump-start on writing or sort through all the photos I have taken. Today there was only one thing on my mind—sleep!

After waking a little early from my nap, I headed down to the kitchen to grab *uno spuntino*—a snack—before my afternoon lesson with Alessandra. I was finishing my second *crostoli* when Nonna came down and convinced me to join her in splitting a potato donut *ciambelline*. Nicola and Jimmy had each eaten several of them earlier today.

Francesca and Stefano woke the rest of the house up—well, Crazy and Cochise did, when they saw them enter the back gate. Their barking brought down Tequila and Brighitta, who joined in the chorus. Alessandra came down shortly afterward as we collected around the kitchen table to watch Francesca pull her purchases from a "Hangar...Authentic Clothes" shopping bag. I don't know why I am so surprised every time I see something American here in Italy, but I am. Besides the music, it is surprising to walk around and see Italians wearing things sporting American names—universities, sports teams, racing names, company names, even city names. I understand seeing Coke, Nike or USA, but when I was in Rome, standing outside the bar, there was a young guy wearing a t-shirt emblazoned with "Memphis High School." The cut of the shirt was form fitting, but I didn't think anything of it at the time. When I asked him if he was American, he gave me a funny look. He didn't speak any English, so when I repeated the question in Italian and pointed at his t-shirt, he explained that he had never been to America—he bought the shirt at a shop in his hometown south of Rome. Since then, I can identify the American logo clothes that were not purchased in America because the cut is definitely European. Most Italians under 30 are thin and wear their clothes very form fitting. American clothes are cut larger because we have bigger waists and, as a culture, don't wear our clothes as tight.

Tonight was another leftovers night. Nonna used the leftover polenta from the other day to make baked polenta layered with mozzarella and Parmigiano-Reggiano and a simple red *sugo*. We started with *antipasti* of the unused speck from lunch today, *mortadella* and five different cheeses. Nonna was clearing out the fridge and mixing the leftovers with some of the things we bought at the store this morning. The baked polenta was so comforting—

hot and gooey with a crunchy top crust. That was rounded out with the usual salad and fruit. It was a simple dinner to prepare and something light to eat after our rather large lunch.

The dinner might have been simple tonight, but there were *fuochi artificiali*—fireworks—during dinner, and not the kind that light up the sky either. Dinner started as usual, with the five of us around the table. Stefano did not stay for dinner; he left as we sat down and said he would be back afterward. Francesca was acting a little odd, but I chalked it up to Stefano not staying for dinner. Lillo poured wine for the two of us and we all helped ourselves to the *antipasti*. There was the usual dinner conversation about the day and Nonna served the polenta.

Francesca started talking about Stefano, Naples and a vacation—it was the fire that lit the fuse. I gathered that she was asking if she could go to Naples with Stefano on a vacation. Well, Lillo and Alessandra were very adamant about not giving their 19-year-old daughter permission to go on a vacation with her boyfriend. As Francesca pleaded her case more, Lillo countered with his concerns and still refused. Francesca then changed her attack and tried a different approach. This time Nonna chimed in, although to begin with I couldn't tell whose side she was taking. Lillo and Alessandra responded to Francesca and to Nonna, too. Things were starting to heat up and alliances had been formed—Francesca and Nonna vs. Lillo and Alessandra.

It doesn't take long for a table of Italians to become impassioned in a discussion. Nonna hit the table with her hand to emphasize her thoughts, and as Lillo started to answer her, Alessandra said, *"Lillo, per favore...,"* and raised her hands as if praying—putting her palms together with the right thumb over the left. This Italian gesture is used to emphatically implore someone, with the help of Heaven, to PLEASE stop what he is doing and listen to you. As you say, *"Per favore,"* you emphasize the gesture by shaking your prayer-positioned hands toward the person. Alessandra's gesture told Lillo, "Please, don't make this worse. I'll take care of this." Lillo sat back and didn't speak. The first firework had exploded at the table.

"Allora, Mamma...," and Alessandra started explaining her reasoning to Nonna. When Nonna answered, it was Alessandra's turn to put her fist down on the table and raise her voice, *"No, mamma!"* Nonna and Alessandra— mother and daughter—were no longer discussing the other daughter at the table—they were arguing about her. Voices were raised, wine glasses shook as fists hit the table and hand gestures became wild exaggerations to punctuate each lady's position.

This is the first time that I have seen a true argument in the house. Had this been the Wild West, these cowboys would have stood up, pistols drawn, and headed out the tavern doors to end it at High Noon in the street. In opera, knives would have appeared from under the table and a dagger fight would have ensued.

Francesca, Lillo and I sat quietly at the table, slowly eating, heads bowed, only looking up from under our brows to see the display before us—and seeing if we might have to jump up and flee for our lives. I couldn't understand a thing at this point and it seemed the argument had turned personal. The tone implied that they had descended into going for the jugular and pushing each other's buttons. And as the volume, table pounding and verbal attacks escalated to a fevered pitch, I was waiting for what should have been the inevitable and logical conclusion to a fight of this nature—the Italian version of "GO TO HELL!" It had gotten to that point. But, suddenly, everything stopped.

Silenzio.

We all sat perfectly still for a moment, as the poisonous air swirled around the table waiting to kill the first person to inhale it.

"Melone, Alessandra?"

Nonna broke the moment, offering the yellow plastic bowl of sliced cantaloupe to Alessandra.

"Certo, mamma. Grazie."

Lillo passed the bowl from Nonna to Alessandra. She took two slices and, with that, the argument was over.

We all breathed a sigh of relief. This is the beauty of Italian passion—the moment of going from fervently pointed exclamations to the silence that brought about the reconciliatory offering of the *melone*. This was not like the numerous arguments my Italian-American uncle had with his father at summertime family functions where my uncle's father would storm off, cursing loudly, after having been proven wrong—followed by weeks of silence between the parties involved. But here—*"Eh."* Life is too short to get caught up in the pettiness of disagreement. The ladies had each made their point—I have no idea what the outcome was—the subject was changed, and we got back to the usual atmosphere around the table.

Stefano came over after dinner and took Alessandra, Francesca and me into town for gelato. Lillo and Nonna stayed home tonight—there was something on TV that they didn't want to miss. It was a fun change of pace going with Stefano and Francesca. There were times when I was certain Francesca was telling Stefano about the fireworks at dinner. I could tell by the way she leaned into him and chatted as they walked slightly ahead of us while we ate our gelatos. Alessandra was taking note of it, too. She misses nothing.

⋘∿⋙

Penne con Prosciutto Crudo e Piselli

Penne with Prosciutto and Peas

This always tastes like a springtime dish to me, especially when the fresh green peas that first appear at the farmer's market are used. The sweet "pop" of the peas is a delicious contrast to the salty flavor of the prosciutto. Substitute the fresh, early peas for the frozen ones, and you will experience the true flavor of simple Italian cooking.

4 tablespoons (½ stick) unsalted butter
1 small onion, finely minced
2 slices (2 ounces) prosciutto, diced into ¼-inch pieces

1½ cups frozen green peas

½ teaspoon salt, or more to taste

½ teaspoon freshly ground black pepper, or more to taste

1 pound *penne rigate*

1 cup heavy cream

¾ cup grated Parmigiano-Reggiano or Grana Padano cheese, or more to taste

Melt the butter in a large skillet over medium-high heat. After the foam starts to subside, add the onion and cook until soft and translucent, 3 to 4 minutes. Add the prosciutto and cook for 1 minute. Add the frozen peas, salt and pepper and cook for 2 to 3 minutes, making sure the peas are well coated with the butter mixture. Remove the skillet from the heat and set aside.

Bring a large pot of water to a boil over high heat. Once boiling, add 2 tablespoons salt and the *penne*. Cook, uncovered, until the pasta is *al dente*—tender, but firm to the bite. Drain the pasta and add it to the pea mixture in the skillet. Return the skillet to low heat, add the cream and mix it together until the pasta is completely coated with the sauce. Stir in the grated Parmigiano-Reggiano and, if needed, adjust the seasoning with additional salt and pepper. Serve immediately, garnished with additional grated cheese to taste.

This makes 6 to 8 servings.

IL GIORNO VENTI (Day Twenty)

I t happened! It finally happened.

Last night I dreamt in Italian.

I found myself, in situation after situation, conversing in perfect Italian. I have no idea what the conversations were about, or even if my Italian was correct, but I do remember that, whether it was in a park, a store, walking down the street or walking along the beach, everything I said seemed to be correct to the others I encountered. I was finally fluent—if only in my dreams.

"Bravo! Marco, bravo!" "Si, si, Bravo!" Alessandra and Nonna congratulated me on my subconscious accomplishment. I was so excited to tell them when I came downstairs that I blurted it out before Alessandra could even ask me how I slept. I'm not sure why I was so excited; I mean, it isn't as if I am now magically fluent when speaking in the conscious world. Maybe it was the fact that I had achieved a milestone, as others have done, while in Viterbo.

"Marco, you are now one step closer to understanding Italian," Alessandra said. I am not so sure about that, but she is the expert.

This morning Nonna and I went grocery shopping at Le Clerc to get things for this weekend's picnic and to get the squid for lunch today. Yes, today is Squid Day! As we entered Le Clerc there was a woman seated behind a table draped in a huge sign for *La Macchina di Santa Rosa*. This was the Viterbo festival that Alessandra was telling me about in my first week—the 100-foot tower that is carried by 100 men through the streets in honor of Viterbo's patron saint, *Santa Rosa*. Nonna said it was an information table and that the woman was selling souvenirs of the event and in support of *i Facchini*—the men's organization that carries the tower. There were the usual souvenir items for sale: small and large *bandiere*—flags—sporting the red and white colors of *i Facchini*, ashtrays, paperweights, replicas of past *la macchina*—towers, and brochures. Nonna was on a mission, so I couldn't stop at the table and get any information—the festival is always on September 3, so I will miss it. I am very sad about that.

The seafood department at Le Clerc amazes me every time I see it. There are so many beautiful, brightly colored and strange looking fish, baby octopi, huge spiney lobsters, whole swordfish heads, mussels, clams, squid and other fish. I was too busy checking out the seafood display to watch Nonna pick the squid; I hope I haven't missed out on important squid-choosing information—every moment is a learning experience.

Le Clerc is always busy: 20 checkout lanes, 5 to 7 customers deep each. While Nonna was taking our items out of the cart and placing them on the checkout belt—*"Busta?" "Sì, per favore."* I was shocked! Nonna was getting bags! Suddenly, the older man standing behind me started talking to me—complaining to me, I think, about *"la donna al tavolo d'informazione per La Macchina"*—as he indicated her, seated at the table just beyond our checkout lane.

His deep basso, whispered tones were very hard to hear, let alone understand. I understood only because he pointed at her, and I barely deciphered "woman," "information table" and "the machine" (in this case, "the tower"). I was about to give him my pat reply of *"Mi dispiace, parlo solo un poco italiano,"* and defer to Nonna to chat with him, but I stopped myself. I thought, "What the hell," and decided that I would see how long I could participate in this conversation before becoming completely lost and discovered as a fraud.

As the man continued talking, it became more apparent that I was not going to be able to understand a thing and that he was the type of person who liked hearing the sound of his own voice, so I decided not to focus on his words so much as to listen to the tone of his conversation. When he seemed to imply his idea was correct, I nodded and agreed with him, *"Si, si, naturalmente!"*—as if I was a like-minded individual. When he seemed to be asking me if I agreed with something he didn't like, I answered, *"No, no."* He really liked that—he was preaching to the choir, or so he thought. *"Davvero?"* was my astonished reply when he seemed to be saying something I perceived as being incredible—"They actually use moon rocks to build the tower." *"Davvero?"* or "They make us pay too many taxes for that ugly eyesore!" *"Davvero!"* I altered my tone with each reply, so I could get the full range of usage out of the single word—"Really?" Naturally, I used sounds— grunts of agreement and gasps of disbelief, head nods and hand gestures to fill in any gaps on my minimal end of the conversation.

We chatted through Nonna checking out and he himself being checked out. We stood for another moment or two at the end of the register with our bags in hand. Nonna was smiling as if waiting for me to introduce her to this long lost friend of mine that I had just met at the store. As suddenly as he had struck up the conversation with me, he grabbed my hand, enthusiastically shook it, said, *"Arrivederci!"* and walked away. As I turned from him to exit the store with Nonna, she stopped me and asked what we had been talking about.

"Nonna, non so. Non lo conosco. Non ho capito niente." —"Nonna, I don't know. I don't know him. I understood nothing."

"Ma, lui ti ha capito? Come?" —"But, he understood you? How?"

"Perchè, Nonna, sono geniale." —"Because, Nonna, I am clever!"

"Si, si, Marco. Mi dispiace, mi sono dimenticata. Bravo!" —"Yes, yes, Mark. I'm sorry, I forgot. Good for you!"— she said, giving me a little Italian wrist wave of disbelief. We both chuckled as we walked past the information table and left the store.

First order of business back at the house was cleaning the squid, which I have seen done many times on TV cooking programs, but now I was about to do first hand. Nonna was impressed that I wanted to jump right in. Cleaning squid sounds like an odd and grotesque job, but it isn't as bad as one might think. Preparing and eating shrimp or crawfish is no worse. With squid, it doesn't really seem that you are cleaning a fish, because it is such a weird, unfamiliar, gelatinous thing—and you have to do many unnatural things: remove the mouth by pinching it out, tear the head and tentacles off, peel the skin from the body and reach inside the body cavity to remove the spine. The spine looks and feels exactly like a hard piece of clear plastic—a clear see-through letter opener—nothing about it resembles a spine. Cutting around the eyes and removing them is pretty gross, but cleaning a newly caught fish is much worse. At least a squid is not bloody—just an ink sack that is removed by gently squeezing it out, making sure that it doesn't break, because that is a huge mess. Imagine breaking a fountain pen in your hand—*"Disastro, Marco. Disastro."*

Nonna diced the heads and tentacles, sautéed them in extra virgin olive oil with garlic and anchovies, and mixed that with egg, bread, parsley and more garlic, raw this time, to create a stuffing. The cleaned body of the squid is a natural pouch, which Nonna showed me how to fill with the stuffing mixture and close by securing the open end with toothpicks. I wanted to overfill the squid, which Nonna said wasn't good to do because as the stuffing cooks, it expands and would rip through the thin-fleshed body of the squid. The stuffed squid—*calamari ripieni*—were browned in olive oil, poached in red wine and then placed in a red *sugo* to cook with cubed potatoes. As the squid simmered with the potatoes in the sauce, we moved on to making the sauce for the pasta course of *rigatoni* with cauliflower.

Cauliflower is one of those things that I never think about using. I enjoy it, but somehow I have relegated it to salad-bar-only status. When looking for a vegetable at the store to replace my usual default choices of broccoli or green beans, I never think of cauliflower and I should. The color green gets stuck in my head, and I forgot about the perfectly delightful flavor of white—cauliflower.

We sautéed onions and garlic before adding a little water and a vegetable bouillon cube. Once the bouillon had dissolved and the onions had become soft, we added diced cauliflower and simmered it on low until the cauliflower was tender. We held off on adding the cooked *rigatoni* until it was time for lunch. Nonna said that another variation of this dish is to puree the cooked cauliflower mixture so that it becomes more like a cream sauce and mix that with pasta. Changing the texture of the cauliflower would give you two separate dishes by using the same recipe. Clever.

My language classes went well today. In writing about class, I haven't really described how we go about the lesson. Alessandra and I have fallen into a routine, just as Nonna and I have a routine when running our morning errands. Some people paying for a language lesson might expect it to be a very sterile and rigid learning environment, but as hard as Alessandra and I try to make it that, we never quite succeed.

When it is time to go into the den for the lesson, I always run upstairs to my room to grab my books, paper and pencils. I could keep them in the den, but I do study some at night—trying to either cement in what I learned earlier in the day or get a jump-start on what lies ahead. While I am getting my stuff, Alessandra pours us each a glass of water and meets me in the den. Tequila always follows me to the den but always stops at the den door. Alessandra and I spend the next minute trying to get him into the room with us—*"Vieni qui." "Tequila, per favore." "Adesso!" "TEQUILA!"* Regardless of how we plead and beg and coddle him, he never wants to come in, so we close the door, shutting him out, and get ourselves set at the formal dining table, which is at one end of the den. Alessandra places the CD/cassette player on the table and opens the window behind her for some fresh air—on hot days she turns on the fan, too. There is a white board on an easel that always needs the previous day's lesson wiped off. With our books open, papers spread, cassette loaded, board clean, birds chirping from the pomegranate tree just outside the window, water at hand and the fan gently blowing the edges of our papers, we are finally prepared to begin.

Scratch.

Scratch, scratch.

Scratch.

"Tequila, no. Seduto."

Scratch. Scratch, scratch, scratch.

"Silenzio."

"Hmmmm." "Hmmmm." Now he starts to whine.

"Tequila! No! Per favore!" and out of frustration, Alessandra gets up and opens the door and lets Tequila into the room.

He circles the table two or three times before lying down at our feet under the table. Brighitta—his silent companion—trots in with tail wagging and curls up in her bed under the sideboard, next to the table. With our canine students now in place, Alessandra shuts the door again, sits down and we start the lesson. That is the routine, twice a day—regardless of how hard we plead with Tequila when we first go into the room, he waits until we are finally seated at the table before he interrupts—he has trained us well, I think.

We are never really left alone during our lessons. Sometimes the interruptions are frequent and drive Alessandra crazy; at other times they just make us laugh. Francesca poked her head through the open window, startling us—*"Francesca, PER FAVORE!"* Alessandra begged, clasping her hands in prayer, caught in the middle of writing something on the board. The phone rings by the kitchen and in the muffled distance I can hear Nonna answer it, *"Pronto"* —knowing full well that a few seconds later there will be a light tapping on the door—*"Alessandra, scusa, ma Lillo è al telephono…"* and through the closed door, she will proceed to tell Alessandra why Lillo is calling. *"Mamma, per favore…"* and giving up, she tells Nonna what to tell Lillo and then, in English to me, but loud enough for Nonna to hear—and not understand—"Why is he calling me now to ask about that? He knows I am in a lesson with you. *Marco, mi dispiace."* That always makes me laugh. Alessandra uses her English as an aside when she doesn't want the Italians in her house to know something, in the same way that immigrant grandparents in America speak in their native tongues in front of their grandchildren. Alessandra can let her inner monologue out without anyone in the house being the wiser.

At times, Alessandra will yell for Nonna, who immediately pokes her head in the door—I think Nonna perches, always at the ready, on the living room sofa just outside the door, listening to our lessons—and answers Alessandra's question about language usage. Nonna has a college degree in literature and helps out with regional language usages—her husband was from Palermo, Sicily, and his Italian was very different from her northern Venetian Italian. Sometimes Nonna will tap on the door and poke her head in if she hears that I am having an unusually difficult time with a concept or pronunciation.

Saying that today's lessons went well really means that they went better than yesterday's, and any improvement on my part is considered "well" by me. We are doing really hard stuff with past tense—"I went to the…," "I said that…," "They were building…," "He told her…," "Last week they traveled…." In Italian there are many forms of the past, and we are only working on one form—the perfect past—the past that is complete and has no condition of time still lingering about it. You might think the past is only what has occurred previous to this moment, but no, there are time considerations and conditions to the past. "We went to the store" is one form of the past; "We would go to the store when she told us to go" is a completely different use of the past because it has conditions. Obviously, the same is true in English, but what makes it more difficult in Italian is that you have to know all the singular and plural forms, plus the gender forms. "I went" uses a different helping verb to express the past than "I said" does. "I went" is a form of motion or movement so you have to use *essere*—the verb for "to be"—as the helping verb to say, *"Sono andato."* ("I went.") You use *avere*—the verb for "to have"—as the helping verb to say, *"Ho detto."* ("I said.") And those are only the forms of those verbs in the singular perfect past, without conditions or gender. Open your mind for this:

I went

  —*Sono andato* (if you are male)

  —*Sono andata* (if you are female)

You (informal) went

  —*Sei andato* (if the person is male)

  —*Sei andata* (if the person is female)

You (formal)/He/She/It went

  —*È andato* (if the subject is masculine)

  —*È andata* (if the subject is feminine)

We went

  —*Siamo andati* (if there is at least one masculine subject in the group)

  —*Siamo andate* (if the subjects are all feminine)

You (plural—as a group) went

  —*Siete andati* (if there is at least one masculine subject)

  —*Siete andate* (if the subjects are all feminine)

They went

  —*Sono andati* (if there is at least one masculine subject)

  —*Sono andate* (if the subjects are all feminine)

Did you notice that the verb form for "I" and for "They" is the same word, *"Sono"*? Also, remember gender does not imply sex: the word for "dog"—*cane*—is masculine, regardless of the sex of the animal, and the word for "pen"—*penna*—is feminine. The informal is used with people you know, while formal is used with strangers and important people.

Now you are living a little of my current life in the past. *Mamma mia!* I deserve a nap.

Dinner tonight was only a slight alteration on lunch, since squid can't really be kept as a leftover for the next day, even though it did qualify for refrigeration between meals. Nonna and I lightly battered and fried strips of zucchini for the first course, we finished off the squid with potatoes as the main course and, as always, followed it with salad and fresh fruit.

During dinner, I asked if there was time in the morning for me to walk into Viterbo and go to the Saturday morning flea market, and then on the way back stop and check out Viterbo's cemetery. Nonna and I have driven past it several times, and it looks pretty cool from what I can see through the gates. I wasn't sure what time we were going to the mountains for our picnic. Nonna offered to drive me into Viterbo and drop me off for the market, giving me more time to walk back to visit the cemetery. Alessandra didn't want to leave for the picnic until closer to lunch, so she assured me that I would have the whole morning for the market and the cemetery.

For a day that started out with dreams, progressed to squid and then moved ahead into the past, it has been a rather simple day compared to some of the others.

I like that.

—⟨⟨⟨⟨∽∾⟩⟩⟩⟩—

Zucchine Fritte

Fried Zucchini

Italians love their contorni—*vegetable side dishes. This classic can be found on* antipasti *buffets across Italy. Make sure you salt the slices immediately after coming out of the pan, while they are still hot. The heat will help the salt adhere to the egg "batter" crust.*

4 small zucchini (1½ - 1¾ pounds)

½ cup all-purpose flour

1 teaspoon salt, plus more to taste

½ teaspoon freshly ground black pepper

2 large eggs

4 tablespoons sunflower oil, divided (extra virgin olive oil may be
   substituted)

Remove and discard the stem end of each zucchini. Expose the flesh of the zucchini for the first slice by removing and discarding a ⅛-inch-thick lengthwise slice of outer skin from one side of the zucchini. Continue slicing the zucchini lengthwise into thicker ¼-inch slices. As with the first slice, expose the flesh on both sides of the last slice by removing and discarding the outside skin on the farthest side. You should get four or five slices from each zucchini.

In a shallow, oblong dish, combine the flour, salt and pepper. In another shallow, oblong dish, beat the eggs well. Place a platter next to the egg dish to hold the battered zucchini before frying and place a second platter with several layers of paper towels near the stovetop.

Put 1 tablespoon of oil into a medium skillet and place over medium heat. While the oil is coming up to temperature, prepare the first batch of four or five zucchini slices by placing them into the seasoned flour, turning to coat both sides, shaking off any excess flour. Place the floured slices into the beaten eggs and, using a fork, turn to coat both sides. Remove each slice with the fork and let any excess egg drip off before placing the battered slice onto the platter.

When the oil is hot, but not smoking, use the fork to put the first batch into the oil—be careful of the oil spattering as you put them in. Cook until nicely browned and tender, 3 to 4 minutes, before flipping over and cooking an additional 2 to 3 minutes on the second side. If the slices are browning too fast, lower the heat.

While the first batch is cooking, prepare the second batch of four to five slices by repeating the flour and egg process, letting them rest on the platter until the batch in the skillet is done.

When the first batch is nicely colored and tender, remove them to the paper towels to drain and sprinkle lightly with salt.

Add 1 tablespoon of oil to the now hot skillet; the oil should quickly come up to temperature. Put in the second batch of battered slices and while cooking, prepare the third batch. Repeat the process until all of the zucchini are cooked—it should take four batches. Remember to lightly salt each cooked batch once it has been placed on the paper towels to drain and remember to add 1 tablespoon of oil to the hot skillet before frying the next batch. Serve warm or at room temperature.

Makes 4 to 6 servings.

IL GIORNO VENTUNO (Day Twenty-one)

There is no easy way to discuss my night last night, but there is no getting around it. Some things in life are unbelievable until you experience them for yourself, and even after experiencing them, it is difficult to find words to capture the truth of that experience. Even in Italy, where the boundaries of life and death are so intertwined, last night would seem miraculous.

I am a moderately religious person—you won't find me watching the Christian Channel, nor will you hear me say that life is a vast collection of coincidences randomly occurring with no shape, focus or plan. Religion is a very private and personal subject—I tend to keep my beliefs to myself. I am not judging the validity of any form of religious expression, or the validity of anyone's views on the subject of religion as a whole. It just happens to be my personal take on the subject, which needs to be stated before I go into details.

Last night, after we finished dinner and our usual lingering around the table drinking *caffè* and *digestivi*—after-dinner drinks, I went upstairs and got ready for bed. I wrote a little, brushed my teeth, made a little plan of action for attacking Saturday, turned out the lights, walked across the room, crawled under the covers and went to sleep.

In the middle of the night, I woke up to find that the bedroom light on the wall to the left of the dresser mirror was on. I was facing that wall when I opened my eyes, and I was surprised to see it on, since I had turned all the lights off before getting into bed. I sat up in bed and something caught my eye on the opposite side of the room—there, in the doorway to my bedroom, stood a woman. It was my friend Carol. Seeing her startled me and I gasped, sitting there for a moment in utter confusion. My friend Carol passed away from cancer just after Christmas in 1997—over seven years ago—and now she was standing in the doorway of my bedroom in Viterbo, Italy.

"Carol?" I asked, disbelievingly.

Silence.

"Carol, what are you ... I mean ... Carol, why ... I don't understand."

Silence.

"Carol ... hi?"

"Hi, Mark," she said, in the happy, smiling tone of one reuniting with a long lost friend.

"But, Carol ... how can you ... I mean ... Carol.... Hi!"

"Hi, Mark." She grinned wider.

I don't believe in these things. This only happens to crazy people on TV. "This isn't happening" should have been the thought running through my mind, or maybe, "Wow, this is one kickass dream I am having!" But neither was the case. I sat there in confusion—not in disbelief, denial or terror. I find it almost impossible to describe how I felt. To say that it was warm and safe and protected would be so far from the truth. On the other hand, there wasn't a cold shiver up my spine and frosty air visibly coming from my nostrils as I exhaled in supreme fright, either.

"Hi, Carol."

"Hi, Mark."

"I don't understand."

She smiled.

"Hi...." It seemed to be all I could think of to say. "Hi," I said again, and laughed as tears started streaming down my face. "Hi!"

"Hi, Mark."

"But ... you're here."

"Tell Kent and Alex I said hello." Her former husband and son.

My alarm clock rang; I bolted up in bed—and cried. I did more than that—I sobbed. I sobbed through my alarm clock ringing louder and louder and LOUDER. It had been a dream—just a dream. I turned my alarm clock off, wiped my eyes and looked at the light next to the mirror.

It was on.

I know I crawled into bed last night in complete darkness, except for the moonlight through the skylights.

It hadn't been a dream. Carol did visit me last night.

I cried more—not from the sadness of the experience or from the remembrance of my lost friend. I cried because there was so much emotion, energy and feeling inside me that my body couldn't contain it. Last night my tears weren't attached to any emotion. I am not sure what caused them. They were just tears streaming down my face, but now I cried in remembering it.

I gathered myself together as best I could: bathed, shaved, brushed my teeth, dressed and got ready to go downstairs for breakfast. I managed to be in control until I rounded the corner of the last flight down and Alessandra asked me, *"Hai dormito bene, Marco?"* It was the feeling of barely composing myself after hearing of a friend's death—that feeling of gathering just enough strength to hold myself together in public and to hold back the waters of the dam. And then there is the moment of running into someone familiar, and the simple act of seeing another friend obliterates all composure and breaks the floodgates again. Alessandra was that friend. Hearing her voice ask me how I slept completely unhinged me and I wept.

Alessandra and Nonna came rushing over to me. I can only imagine what a crazy sight I must have been—a grown man comes downstairs, and when asked how he slept, he starts bawling. They guided me to a chair at the kitchen table and sat me down. "Marco, what is the matter?" Alessandra asked, rubbing my arm as Nonna patted my back. There is something inherently comforting about maternal love.

Through my tears and sobs, I told them about Carol, our friendship, her death and how she came to me last night and how the light was on. "The light was on!"

I asked them if anyone had been up to my room in the middle of the night and turned my light on to get something or if that switch was known to have a short in it. Of course, an electrical short wouldn't explain how the switch itself had gotten moved into the "ON" position, but I still asked. They said that they had never had any problems with the light or switch before.

"So, why did she come and visit me last night?"

"Because, Marco, it is simple. The night before you dreamed all in Italian. Your mind and soul are wide open right now. This morning you have plans to go visit the cemetery here in Viterbo. It is a place of many, many memories of many, many souls. Your friend Carol came to you last night to see you and to let you know that she is always with you. Also, she has given you an important message to give to her family," Alessandra said. She translated for Nonna, who whole-heartedly agreed and added, "Si, si. È vero." —"It's true."

There was no disbelief on either of their parts. For them, it was perfectly logical that Carol would come and visit me. In Italy, all things are possible and all things are true. I'm not sure how this experience will change me, but I do know I will never be the same for having had it.

"Stai bene, Marco?" —"Are you alright?"— Nonna asked.

"Si, si, sono pazzo solo!" —"Yes, I'm only crazy!"

I laughed while wiping my eyes with Nonna's hanky; they chuckled and comforted me with the usual *"No, no, no,"* and embraced me. Our group hug helped me to compose myself yet again and the three of us ate breakfast before Nonna dropped me off in Viterbo at the farmer's market.

The huge parking lot of the Piazza Martiri d'Ungheria, opposite the bus station, had been turned into a tented flea market, a city of makeshift streets between rows of vendors' carts and tents. Items hung from tent edges beckoning you under the awning to see even more tempting offerings, household items from pots and pans to linens, clothing of all styles and sizes, toys for the kids, CDs and DVDs and electronics and the items went on and on. The thing I wanted to see most, but was surprisingly missing from this flea market, was food—there was no locally grown produce, cheese, sausages or baked items here.

It was fun to see the variety and check out the locals who were out shopping in full force. I didn't buy anything—nothing really caught my eye, and I wasn't up for lugging around the bags. I walked up into the historic neighborhood of San Pellegrino and did some window-shopping. There were a couple of antiques that might end up in my suitcase if I get back here during the week when the shops are open. I haven't purchased anything for myself—no keepsake to remind me of my time in Viterbo, although I have taken about 500 photos so far. Those and my memories might just have to suffice as my keepsakes.

Un gelato was in order before my trek to the cemetery, which lies about halfway between the historic center of Viterbo and the house. It was a glorious day for a walk, and although the walk wasn't really scenic—mostly walking alongside a very busy road—I did have my gelato, and that is all one needs in life.

Viterbo's cemetery is a gated fortress, or so it seems. The inhabitants are well protected behind 20-foot stone walls with heavy iron gates guarding arched entrances. Today the central gate was open and, before entering, I stopped at the flower vendor's stand outside the gate to see what the selection was. It is pretty cool that there are flowers for sale right outside the main gate to the cemetery, and the selection of flowers was amazing. I thought it might only be carnations and gladiolus, the usual "funeralizing" flowers, but it wasn't. There were at least a hundred varieties of flowers and plants in all shapes, sizes and colors.

Once inside, the cemetery is more art museum than a land of the dead. Headstones are works of art, monuments to the deceased: the winged Angel of Death embraces a woman with his skeleton fingers while his bony skull kisses her on the forehead as she looks up in ecstasy; the contemplative nude figure of a man sitting on a grave; a huge pyramid bearing a crucifix; carved floral sculptures—one with a little owl hidden amongst the carved stone lilies; maidens and angels, draped over headstones, mourning or silently guarding a deceased soul.

The most remarkable thing was that almost every headstone, mausoleum marker, sculpture, work of art and funereal urn bears an oval photo, usually black and white and protected behind a glass cover, of the deceased. The photos show a wide variety of ages, social and economic classes, and fashions. Sometimes the photo shows a recent image before their death—grandparents, children, soldiers and military officers. Other times, the photo shows the deceased earlier in life and more energetic—one of my favorites was of a woman who had died in her late 80s, but her photo showed her in her youth—glamorous, lipsticked, bright wide smile, sporting a 1940s hairstyle. She looked liked the life of the party; I was a little sad that I'd never get to meet her. The oldest photo I could find was from the late 1800s, while the rest started after the turn of the 20th century.

It was very peaceful here, as one would expect, and there were not many visitors. I found a bench under a shady tree and took a moment to enjoy my time here—not only my time amongst the deceased, but also my time in Viterbo with the very much alive. Sitting on the bench, I thought about Carol. I felt comforted by her visit, and it no longer wrecked me to think of it or of all the joyous moments we shared as friends. At its best, isn't that what a cemetery is about—remembering and celebrating the lives of those no longer with us—a place of eternal keepsakes.

I walked in the door carrying a bouquet of flowers. I hope it isn't too creepy to buy flowers from a cemetery florist to bring home for a vase on the living room coffee table. Nonna, Alessandra and Francesca were thrilled to get flowers, and we were just waiting for Stefano to arrive before heading off into the mountains. I had been a little nervous that they were all going to be waiting for me, but I timed it well, and within moments, Stefano with his dog Neo (named after the character in the movie *The Matrix*—American culture at work again!) arrived, and we regrouped and headed out the door. Lillo was off in the country taking care of the cows and horses, so it was just the five of us plus Neo. Nonna drove her car with me riding shotgun and Alessandra in back holding her hair, as usual. Francesca and Neo went with Stefano in his Jeep.

We drove to the nearby national park—*Riserva Naturale del Lago di Vico*—and more specifically to Monte Cimino where there are picnic areas in the vast beech forest. Alessandra told me that folklore claims Hercules created the lake and the mountains surrounding it by showing his sheer strength—he threw a huge tree trunk into the ground creating a hole big enough to form a lake in the midst of the mountains. She went on to tell me that, in reality, the area was created by an ancient volcano, which has long since been dormant.

Nonna followed Stefano as we twisted our way up the mountain, going deeper and deeper into the thickening forest. The further up we went, the cooler it became under the canopy of ancient beech. The graveled parking lot we pulled into was not shaded, so when I climbed out of the car I expected it to be hot and sunny. Instead, the sky had become overcast with a thin veil of clouds, not storm clouds, but the kind of clouds that turn an otherwise perfect day into a shaded grey day. There were lots of families spending the day on Hercules' shaded mountain—we were not the only ones who thought today would be a good day for a picnic. As we unloaded the car, I asked Alessandra what the Italian word is for picnic, *"Come si dice "picnic" in italiano?"* *"Picnic, Marco."* Alessandra explained that the term comes from the French term *"picque-nique,"* and the Italians, as do the English and Germans, use the modern derivative of the French word.

Quick Italian lesson: Words that are from another language—such as "picnic" or "bar" are automatically considered masculine words, because there isn't a vowel on the end to help distinguish the gender of the word. So, when trying to determine how to use words like "computer," "internet" or "weekend," it is easy because they are always masculine. Also, you can tell which words have infiltrated the Italian language from another culture if the words start with or include a "J," "K," "W," "X" or "Y," because those letters do not exist in the Italian alphabet—it contains only 21 letters compared to our 26.

We hauled our things down one of the many trails from the parking lot past many occupied picnic sites. I was getting a little concerned that we were going to be walking halfway down the mountain, which was fine now, but who wants to haul picnic items back up a mountain after eating? It was a lovely hike, and the forest was beautiful, but it was eerily silent. The only sounds in the forest were the other picnickers—no birds chirping or bugs buzzing, none of the nature sounds I associate with a summer picnic outside.

We found a table down a secluded path off of the main trail and unpacked lunch. We had salami, prosciutto, pecorino and asiago cheese, a freshly made tomato, mozzarella, basil and *penne* pasta salad and *una l'insalata di Russo*—Russian salad, made of green peas, potatoes, carrots (Nonna used a premixed blend from the freezer section of Le Clerc), a little mayonnaise and chopped dill pickle. It actually wasn't bad, considering I am still not a big fan of green peas. Stefano brought a big liter bottle of Coke, but unlike every American picnic that I have ever been to, there was no cooler full of ice. So, once again, we drank our Coke warm. Yikes!

While the ladies set out the spread, Stefano and I tossed the ball, playing fetch with Neo, a medium-size mutt mix with the coloring of a German shepherd but the shorthaired coat of a hound variety. Neo is very sweet, and unlike Crazy and Cochise, he is well trained and absolutely dotes on Stefano. Stefano is a handsome guy—a slender but athletic build, tall, his dark hair almost always pulled back into a ponytail. He is Brazilian by birth but was adopted from an orphanage and brought to Italy with his new parents when he was very young. Being Brazilian, and given the fact that it is August, and that he is a Forestry Management student at the university in Viterbo, his skin is chestnut brown, dark even by Italian standards.

This is the most time I have spent with Stefano, and he does speak some English, so it was a little easier for us to chat while throwing the ball for Neo—my pidgin Italian and his better than pidgin English kept us in good stead. Stefano seems like a very nice guy, and he certainly knows how to flirt with Nonna and Alessandra in the way that well-mannered men are trained by their mothers—he is always bringing some type of food gift to the house when he visits. It is usually fruit from his family's farm, but the other day it was his family's extra virgin olive oil that had just received its DOP rating for meeting very specific and stringent governmental standards—something that he is very proud of because it is not an easy thing to achieve. Today's gift was a *crostata di friutta*—a fruit tart—made by his mother's friend. He's a smart one. I get the sense that there is a little something of the kiss-ass about him—the kind of person who does and says all the correct things to authority figures, but when their backs are turned, his true devilish nature comes out. But it's only a feeling I have.

While we were sitting at the picnic table, Francesca brought up the subject of the trip to Naples. As soon as she mentioned *"Napoli,"* I could see

Alessandra and Nonna's bodies shift in anticipation of yet another heated discussion. Stefano noticed it, too, and before either lady could speak he jumped in and said that Francesca's parents had made the right decision in saying "No" to their going on a vacation alone. He could understand their concerns over the fact that he and Francesca had only been dating a relatively short period of time. Francesca looked as if she had been taken off guard—it seems she brought the subject up to get a rise from people, but Stefano put out that fire as soon as Francesca struck the match. Alessandra thanked Stefano for being so mature and understanding. He is a smart one, isn't he?

The picnic was perfect—a beautiful setting in an ancient forest, simple food, delightful conversation and no bugs! What more could one ask of a picnic?

It was siesta time when we got back to the house. Nonna, Alessandra and I headed upstairs to nap, while Francesca and Stefano regrouped to go horseback riding and camping with Marianna and Marco out at the family's farm in Blera. Marianna grabbed the jar of *zuppa di gatti* off the counter, and Nonna nudged me for noticing it. Some things do not change.

When I came downstairs after my siesta, Nonna was waiting for me with the car keys out and her purse in hand. She had spent her siesta trying to think of what to make for dinner, and we were now off to get it. We went to the medium-size grocery store and grabbed a bag of mixed mushrooms from the freezer section. I have never heard of frozen mushrooms before. TV cooks always talk about how rinsing off mushrooms to clean them destroys the flavor, since mushrooms act like little sponges and would soak up water. I assumed buying them from the freezer section would do the same thing.

"*Questi sono buoni, Nonna?*"

"*Si, Marco. Perchè?*"

"*Perchè dell'acqua.*" I really wanted to say "moisture," but I don't know that word, and I figured Nonna would make the logical deduction of my question, and she did.

"*No, Marco, questi funghi sono molto buoni. Credimi.*" —"No, these, mushrooms are very good. Believe me." Why would I ever doubt her?

From the freezer section, we made our way over to the bakery. The usual bread guy wasn't behind the counter; maybe he has Saturdays off. There was an attractive woman, mid-to-late 30s, working behind the counter today.

"*Prego?*"

"*Si, si. Vorremo del pane.*" —"Yes, we'd like some bread."

The woman grabbed a loaf from a stack of oblong-shaped loaves, holding it out for Nonna to visually inspect.

"*Questo?*"

"*Mmmm, un'altro, per favore,*" Nonna said, pointing back to the stack of loaves.

The woman obliged and grabbed a second loaf with her other hand and held them side-by-side for Nonna to compare. The woman caught my eye and smiled. I smiled back. Everyone at this store is always so friendly.

"*Mi dia quel pane li a destra. È bello.*" —"I'll take the bread on the right. It's beautiful."

"*Si, si. Vorrei prendere anch'io uno di quei pani li a destra. Un bel pane a destra per il bell'uomo a destra.*"

Nonna heard this and immediately started poking me in the ribs, "*Capito, Marco?*"

"*No, Nonna, mi dispiace, non capisco!*" I know she didn't believe that I couldn't understand the woman behind the counter. For one thing, I had to understand—I was blushing.

When Nonna said that she'd take the bread on the right because it was beautiful, the woman replied, "I'd like to take the one on the right, too. A beautiful bread on the right for a beautiful man on the right." I was standing on the right side of Nonna. The woman was shamelessly flirting with me—with Nonna right there.

"*Ehhh? Capito, Marco?*" Nonna said again, grinning wide and winking at me.

"Nonna, no! Mi dispiace." I was turning my fourth shade of red by now and trying to get Nonna to knock it off—the woman smiled and winked at me as she handed the wrapped bread to Nonna.

"*Grazie, Signora ... e Signore, anche,*" she said as Nonna took the bread from her, while winking at me one last time as we walked away.

I was embarrassed for two reasons. First, the fact that someone flattered me enough to make me blush, but secondly, Nonna not knowing that I am gay and egging me on made it even worse. I can completely see Nonna setting me up on a blind date and my not having a clue that she was doing it. One night the back gate would buzz and in would walk the *la Donna di Pane*—the Bread Lady—looking for a hot loaf. All the dogs would be barking, Nonna and Alessandra would be standing with linked arms, nodding in approval, while Lillo would be slapping me on the back and wishing me, "*In bocca al lupo!*" Can you imagine how awkward that would be? How in the world would I ever talk my way out of it? *Sono un carne*—I am a meat—remember?!

I pushed the cart as Nonna led me toward the canned vegetable aisle— she needed beans. Not pardoning the pun, she kept giving me the beans the entire way—smiling at me, nudging me, saying, "*Capito, Marco?*" and then laughing. I continued to blush and shake my head "No, Nonna. No." It continued from there to the dairy department, then to the check out—where she asked the cashier if she thought I was handsome, and when the woman said, "*Naturalmente,*" causing me to turn red again, Nonna giggled like a schoolgirl—then out to the car and on the way home, too.

"*Nonna, PER FAVORE!*"—my hands in prayer, desperately pleading with her to stop.

"*Ok, Marco. Mi dispiace,*" and we parked the car at the house.

I wasn't offended by her teasing me, nothing like that. It just made me feel thirteen all over again—awkward about the truth of the situation and goofy about someone flirting with me in front of family. I felt this way in 7th grade when the minister's daughter called me on the telephone after confirmation class to ask if I wanted to go out to the movies with her. I politely declined then, and now it was easier not to understand—*"Non capito."*

Dinner was kept to a minimum for the four of us, since the girls were off camping for the night. We made two different types of bruschetta: the traditional tomato, basil, extra virgin olive oil version and we used the frozen mushrooms for a different version. The bag of mushrooms was actually a blend of five different varieties, including porcini—the king of Italian mushrooms—a short, fat, brown, squatty-looking mushroom that could be in a fairytale story involving a troll or a frog or a spritely perched pixie. The mushrooms were diced and stewed more than sautéed in a little water with onions, garlic and mushroom stock—Nonna used a tablespoon of it from a jar in the fridge door.

We went on to make *fagioli e cipolle con pomodoro*—borlotti beans (a pinkish kidney bean) and onions with tomato. Lillo walked in the door with some porchetta from his favorite place in Blera. In a way, we were having the Italian version of a summer BBQ—smoked pork served with baked beans; we only needed cole slaw, potato salad, sweet tea and corn bread to make it Southern. He said he had seen the girls up at the farm before he left, so he knew they were going to be okay.

We started with the bruschetta, but we really never stopped eating them. At one point, having supposedly moved on to the porchetta, we were putting the fagioli on the bread, too. They weren't made for that purpose, but hell, when a piece of bread is around, just about anything can go on it. I think what makes bruschetta so good in Italy is that they rub a cut clove of garlic on the grilled bread before putting on the topping. The heat of the freshly grilled bread literally melts the garlic onto the surface of the bread, and once topped, the otherwise pungent flavor of garlic becomes a subtle backdrop for the topping. Freshly baked bread plays a huge role in the Italian diet; I guess you could say the same thing about the French, although I think Jimmy would say that his country's was far superior. When I think about it, I don't think I have seen sliced bread in plastic bags at the grocery store.

There is no vast bread aisle where the loaves are suffocatingly wrapped and stacked. I may be craving a hamburger now and then, but there is nothing better when it comes to the baked bread in Italy.

Nonna could not resist telling Lillo and Alessandra about my bread "date." As she told the story, aided by hand gestures, I think she was embellishing it, because it sounded and looked a lot more complicated than it should have. Lillo and Alessandra laughed at every twist and turn in her tale—especially Lillo, who kept looking at me as if I had missed out on getting some action with the Bread Lady. His eyes would widen and he would look at me surprised, which only encouraged Nonna to gild the lily. Alessandra, who always sits to my right, giggled and poked my arm as if I had been caught on the playground kissing a girl during recess. When she got to the punch line, "A beautiful bread on the right for a beautiful man on the right," the table erupted with laughter and applause—as I sat there bathed in red. I told Alessandra to tell them, "If I am so beautiful, why wasn't the bread free—we still had to pay for it!" That really brought the house down. Alessandra said not to worry because "that woman has been married three times before and has several children"—implying that the Bread Lady was a little fast and would soon be on to newer, more freshly baked goods.

We are still having fun with *la persona molto importante dall'America.*

Bruschetta con Fagioli e Cipolle
Bean and Onion Bruschetta

Rubbing the sliced end of a garlic clove over the toasted and warm cut side of the bread adds a spicy heat to this appetizer. A one-slice serving makes a filling antipasto.

For the topping:

1 tablespoon extra virgin olive oil

1 small onion, sliced into half-rounds

1 tablespoon tomato paste

½ teaspoon salt

¼ teaspoon freshly ground black pepper

½ cup plus 2 tablespoons low-sodium canned chicken broth (water may be substituted)

1 (15.5-ounce) can borlotti beans, drained and rinsed —also known as cranberry beans or Roman beans (pinto beans or cannellini beans may be substituted) *

Heat the olive oil in a medium saucepan over medium heat. When the oil is hot, add the onions and sauté until they are soft and translucent, 3 to 5 minutes. Add the tomato paste, stirring until it is well blended with the onions, 1 to 2 minutes. Add the salt and pepper, stirring until combined. Add ½ cup of chicken broth and the drained and rinsed beans, stirring to combine.

Cook the beans over medium heat until they start to boil, 2 to 3 minutes. Once boiling, cover the pan, reduce heat to low and simmer until the beans are tender but still retain their shape, 18 to 20 minutes, stirring occasionally. If the beans start to become too dry, add the additional 2 tablespoons of broth and stir until well combined. Remove pan from heat and set aside, covered, while the bread is prepared.

For the bruschetta:

4 slices Italian bread (¾-inch-thick slices of a Tuscan boule or similar
   bread)

1 large clove garlic, skin removed and cut in half

1 to 2 tablespoons extra virgin olive oil

Cut the slices of bread in half and toast the 8 half-slices on the stovetop
using a grill pan over medium heat, turning the slices to toast both sides to
a golden brown. Or, toast on a baking sheet on the top rack of a 450-degree
oven, turning the slices to brown both sides.

Remove the toasted slices to a serving platter. While the bread is still hot,
rub the cut side of the garlic halves over the top surface of the toasted bread.

Drizzle the top of each slice with olive oil and, using a tablespoon, evenly
distribute the bean mixture on top of the toasted slices. Serve warm.

Makes 8 bruschetta.

★ *Note: Borlotti beans are difficult to find, but may be found in Italian specialty
food markets. I use canned Roman beans, Goya brand, which can be found in most
regular supermarkets across the country. Look for them with the other canned
beans or, sometimes, they can be found in the Mexican food aisle.*

IL GIORNO VENTIDUE (Day Twenty-two)

This morning I walked to *il centro* of Viterbo and wandered through its ancient streets hoping to discover some hidden treasures. *Il centro* has become very familiar to me at night, since we come into town often for late night gelato, but during the day it seems like a new and completely different city. I never bring my camera with me at night, so I took advantage of the beautiful sunny weather to catch up on my photos.

It's Sunday, so my first destination was to find *La Chiesa di Santa Rosa*—the church of *Santa Rosa*. Since my first gelato trip with Alessandra and Lillo on my second night in Viterbo, I have not been able to get the image of *La Macchina di Santa Rosa* out of my mind. How is it possible for 130 men—*i Facchini*—to carry a five-ton, 100-foot tower on their backs? And who was this saintly woman in whose honor *i Facchini* performed this *spettacolo*?

I stopped some people and asked for directions to the church—some of which I understood. I was thankful for the people who pointed; that clarified a lot. I stopped at a *caffè* to grab a morning cappuccino—something Italians won't drink after breakfast time. If you want to be immediately pegged as an American tourist, order a cappuccino after 10:00 a.m. and watch the Italians roll their eyes in disbelief. It is also much more fashionable to stand at the counter and drink one's *caffè*—usually a single shot of espresso—than it is to walk down the street carrying a to-go coffee cup. In a *caffè* you always drink out of a ceramic "real" coffee cup, not a paper one. Besides being more fashionable, the counter is quicker and cheaper than sitting at a table because you have to pay a linen charge to sit at a table—most Italians stand at the counter. There must be coffee to go, but I have never noticed it.

I put my cup down, asked, *"Dov'è la Chiesa di Santa Rosa?"* and was pointed up the street. I found *via di Santa Rosa* and looked up the very steep road to see only the dome of a church. The road was steep enough to block the bottom half of the church from view. There is a tiny *piazza* at the top of the street in front of the church, the final resting place of *La Macchina*.

I peeked in the front door; I didn't want to interrupt a mass if it was in full swing, but the church was empty. I must have missed the morning service. The church is large, all white and simply appointed. I walked toward the altar and stopped under the *cupola*—dome—and looked up. It wasn't a particularly amazing fresco, but WOW—was it colorful. On a background of blue, in the center of the dome, was a lamb with a golden halo seated on a golden, tasseled pillow surrounded by stars in the center of a large red and golden sunburst. Surrounding that was a ring of *putti*, or cherubs; some were only haloed heads with red wings, some had complete bodies. The full-figured *putti* sported three sets of red wings. The highest set was opened fully, the middle opened to the sides behind their outstretched arms, and the third discreetly crossed and draped in front of their naked bodies. A burst of fire shot straight up from their golden halos. Coming farther down the dome, surrounding the flaming *putti*, were saints, angels, a winged lion and a winged bull all holding scripture written on opened books, sheets of parchment or long unfurled scrolls.

I had to take a picture of this *cupola*. I looked around, and since I was alone, decided to lie down on the floor directly under the center of the dome. I know it was probably uncouth to be on the floor, on my back, in the middle of a Catholic church, but how often would I get this chance? When I got up, there on the right side of the nave was *Santa Rosa's* chapel. I had been so taken with the dome that for a second I had forgotten why I was here in the first place—to see *Santa Rosa*.

Legend has it that *Santa Rosa* gained her sainthood by performing several miracles—raising an aunt from the dead, standing in a fire for several hours to prove her devotion, being healed of an illness by the Virgin Mary, and after having some disagreements with the then emperor, being exiled by him and shortly thereafter predicting his death and returning to Viterbo along with papal power—all before her death at age 17. Young Italian women were busy back in the Middle Ages.

When I say I came to see *Santa Rosa* I mean just that—to SEE her. In her chapel, displayed in a glass box inside her shrine, is the actual corpse of *Santa Rosa*, who died in 1252. Yes, she is preserved—looking like a very tanned piece of leather and dressed simply in a nun's white habit, much like Mother Teresa. Some people may think this is disturbing—a 753-year-old corpse displayed for all to see. I think it is kind of sweet. She looks like she is smiling, which probably has more to do with the preservation process than her actual eternal bliss, but maybe I am wrong.

What I like most about *Santa Rosa's* story is that upon her return to Viterbo from exile she tried to join the monastery of Saint Mary's of the Roses, but was denied acceptance because she was so poor. In 1850 *La Chiesa di Santa Rosa* was built on the remains of the very monastery that rejected her, and she has been enshrined there ever since. As I stood at her shrine, reading about her life, I wondered if maybe that was why she was grinning, just a little.

I returned to the house at the same time as Lillo, Alessandra and Nonna. They were all very smartly dressed and had gone to church. For a brief second I felt as if I had been left out of a family event and wished I could have gone with them, but ultimately, since I am not Catholic I wouldn't have understood much of the service anyway. My time was probably better spent marveling over *Santa Rosa* and her church. Francesca, Stefano and Neo arrived just in time for lunch, which Nonna had prepared before going to church—chicken cooked in a mixture of herbs and broth and spaghetti in a sauce made of fresh San Marzano tomatoes and basil, topped with bread crumbs toasted in olive oil.

There were no siestas today. Lillo headed out to the farm to check on the cows and horses, Francesca and Stefano left Neo at the house and went over to visit Marianna and Marco, while Nonna, Alessandra and I headed out for some gelato. Instead of going into *il centro*, the ladies decided that they wanted to take me around *il Lago di Bolsena* to the town of Bolsena itself.

As we drove north, Alessandra and Nonna were speaking about a cemetery—*un cimitero*. For the life of me I couldn't figure out why they would be talking about that of all things. There was much discussion back and forth, and just as my curiosity could take no more, Alessandra said, "There is a place that Nonna and I have been wanting to visit but we have never taken the time to go, and since you are with us we hope that you will want to go, too."

"*Certo, Alessandra, dove?*"

"Well, Marco, it is a World War II cemetery and memorial of the soldiers who were killed in this area. It is supposed to be very beautiful and we have never been to see it. Would you like to go?"

"*Naturalmente, Alessandra.* My grandfather was in the war, and although he was stationed in England, I would enjoy seeing it with the two of you, so *andiamo*—let's go!" Nonna punched the gas and off we flew.

We drove around the east side of the lake, winding our way higher and higher along the ridge of the ancient volcanic crater that created it. *Il lago* came into view over Nonna's left shoulder through her opened window. The lake glistened in the distance below meticulously manicured vineyards, flickering in and out of view behind random thickets of trees along the road.

Nonna reminded Alessandra that somewhere in the woods around here American soldiers had used large timbers to build a church during the war. As Alessandra translated for me, Nonna could not help throwing in *"È una bella chiesa. Bellissima!"* I asked if it was part of the memorial and cemetery, but was told it wasn't.

"Marco, I hope we have time to find this church and show it to you, but we are not exactly sure where it is around here."

"Non c'è una problema. I am sure the cemetery and the memorial will be beautiful enough."

"I hope so, Marco."

We zoomed by some cars parked along the opposite side of the road and I could see some type of monument amongst them. Nonna quickly slowed down, pulled off onto the right shoulder and, as I placed a hand on the dashboard to steady myself, whipped the car around to put us in the other lane to go back toward the parked cars. *"Mamma! Per favore,"* Alessandra chided from the back seat. Nonna just grinned at me.

We pulled behind one of the several cars parked single-file just off the road. *"Attento Mamma,"* warned Alessandra as Nonna had to wait for passing cars to clear before opening the driver's side door to get out. We were parked so close to the road that I knew the next passing truck would rip off the mirror. Nonna closed her door and pushed the mirror flat against the side of the car—obviously she was worried, too.

We grew silent as we approached the roadside monument. Atop the stone block monument, a large rampant lion was standing on top of a vanquished dragon whose head was held tightly in the grasp of the lion's rear claws, the dragon's forked tongue lifelessly dangling from its mouth. It was a nice monument, powerful in its imagery, but as we stood there admiring it, I thought, "Well, is this it?" Nonna tapped me on the shoulder and motioned for the two of us to follow her.

To the left of the monument, a steep stone staircase went down the hillside from the road and led to a wide cement path that disappeared into the distance. It was breezy as we walked along the path—a wide pasture of grass bordered the path to the left and to the right, row after row of vines dripping with green furry kiwi. For some reason I thought kiwi grew on trees. I stopped and stared at the vast kiwi orchard to my right. "*Stupefacente!*" I said to the ladies and they nodded in agreement. It was a long way down the path before it curved to the right, disappearing behind the orchard and opening onto the cemetery and the actual memorial. There before us was a large white marble pedestal topped with a huge white marble cross. Centered in the face of the cross was a large metal sword. There was something so chivalrous, stately, knightly and proud about it—very fitting for a war cemetery.

Behind the cross, stone columns marked the entrance into the cemetery through a manicured hedge. To the left were rows and rows of white marble headstones in front of which were planted red roses, now in full bloom. It was striking to see the rows of perfectly spaced white marble markers fronted by blood red roses, backed by the green orchard, and surrounded by a lush and manicured lawn. This morning, *Santa Rosa's* church had been red, white and blue, and here the image was red, white and green. Trees dotted the landscape and provided much needed shade to this somber place.

The three of us split up to wander the grounds individually. I am sure this place had a special meaning for Nonna, who had lived through the war. Each marker was a piece of art unto itself. Carved into the top of the marble was a symbol representing each soldier's service: elaborate anchors identified sailors, the Royal Army Service Corps medallion identified British soldiers, round-shaped bombs with flames shooting out the top marked Grenadier Guards. Most of the markers had the names of the deceased and the dates of their birth and death carved into them, but some only said "A Sailor." Besides Brits and Americans, there were other nationalities here—South Africans, Yugoslavians—and I noticed one Star of David amongst the sea of crosses.

Several rows away from me, a woman, roughly my age and dressed in casual black clothes, was kneeling in front of one of the markers. While she spoke directly to the name on the marker, reaching out and touching it at times, wiping tears from her eyes, a tall gentleman in more typical vacation clothes stood slightly away from her. Two pre-adolescent kids would come running up to the man, and the three of them would stand in silence, watching the kneeling woman. After a moment the man would shoo the kids away to go play in another part of the cemetery. I stood in silence watching this family, and after a moment, when the woman got up, I quickly diverted my attention to other markers and changed rows. I wasn't snooping or staring; her emotion had intrigued me. I continued down the row before Nonna caught my eye and waved me over to a small stone pavilion on the grounds.

Alessandra explained that there was a guest book here that I needed to sign and there was a chart, which showed by name the location of each marker. The woman that I had been watching was signing the guest book as I approached. She stepped away, caught my eye, and we both politely grinned and nodded to each other. As I was signing the book under her name, I noticed that she listed her hometown as "Skokie, IL"—a suburb of Chicago. Inevitably, when traveling overseas you bump into other Americans and there is a wave of curiosity—an urge—that forces you to ask where they are from and why they are traveling. It is an urge that I try hard not to indulge, but sometimes it cannot be pushed aside or ignored; it is as if you cannot believe that someone from America would be out of the country at the same time as you, so you have to get the details of their escape. I turned around, walked up to her and said, "Excuse me, I noticed from the book that you are from Skokie. I am from Chicago, too … well, I grew up in the far north suburbs of Chicago."

She smiled politely without speaking. I felt compelled to keep talking.

"So, why are you here at this memorial? I am here studying in Italy for a month and the family I am with brought me here today." I pointed over my shoulder to Alessandra and Nonna who waved at the couple. "My grandfather was in World War II, and they thought I would find this place interesting, and they themselves have never been here to see it either. I think my grandfather will get a kick out of hearing that I was here, even though he was stationed in England during the war."

There was a brief pause and the woman's eyes started to well up with tears.

"My grandfather was in the war, too. He is buried here and I never got to meet him … until today."

"Oh … I'm sorry."

"Thank you."

For a moment, I thought I had said something wrong, but after a brief pause, she continued.

"This is a good trip, actually. I've always wanted to come and see where he is buried and visit his grave. I'm the only one in the family who has been here to see it. I'm happy, and sad too, of course. He is one of only two Jewish men buried here."

"How wonderful that you have this beautiful day to spend time with him and honor his memory."

"Yes, it is a beautiful day to be here," she said, wiping her eyes before they could flood. "Well, have a wonderful day and enjoy your time here studying."

"Thank you, I will. *Buona giornata!*" I said.

"You, too." And off they walked, gathering their kids and heading back up the path.

"Marco, do you know those people?" Alessandra asked me.

"No, I don't, but they are from a suburb of Chicago, so I had to say hello." I told Alessandra and Nonna the woman's story.

"She is a very good granddaughter to travel all this way to visit her grandfather," said Alessandra. *"Si, lei è una buona nipote,"* agreed Nonna.

We stood there a moment facing the grounds. It dawned on me that these marble markers not only represented an individual person, but a family— and not only the family at the time of the person's death, but the entire family, immediate and extended, that was yet to be in the future, too. Her grandfather may have passed away 60 years ago, but the loss of his soul was still being wept over today, in this moment of time.

"*OK, andiamo a Bolsena,*" I said, before I could start crying, too.

Bolsena is a lakeside resort town with two distinct personalities. The modern part of Bolsena bordering the shore of the lake was slammed with tourists—campgrounds filled with travel trailers and tents, balconies of small hotels covered with drying beach towels, crowded rows of vacation bungalows hidden behind clotheslines of billowing laundry and tour buses dropping off and picking up crowds of visitors. It was quite the scene, but Nonna skillfully drove the car through the obstacle course of people crossing the main drag, coming and going from the beach. She pulled into a crowded parking lot, double-parked and told us to get out. She was going to stay with the car and keep moving until she found a place to park, while Alessandra and I made our way up the hill into the historic center of ancient Bolsena. We agreed to meet Nonna later on the nearby street corner.

As with so many old cities in Italy, Bolsena was built on a hilltop and had a *rocca*—fortress—inside its stone walls. *Il centro di Bolsena* was similar to Viterbo's—narrow, twisting and turning medieval cobblestone streets filled with stone houses and churches, but here the stone wall surrounding *il centro* had archers' portals that overlooked the lake below. As we walked the steeply inclined streets, Alessandra told me stories of Bolsena, but I was so distracted by the beauty of the stone buildings and the hidden views of the lake that magically appeared when looking down a street or through a portal, that I didn't really pay a lot of attention to what she was saying. At one point, we stopped along a walkway that overlooked the tiled rooftops below to admire the lake glistening in the late afternoon sun.

"*Bellissima, Marco, no?*"

"*Bellissima, Alessandra, si!*"

La Rocca was closed, but at the top of the hill we found a church. It was old on the outside—beautiful—and completely modern on the inside—

not so beautiful. Modern, vibrantly colored ecclesiastical paintings filled the white plastered walls. Alessandra and I looked at each other, scrunched up our noses and walked out. *"Brutta."* —"Ugly". We both agreed.

Back at the bottom of the hill, we found Nonna on the corner chatting with a couple of fellow retirees. She waved at us, said her goodbyes to her newfound friends and crossed the street to meet us.

"Gelato, Marco?"

"Si, Nonna, si!" And off we went, Nonna leading the way.

We sat at a little table outside and ate our gelati while we watched the tourists passing by. I noticed that there didn't seem to be a lot of Italians in Bolsena. Alessandra said that Bolsena was a very popular vacation town for Germans, and she was right. Down here in the modern part of Bolsena—the lakeside part—I heard only German being spoken. Inside *il centro* is where I heard Italian. I had wondered why the girl who was working the counter of the *gelateria* said hello to me in German when I first walked in. Here they see more Germans than Americans, so naturally German was the default language when encountering a foreigner, but the minute she saw the ladies with me, she immediately spoke in her native Italian.

We had a great time people watching. On our way to the car, we stopped by a church famous for its grotto of Saint Christina (dating back to the 9th century). It seems a Eucharistic miracle happened to a German priest here in the mid-13th century while he was performing a Holy Mass, so Saint Christina's church is a very popular stop on pilgrimages. Before becoming martyred, Saint Christina was a feisty young girl—her pagan father tried to drown her in Lake Bolsena (he attached a huge stone to her neck before throwing her in), a government official had her tongue cut out, she then survived being burned in a five-day fire and was eventually martyred when she was shot full of arrows. Italian girls are tough!

On the way home we discussed keeping dinner simple and having the leftover chicken from lunch; however, either Tequila or Neo got hungry while we were gone and ate all of the chicken, right out of the pan on top of the stove. Brighitta was the only one wagging her tail when we entered the back door; the other two hanged their heads in shame—it was easy to tell who was guilty. The pan had been knocked on the floor and everything had been licked clean. Nonna was furious—*"Disastro! Disastro! Mamma mia, disastro!"* Luckily for Tequila and Neo, Nonna does not have any recipes involving dog, although she was mad enough to make *zuppa di gatti* out of them. Nonna panicked about what we were going to have for dinner now that the second course had been eaten, but we calmed her down, forged ahead and cleaned out the fridge. And I have to say for having "nothing" to eat, I was stuffed! Nonna made a *frittata di patate* and an English pea, potato and pasta soup. We also had leftover salami, prosciutto and the last of the salad from Saturday's picnic, along with bread. It was a feast.

When Stefano and Francesca returned to the house, Stefano explained to Alessandra and Lillo that his parents weren't thrilled with the idea of he and Francesca going to Naples alone either, so they offered to go on the trip as chaperones—but only if the Stefanis approved. By Francesca's overjoyed reaction you would have thought the Stefanis had agreed to a marriage proposal by Stefano and not just to a chaperoned vacation to Naples. Lillo said he wanted to talk to Stefano's parents directly to make sure everything was okay with them and, after a brief phone call, Francesca was bouncing off the walls with happiness when Lillo and Alessandra gave the final okay.

This week has been Shakespearean: a celebration of a long-awaited and unexpected victory, the excursion of young love first vehemently argued over and denied, only later to be approved through some crafty negotiations, and a weekend of discoveries, dreams, death and memorials. From Carol's unearthly visit, seeing the preserved *Santa Rosa* and witnessing a woman connect with her grandfather for the first time at a lakeside cemetery—it has been an intertwining of this world and the world beyond, resulting in one affirmative thing … life.

Minestra di Patate, Piselli e Tubettini

Potato, Pea and Pasta Soup

In the best of all possible worlds, use homemade chicken stock for this dish instead of the canned and you might think that Nonna has prepared this for you herself. Because I don't readily keep a supply of homemade chicken stock in my freezer, the low-sodium canned or cartoned variety will do just fine. If you are a vegetarian, substitute vegetable broth for the chicken broth and you will have an easy, meat-free soup.

2 tablespoons extra virgin olive oil

1 medium onion, finely minced

1 medium potato, peeled and diced into ½-inch cubes

½ teaspoon salt, or more to taste

½ teaspoon freshly ground black pepper, or more to taste

8 cups low-sodium canned chicken broth

1 cup tubettini (or another small tube pasta, such as ditalini) *

1 cup frozen peas

¼ cup chopped fresh Italian flat-leaf parsley

½ cup grated Parmigiano-Reggiano cheese for garnish

In a large pot, heat the oil over medium heat. Add the onion and cook, stirring, until it starts to turn golden, 5 to 6 minutes. Add the potatoes, salt and pepper and stir until well combined. Add the broth, cover and bring to a boil.

Once boiling, uncover the pot and boil the potatoes for 5 minutes. Add the pasta and, stirring occasionally, cook until *al dente*—tender but firm to the bite, about 10 to 12 minutes. Add the frozen peas, stirring until well combined. Let cook for one minute. Turn off the heat, add the parsley, stir until well mixed and let the soup rest for a couple of minutes. Taste and adjust the seasonings. Serve with a tablespoon of grated Parmigiano-Reggiano sprinkled over the top of each serving.

This makes 8 one-cup servings.

---

* *Note: There are many small-shaped pastas to choose from besides tubettini (small tubes) and ditalini (small thimbles). Regardless of our age, we are all still children at heart, so look for these other fun, small shapes to add some childlike discovery to this soup: Acini di pepe (peppercorn shaped), Alfabeto (letters of the alphabet), Anellini (small rings), Conchigliette (small shells), Filini (little threads), Gomito (bent tubes), Orzo (rice shaped), and Pearl Pasta (which is slightly larger than Acini di pepe).*

LUN. · 22 AGO

IL GIORNO VENTITRE

"*Marco, dov'è il tuo bucato?*" —Mark, where is your laundry?"— Nonna yelled up to me from the kitchen. Mondays are laundry day and from the very first Nonna has insisted on doing mine. I have tried, repeatedly, to talk her out of it—"*Nonna, no. Posso lavare il mio bucato, per favore*"—but regardless of my attempts there is no changing her mind. She is doing my laundry every Monday whether it makes me feel like a spoiled college student coming home for the weekend or not.

"*Nonna, vengo giù con il bucato.*" —"Nonna, I'm coming down with the laundry."

She met me at the bottom of the stairs and took my armful of clothes off to the laundry room in the downstairs bathroom.

"*Nonna, per favore....*"

"*Marco, no, no, no!*" And she disappeared around the corner.

I know most people would relish having someone do their laundry every week, but because there is only a washing machine here and no dryer, the laundry dries on a clothesline in the backyard. I was shocked one afternoon when I went into the backyard to chat with Nonna, Alessandra, Marianna, Francesca and Marco only to discover my underwear hanging on the line right up front. My skivvies were blowing in the breeze for all to see. *"Disastro!"* I thought to myself and turned three shades of red. No one else was paying attention to what was on the line—they are used to seeing clothes drying in the backyard. I wanted to say something, but I had no clue how to explain my embarrassment in Italian, and I couldn't hurt Nonna's feelings by saying, "Oh my God, you put my underwear right up front for everyone to see." She has been incredibly kind by doing my laundry, so I have avoided the weekly embarrassment by steering clear of the backyard on laundry day. Whether it makes sense or not, my rationale is "What I don't know won't hurt me."

After starting my laundry, Nonna returned to the kitchen to finish making a batch of *marmellata* with the remaining yellow plums from the backyard. *"Marco, prendi qualche marmellata a casa."* —"Mark, you can take some jam home."— Nonna said, filling a large quart jar with the hot pale-orange preserves. *"Certo, Nonna. Grazie!"* What a great souvenir that will be.

My final week here is going to be a busy one and it is going to be over before I know it. According to Nonna and Alessandra, we have a lot of food on our "must cook" list—tiramisù, *amaretti* cookies, potato *gnocchi, fettuccine di Blera* are only a few. And I am starting to learn future tense—"I will be going...," "We should plan on...," "You'll read my...." I told Alessandra that I can barely grasp and remember the present and the past—and now we are moving onto the future?

"Davvero, Alessandra? Mamma mia!"

"Si, si, Mark, davvero. Coraggio!" —"Yes, yes, Mark, really. Courage!"

It is going to be a big week—both cognitively and digestively. Hopefully, I'll remember where I packed my thinking cap and my second stomach.

Per il pranzo, we had a roast that had been marinated in red wine and garlic overnight. Actually, it was more like 12 hours—Nonna started it last night right after dinner. The roast was served with a red wine *risotto,* and for dessert we made a *frutta in crosta,* which is an American fruit cobbler. It was pretty much the same recipe, not quite as much sugar, as a cobbler—we used pears from Stefano's parents' farm. Nonna was a little disappointed that I already knew how to make a *frutta in crosta.* I think she was ready to impress me with this different type of dessert, but when I said, *"So questo ricetta e la faccio a casa,"* —"I know this recipe and I make it at home,"— I could see her deflate a little—*"Ah ... buono, Marco ... buono."*

I enjoyed having a roast on a Monday, even though I still think of it as something you eat on a Sunday—that way you can eat all you want and take a nap afterward. Luckily, I could eat as if today was a Sunday because lunch every day here is followed by a siesta. I am going to miss my afternoon siestas—a lot!

The future has me all confused and after my lesson this afternoon, Alessandra and I decided that maybe we will save the future for the future. We have more than enough things for me to work on and learn without moving ahead in time. There is something poetic about us abandoning the future during my last week here. Maybe it is best to spend the remainder of my time firmly in the present and joyfully looking back on the past.

Tap, tap, tap.

"Scusa, Alessandra e Marco," Nonna said, as she opened the den door and poked her head in. *"Alessandra, è Francesca al telefono."*

"Marco, scusa." In a flash Alessandra was up and on the kitchen phone with Francesca.

Francesca and Stefano left early this morning for their *vacanza di Napoli.* This is Francesca's first non-family, away from home vacation—and with her boyfriend and his parents, no less—so there have been a lot of phone calls back and forth this morning. Our morning lesson was interrupted twice by Francesca calling Alessandra's *telefonino*—cell phone. The kitchen phone had been called earlier, too, while Nonna and I were preparing the *risotto*. Each phone call centers around where the lovebirds are in their travels—arriving at Stefano's parents' house south of Rome, the trip from their house back to Rome and to the Termini—the central train station where I had checked my bags when I first arrived three weeks ago, the interminable wait for the train or so it seemed to Francesca, and this latest one was midway on the train ride to Naples. Every time Francesca calls, Nonna and Alessandra act like giddy schoolgirls—giggling and relishing every detail of her trip. They are having as much fun as Francesca and this trip has turned them into 19-year-old girls, too.

The kitchen phone rang again tonight in the middle of dinner. Nonna was the first to leap up and answer it—*"Pronto... Aaa, Francesca...."* We each took our turn on the phone with her; I chatted with her briefly after Lillo finished. She and Stefano left this morning before I came downstairs and I didn't get to say my goodbyes. I'll be gone before they return from Naples. You could hear the excitement in her voice as she told me about the ferry ride out into the bay, the moon, Stefano and the view of Naples. I could only understand a word here and there, but the joy in her voice said it all. I said my goodbyes and thanked her for everything during my time in Viterbo, and we wished each other *buon viaggio*—safe travels—as I handed the phone to Alessandra.

There was a moment of silence after Alessandra returned to the table and resumed eating. Ah, to be 19 and standing on a ferry in the middle of the Bay of Naples in the arms of your beloved, under a moon reflecting light back toward the coast, and looking at that ancient city and its lights twinkling in the distance.

Our conversation was all about her phone call, and we decided that the only way to accurately describe what a great time she must be having was not to describe it with words but with a single gesture. Holding your right hand up with the back of your hand facing away from you, touch your thumb to your first two fingers and shake your hand back and forth at the wrist. This

Italian hand gesture means nothing could be better and there are no words to explain how amazing, incredible, beautiful or delicious the experience is. With a knowing look and an implied depth of knowledge, Nonna does the gesture best. Lillo is a tight second.

For dinner, I helped Nonna make a *pasticcio di zucchine*—a zucchini and egg casserole with pecorino cheese, thyme and mint. I forgot how wonderful mint is when used as a savory herb instead of a sweet one. While helping me prepare the *pasticcio*, Nonna also made a lentil and orzo soup. The weather has cooled off here lately and we have been having more rain, so Nonna thought an autumn-type soup would be good.

After dinner and a final phone call from Francesca, I headed upstairs to bed, stuffed from dinner and looking forward to the rest of the week.

Pasticcio di Zucchine

Zucchini Casserole with Thyme and Mint

Using cream and milk with cornstarch gives this dish a frothy consistency, much lighter than an omelet and almost bordering on a soufflé. Pairing thyme and mint with zucchini is an Italian classic.

2 tablespoons extra virgin olive oil

3 medium zucchini (1¼ -1½ pounds), sliced into ¼-inch-thick rounds

1 small yellow onion, thinly sliced into half-rounds

1 teaspoon salt, divided

½ teaspoon freshly ground black pepper, divided

1 cup whole milk

2 tablespoons cornstarch

1 cup whipping cream

2 whole eggs plus 2 egg yolks, slightly beaten

2 tablespoons grated Parmigiano-Reggiano cheese (Grana Padano may be substituted)

4 ounces ricotta salata, cut into ¼-inch-thick slices (provolone or fontina may be substituted)

¼ teaspoon dried thyme

10 small to medium-sized fresh mint leaves

Preheat oven to 300 degrees.

In a large pan, heat the oil over medium heat. Stir in the zucchini, onion, ½ teaspoon salt, ¼ teaspoon black pepper and sauté until the onions are golden brown and the zucchini is tender, 10 to 12 minutes, stirring occasionally. Remove pan from heat and let cool.

In a medium bowl, whisk together the milk and cornstarch. Whisk in the cream, beaten eggs and yolks, Parmigiano-Reggiano, ½ teaspoon salt and ¼ teaspoon black pepper.

Grease a shallow, 10-inch round baking dish with olive oil. Evenly distribute the zucchini/onion mixture in the dish. Pour the milk/egg mixture over the zucchini. Arrange the sliced ricotta salata across the top. Sprinkle with thyme and decorate the top with mint leaves, making sure that the mint is placed on the eggs and not the cheese.

Bake for 52 to 55 minutes, until the eggs have set and the top starts to lightly brown.

Let rest for 5 to 10 minutes before slicing and serving warm, or let cool completely and serve at room temperature.

Makes 6 to 8 servings.

In Italy, mint is not just a sweet herb to be used for desserts. It is also used in savory dishes. Being in the same family, mint and basil are often used together or interchangeably in savory dishes, especially when using tomatoes.

IL GIORNO VENTIQUATTRO

"*G*OOOOL!*"* I cried, dropping my spoon into my cereal.

I was startled by a huge crash of pots and pans behind me. Nonna was digging around in one of the kitchen cabinets and pulled out a stack of pots and pans that got away from her and crashed onto the floor.

"*GOL!*" Nonna replied, laughingly.

"*Mamma, attenta, per favore,*" Alessandra pleaded.

"*Si, si, Alessandra.*"

There are times when things get away from Nonna. Honestly, there are times when things get away from all of us, but when it happens to Nonna everyone in the family gets a little concerned. I noticed it the first day I arrived when Nonna was slicing some bread and dropped the knife on the floor. "*Mamma, attenta,*" Alessandra said, casually scolding Nonna, more out of concern for Nonna's well being than out of anger. After the third day of bottles clanking, pans banging and misplaced cell phones, I decided to turn what would sometimes be an awkward situation into a funny one. I yelled *"Gol—*Goal!" any time that Nonna did something that made a loud noise that might cause everyone to roll their eyes and say *"Nonna, attenta!"* *"Gol!"* is a soccer term that is yelled whenever someone scores a goal. Usually the vowel sound is held out long as the scoring player runs away from the net with his hands held high—*"GOOOOL!"*

Around the house back in Alabama, whenever there is a loud crashing noise—a dropped lid, a knocked over box or a slammed cabinet door, Richard yells "And stay out!" as if the noise were in reaction to throwing someone out of the house and slamming the door behind them. I don't know how to say "And stay out!" in Italian, so I came up with the first thing that entered my head and that was *"Gol!"* People were yelling it at the beach soccer game my first trip into Viterbo three weeks ago and it stuck with me. It certainly seems to lighten the mood around crashing sounds and simple foibles. So when things go awry for any of us and a crashing sound occurs—*"GOOOOL!"* can be heard throughout the house.

Nonna is certainly not losing her faculties and she isn't any clumsier than the rest of us—I almost pulled the deep fat fryer off the counter the first night we used it; want to talk about a *disastro* if that would have happened?! Everyone's reaction to a noise when Nonna makes it implies impatience and a heightened concern on their part. Maybe that is just the natural worry a person has for an aging parent.

On our shopping rounds this morning Nonna stopped by the bakery and we purchased some *pizza bianca*. Standing in line at the counter, I realized that this is the one food that I will miss most from Italy. There is an unending list of really great food and meals that I will miss, but the one thing that I know I will not be able to find or make for myself is *pizza bianca*.

"Voremmo quattro pezzi di pizza bianca, croccante, per favore." This might be the last time I get to hear Nonna speak those magical words—*pizza bianca croccante*. We dove into the olive oil stained bag the instant we closed the car

doors. Second only to gelato, this is my favorite thing, and eating it alone with Nonna in the car makes it all the more special. Being with Nonna reminds me of being with my great-grandmother.

From as far back as I can remember until my junior year of high school, every summer we would travel to Ohio to visit my dad's side of the family, and for those two weeks we stayed with my great-grandmother, Big Gram. My father lived with her and my great-grandfather after my father's parents divorced when he was 13, so there was a deeper bond between him and his grandparents than one might have otherwise. I never knew my great-grandfather, who passed away before I was born, but Big Gram spoiled us rotten when we visited. She was short and round, though not obese, a wonderful cook and the type of person who lived in the kitchen and cooked all day long. When we first arrived at her house she would have already prepared our favorite cookies—peanut butter cookies for my brother, chocolate chip for my sister, oatmeal for me, and besides cookies, there would be homemade pies waiting—lemon meringue for my father, apple for my mother, chocolate for us kids and a cherry pie for just in case. For breakfast she would have our favorite cereals on hand, and there was always watermelon for my brother who did not like cantaloupe for breakfast.

Every morning I would wake up early and lie in the raised box-springed bed in the bedroom just off the dining room, which was adjacent to the kitchen, listening to my Uncle Danny and Big Gram chat as she cooked him breakfast. I never heard him come into the house, but was always awakened by their muffled voices, not their actual words, through the closed swinging kitchen door, and even though the bedrooms of Big Gram's house did not have doors on them, the curtains hanging in the doorways were heavy enough to muffle conversations but not sound. I could smell and hear the crackling of bacon as she fried it in a cast iron skillet before making his eggs. In the early morning stillness that loomed over the rest of the house, my uncle, who was 20 at the time, would tell her stories, making her whoop and snort with laughter before she quieted down after he shooshed her. I would move to the foot of the bed and move the curtain away from the doorframe just enough to let me see the light streaming from under the swinging door. I tried to understand their conversations, but I never could. Her laughter and the rhythmic tone of his voice made me want to get up and join them in the kitchen, but this seemed a very special, intimate, private time between them and I never had the nerve to interrupt them. That is how I feel about my morning errands with Nonna. It is a time that only we share, and even though she isn't making bacon and eggs in the car, we are laughing and eating something just as special—*pizza bianca.*

The morning's cooking lesson started with *pasta al forno Pugliese*—a baked casserole-style dish of pasta and tomatoes from the Puglia region— the heel of Italy's boot. It consisted of a layer of fresh plum tomatoes sliced in half, topped by *penne* pasta, bread crumbs and fresh basil, which in turn was topped by the other half of the sliced tomatoes. It was baked in the toaster oven; even though the weather has cooled off here it is still too hot to turn on the oven. For dessert we made a rice and lemon *torta*— a kind of lemon-flavored tapioca tart. Of course there was a meat course between the pasta and dessert. Nonna rubbed pork chops with ground fennel seed, salt and pepper, rolled them in flour and cooked them on top of the stove in a little bit of olive oil.

Since Alessandra and I have given up on the future, we are now free to do things out of the box and mix up my lessons. Today was all about music—and, no, we were not singing or listening to American music. Francesca had copied music onto a cassette and typed out the lyrics for each song. I'm not sure if she did this specifically for my lessons before leaving on vacation or if this is something that Alessandra has used with other students. Considering I am *una persona molto importante dall'America*, let's imagine that she did this just for me.

Alessandra and I settled ourselves at the table in the den—after we played the customary "in or out" game with Tequila and Brighitta. Brighitta settled in her bed under the sideboard, and Tequila spread himself out under the table on the cool tiled floor. The first song Alessandra played was *"Vivo per Lei"*

("I Live for You"), a duet sung by Andrea Bocelli, the internationally famous blind Italian singer, and Giorgia, a famous female Italian singer. We listened to the song, and even though Andrea Bocelli isn't one of my favorite singers (I watched him perform once on Oprah), I was thrilled to be finally listening to actual Italian music in Italy. This was a first for me and it is my fourth week here—I guess better late than never. Alessandra loves Andrea, and I think I enjoyed seeing her enjoyment with the song more than the song itself.

"Marco, isn't that a beautiful song—*una bella canzone?*"

"*Si, si, Alessandra.*"

"Let's listen to it again and we can go over the words of the song ... um ... what is that called?"

"You mean the lyrics, Alessandra?"

"*Si, si.* We can listen to the song again and go through the lyrics." And with that, she pulled out the typed lyric sheets.

We listened a second time and I followed along with the words in front of me. It helped to see the words. Frankly, it would be nice to have the words in front of me when I listen to some music in English, too. "*Che bella canzone,*" Alessandra sighed, after the song ended. Now it was time for me to read the lyrics out loud. Alessandra has convinced me that the more I read out loud and perfect my pronunciation, the better at understanding Italian I'll become.

"*E'una musa che ti invita ... A sfiorarla con le dita ... Attraverso un pianoforte, la morte è lontana.*"—"And the music invites us ... touched softly with fingers ... through a piano, death is far away." After I read through the lyrics, my next task was to translate as much of the song as I could. Of course, there were words that I have yet to learn and translating music is a little harder because it is like poetry. Sentences and ideas are not always written in a logical order; they are presented in a style that fits a rhyme or a particular metaphor. Still, it was a new way to look at the language and something completely different from what we have done before. We listened to the song one last time as I followed along with my lyric sheet, now scribbled upon with circles and lines pointing to translated words and ideas. Alessandra's response was the same after the song ended this third time—*"Una bella canzone, no?"*

Next we listened, read, listened, translated and listened to three songs by Laura Pausini. I really enjoyed her songs: *"E Ritorno da Te"* ("I Return to You"), *"Incancellabile"* ("Unforgettable," which really means something more like "indelible" or "unremovable"), and *"Strani Amori"* ("Strange Loves.") Alessandra was a little surprised that I had never heard of Laura Pausini. She is an Italian singer with a large international following and career. I guess she hasn't hit America yet. Alessandra compared her to Madonna, even though there is nothing similar about their music. Maybe she'll make the transition to America soon.

The final song was a duet between Luciano Pavarotti and Andrea Bocelli entitled *"Miserere. Zucchero"* ("Misery. Sweet"), although *miserere* doesn't literally mean "misery;" it really means something more like "to be in one's last hours" or "God's pity." Neither Alessandra nor I could figure out an English word that evoked the same feeling—some things cannot be translated directly. It was a beautiful song full of metaphors and images of life, death, pity and possible joy. There was something Italian about the philosophy of this song—life and death, pity and joy—maybe that is why we couldn't arrive at a direct translation for me. It was intrinsically Italian. Regardless, I am thrilled to be listening to Italian music by Italian artists in an Italian house while sitting opposite an Italian woman sighing, *"Una bella canzone, no?"*

Marianna stopped by at the end of lunch. There is always such fervor around Marianna's visits—mostly from the dogs, who go crazy when they see her. She brought over her friend Silvia's tiramisù recipe and invited all of us over to her apartment tomorrow night for dinner. I think Marianna is missing Nonna's cooking, because she asked Nonna if she would cook something for tomorrow's dinner. Nonna told her not to worry and that she and her assistant (meaning me) would figure out what to make. I took that as a compliment.

For a while there was talk about skipping our siesta and going into town to do some shopping this afternoon, but I decided that I could wait until later in the week to do some final souvenir shopping. I have had more than enough treasures on this trip with memories and recipes, so I might give up on souvenirs altogether. Besides, I was really looking forward to a nap.

Dinner started with the classic *pasta fagioli alla Veneta*—pasta and beans Venetian style. Often, Italian-Americans refer to this dish as pasta "fazool." Italian borlotti beans, known in America as cranberry beans, are cooked with onions, tomatoes and *fettuccine* in a light broth. *Crespelle con funghi*—crepes with mushrooms—was the main course, and I have really grown fond of *crespelle*. These were filled with a mixture of mushrooms in a béchamel sauce, topped with Parmigiano-Reggiano and baked in the toaster oven until hot, browned and bubbly. There was still some of the lemon and risotto *torta* leftover from lunch, so we had that for dessert tonight, too. No complaints here!

⚯

Pasta e Fagioli alla Veneta

Venetian Pasta and Beans

This Italian classic survived the immigration to America and has become a classic here, too. Most Italian-Americans, especially from the East Coast, will know this dish as "Pasta Fazool." The dish may have survived the boat ride—the pronunciation did not.

2 tablespoons extra virgin olive oil

1 small onion, finely minced

2 tablespoons all-purpose flour

2 cups plus 2 tablespoons low-sodium canned chicken broth (water may be
   substituted)

1 (15.5-ounce) can borlotti beans—also known as cranberry beans, or
   Roman beans (pinto beans or cannellini beans may be substituted) *

4 large fresh sage leaves

1 tablespoon tomato paste

½ teaspoon salt, or more to taste

¼ teaspoon freshly ground black pepper, or more to taste

5 ounces fresh egg fettuccine, cut into 4-inch pieces (dried, factory-produced fettuccine may be substituted, broken into thirds)

Heat the oil in a large saucepan over medium heat. When the oil is hot, add the onion and sauté until it is soft and translucent, 2 to 3 minutes (if the onions are cooking too fast, add 1 tablespoon water and cook until almost evaporated, then proceed with recipe). Add the flour, mixing thoroughly, and cook until the flour mixture starts to turn a golden brown, about 1 minute. While stirring, slowly pour in the chicken broth until well combined. Allow to cook and thicken, stirring occasionally to remove any lumps of flour, and bring to a slow boil, 3 to 5 minutes.

When boiling, add the canned beans with their liquid, whole sage leaves, tomato paste, salt and pepper, stirring until the tomato paste has dissolved and the mixture returns to a boil, 2 to 3 minutes. Add the uncooked pasta, previously broken into small pieces, stirring frequently to make sure the pasta does not stick together. Cook until the pasta is al dente—tender, but firm to the bite, 7 to 9 minutes. Adjust the seasonings and remove the pan from the heat. Ladle into bowls and serve hot with a drizzle of extra virgin olive oil.

This makes 4 to 6 servings.

* Note: Borlotti beans are difficult to find, but may be found in Italian specialty food markets. I use canned Roman beans, Goya brand, which can be found in most regular supermarkets across the country. Look for them with the other canned beans or, sometimes, they can be found in the Mexican food aisle.

MER. · 24 AGO

IL GIORNO VENTICINQUE

*T*iramisù, which translates as "pick me up," is a Venetian dessert and I can safely say it is the most famous of all Italian desserts. There is no comparison between the tiramisù that I have ordered at restaurants back home and the Italian original, which is a relatively new creation dating from the 1970s-early 1980s. Silvia's recipe uses Martini Bianco, Italian white vermouth; however, Nonna insists that it should never be made with liquor or a liqueur. Most versions that I have tasted in America have some type of alcohol in them, and it tends to be too strong of a flavor in the dessert. Marianna said that she likes Silvia's version, but Nonna insists that her recipe is the best. Regardless, if you prefer it with liquor or not, the biggest secret to achieving perfection is to use Italian ladyfinger biscuits and espresso—instead of sponge cake and coffee.

At the grocery store we bought Pavesini brand ladyfingers, very thin biscuits which are extremely dry. Nonna says that the thinner biscuits don't need to be used with as much filling so the finished dessert is thinner, which is why she prefers using them. Nonna pointed out brands where the ladyfingers were thicker, and those seemed to have a sugary coating on the top. She said either one would work, but that the thicker ones would need a double batch of filling.

Back at the house Nonna pulled out several mixing bowls and a foil pan to assemble it in. There is going to be nothing glamorous about how we serve this tiramisù. Alessandra started making espresso and Nonna guided me through the recipe. I separated egg yolks into one bowl and the whites into another and began the long, arduous process of creaming things together by hand with a wire whisk. Nonna added sugar to the yolks and told me to whisk them together until the yolks turned a very pale yellow and the sugar, which was added in batches, had fully dissolved into the yolks.

"Ancora," —"More,"— Nonna said, after checking the mixture. I had been whisking it for five minutes and my arm was getting tired and it looked pretty good to me, but no—*"Ancora, Marco."*

"Marco, if the *zucchero* is not completely dissolved into the yolks, then the filling will not have a very good texture. It must be smooth now, since the tiramisù doesn't get cooked," Alessandra said, trying to explain why I needed to continue whisking. "Besides, you are a strong man and this should be easy for you," implying that normally a woman would be doing this task, and since I am of the stronger sex this should be simple. I wanted to remind her that there is a reason why women are the ones who give birth—men could never handle the pain. So, on I whisked for what seemed to be 20 minutes before Nonna finally said that I had achieved the correct texture—a perfectly smooth, pale yellow ribbon of batter drizzled off the whisk as she inspected my work.

"Perfetto. Adesso, aggiungere e mescolare il mascarpone ... a mano,"—"Perfect. Now, add and stir in the mascarpone ... by hand,"— Nonna said, smiling at me, already knowing what my response would be.

"A mano, davvero?"

"*Si, si, Marco, a mano.*"

"Okay," I said and slowly started whisking in the mascarpone cheese in batches.

My arm was throbbing with pain and I expected it to twist off and go flying across the room at any moment, at which point I am not sure if I would have yelled "*GOOOL!*" or "*Disastro!*" I guess that would have depended on whether or not my disembodied arm, still clutching the whisk, had hit something that would make a crashing sound—"*GOOOL!*" But should it only fly off and hit the floor, well, then, "*Disastro!*" would be more appropriate.

The egg whites were the next thing to be whisked. I have vivid memories of my great-grandmother, in her very late 70s, whisking egg whites by hand in a copper bowl with a wire whisk when making meringue for a pie. The back of her arm would flap wildly as she whisked those egg whites into a mountain of frothy, hard peaks, but my arm was worn out. I had great respect for Big Gram at this moment, and before I could protest about whisking egg whites *a mano*, Nonna pulled out a hand-held electric mixer. "*Marco, questa usi.*" —"Mark, use this."

"Alessandra, is there a reason why I couldn't have used a mixer before now? I mean, could I have been creaming the sugar and mixing in the mascarpone with a mixer instead of doing it by hand?"

Alessandra and Nonna chatted a moment before Alessandra told me, "No, you could use an electric mixer."

I looked at her in disbelief.

"Marco, Nonna only uses an electric mixer for egg whites. She forgot about it."

"*Mi dispiace, Marco,*" Nonna said, being truly sorry for not thinking of the hand mixer sooner.

"*Non c'è problema, Nonna.*" I guess Nonna and I are finally even for the lost 2-euro coin from our first shopping trip.

The egg whites, followed by the heavy cream, were quickly whipped by the hand mixer and slowly stirred into the mascarpone/egg mixture. The resulting filling was smooth, light and creamy. The only thing left to do now was assemble the tiramisù.

First, we spread a little of the filling inside the bottom of the foil pan. "Marco, it is most important to use *caffè* that is *freddo*—cold—otherwise the Pavesini will drink up too much," Alessandra said, bringing over the espresso, which had been allowed to cool in a shallow dish. She was my dipping instructor and showed me how to quickly dip each biscuit into the espresso, flip it over, and quickly remove it, shaking off any excess espresso before placing it side-by-side in rows on top of the filling in the pan. Dip, flip, shake and place. The Pavesini are so dry that if you leave them in the espresso for more than a second they get too soggy and fall apart. *"Disastro!"* With the first layer of soaked Pavesini in the pan, we added another layer of filling and started a second layer of biscuits, running the rows in the opposite direction.

We dipped, filled and stacked four layers of Pavesini before finishing the top with the final layer of filling and dusting that with a coating of unsweetened, dark cocoa powder. Nonna carefully covered the top with plastic wrap and then foil before placing the completed tiramisù in the fridge to chill, which allows the Pavesini to absorb a little of the filling, too. I was very happy with the result and, even though it felt as if I would have to eat left-handed today because my right arm was useless from all the whisking, I was looking forward to tasting it later tonight at the party.

Our next order of business in the kitchen was to prepare lunch. We started with the *sugo* for *penne all'arrabbiata con panna*—*penne* pasta in a spicy tomato and cream sauce. *"Arrabbiata"* stems from the verb *"arrabbiare"* meaning "to go mad" when talking about rabid dogs or it can mean "to become angry" when talking about people. I love the idea that we are making "rabid dog" pasta—Grrrrrrrrrrrrrrr! The "rabid" part comes from the use of several small, dried red *peperoncino*—peppers. I don't care for really spicy food and I know Nonna's ulcer cannot take a lot of heat so I'm sure our "dogs" will be more of the barking variety than the foaming-at-the-mouth kind implied by the name.

The rest of lunch had to be prepared once we sat down to eat, so I headed off to my language lesson in the den. Lillo came downstairs looking very under the weather. He surprised me, because I thought he was at work.

"*Lillo, come stai?*"

"*Marco, non sto bene,*" he said, holding his back and heading toward the kitchen.

"Lillo has a kidney stone and it is bothering him today," Alessandra said, following him down the stairs and into the kitchen.

Nonna poured Lillo a glass of cold water from the fridge and he drank it straight down before pouring himself another and heading back upstairs. He smiled as he passed back by me. I could tell he was in pain but was still trying to be pleasant about it all.

"*Spero che senti migliore,*"—"I hope you feel better,"— I said. He nodded his head, turned at the landing, smiled at me and disappeared upstairs.

"*Povero Lillo.*"

"*Si, si, Marco.* The doctor says he needs to drink more water," Alessandra said, heading up the stairs with the bottle of water from the fridge.

"I hope he can go with us tonight to Marianna and Marco's."

"*Spero, anch'io. Ritorno subito per la noi lezione,*"—"I hope so, too. I'll be right back for our lesson,"— she said, disappearing upstairs, too.

Lillo managed to bring himself down for lunch, but he was unusually quiet and only drank water—VERY unusual for Lillo. I was going to drink only water too, but Lillo waved me off of water and insisted that I have wine with lunch, as we usually did. I'm not sure if he wanted to drink vicariously through me or if he didn't want me to feel sorry for him by drinking water, too. Whatever the reason, Lillo made sure that my glass was never more than half empty at lunch today. I think I drank more at lunch today than ever before. *Mamma mia!*

Besides the "mad dog" *penne*, Nonna made *carne in fricassea*, a Tuscan recipe where cutlets of turkey, pork or veal are cooked with onions before lemon juice and an egg are added to the pan. Nonna used turkey and veal cutlets today—I am still surprised by how much turkey we eat here. I would never have imagined Italians eating turkey; it seems like such an American food item. The dish takes no time to prepare and must be served and eaten immediately from the pan, so I had to get up from the end of my pasta course in order to watch Nonna whip it up moments before she served it. She added the lemon juice and egg to the pan, whisking them quickly to prevent the egg from scrambling, which allowed the egg to be used as a thickener—making a simple Hollandaise sauce right in the pan. Before heading upstairs for our siestas, we finished off the lemon and risotto *torta* for dessert.

Nonna rushed me from my afternoon *lezione di lingua* into the kitchen to help her make *sfincione*—Sicilian pizza. Since we had (I had) gone through all that effort to make tiramisù for tonight, Nonna thought we should make something as simple as pizza to take over to Marianna and Marco's. Of course, there is no competing with Marco's mom, Anna, when it comes to making pizza, especially since his parents have a wood-fired oven, so Nonna is being very smart by making a thick-crust Sicilian pizza instead—something completely different from the style of pizza Anna makes.

Sfincione, pronounced "sfin-choe-nay," is famous in Palermo, Sicily, where street vendors hawk it from carts by yelling its name. Nonna threw her head back and demonstrated the sales pitch. I repeated the word, but Nonna said I was not doing it correctly. Again, she threw her head back and at the top of her lungs called out, "*SFINCIOOOOOOOOOOONE!*" I had not gotten the ballpark vendor quality in my first attempt, so when Nonna prompted me to do it again—"*Ripeta*"—I threw my head back and yelled "*SFINCIOOOOOOOOOOOOONE!*" causing Tequila and the rest of the dogs to bark, and Alessandra to come from the den and chide us for being so loud. "*Per favore, Lillo non si sente bene,*" she said, pointing upstairs.

Oops! "*Ci dispiace,*" I said.

The crust is made with flour, yeast, water, extra virgin olive oil and cooked potatoes that have been put through a ricer. I kneaded *a mano* for at least 15 minutes before dividing it between two large baking sheets and allowing it to rise. My right arm survived the kneading.

The *sugo* simply consisted of lots of onions, thinly sliced into half rounds, sautéed in olive oil until they were soft and translucent and strained tomatoes—no salt, pepper, oregano or any other spice. Once the crusts had risen, they were topped with the *sugo*, a drizzle of olive oil and grated pecorino cheese. There was no meat on this pizza. Once assembled, we covered the two *sfincioni* with plastic wrap and got ourselves cleaned up for dinner.

The four of us—yes, Lillo was feeling well enough to come along and drive—piled into Nonna's car with me riding shotgun and holding the tiramisù, while Nonna and Alessandra, each holding a *sfincione* in her lap, sat in the back seat. "If we get into an accident, there is going to be such a huge mess inside this car. There will be cocoa topped cream, espresso-soaked ladyfingers, raw dough and red sauce with onions all over everything," I thought to myself as Lillo pulled away from the curb. *"Attento, Lillo,"* Alessandra piped up from the back seat. She must have been thinking of the same thing.

Surprise, surprise! Nicola and Jimmy were at the apartment when we arrived. Tonight is their last night in town before heading back to France—Dijon—to get ready for their second year at university in October. I headed to the kitchen where Silvia helped me find room in Marianna's fridge for the tiramisù and Marianna helped Nonna and Alessandra put the *pizze* right into the oven. I was thrilled to finally get to meet Silvia, Marianna's cute, blonde friend. Our arrival had caught Silvia and Marianna in the middle of slicing *ananas*—pineapple—for dinner.

"Rimani per la cena stasera?" —"Are you staying for dinner tonight?"— I asked Silvia.

"No, non posso. Vorrei rimanere e mangiare pizza e tiramisù, ma devo andare a presto." —"No, I can't. I'd like to stay and eat pizza and tiramisù, but I have to go soon."

"Mi dispiace. Desidero che rimani per la cena." —"I wish you could stay for dinner."

"Anch'io." —"Me, too."

There was the usual hubbub as we all got our drinks and settled into conversations throughout the apartment. I told myself that I was going to try and speak only in Italian tonight, so I stayed in the kitchen trying to chat with the girls as they finished slicing the *ananas*.

"Marianna, mi piace il cavallo là," I said, pointing to the black magnet of a running horse that was stuck on the exhaust hood above the stove top.

"Grazie. Silvia lo ha comprato per me." —"Thanks. Silvia bought it for me." *"Brava, Silvia!"*

"Grazie, Marco," Silvia said, giggling. I think she found it funny that I was giving such high praise to a magnet of a horse.

I decided to head outside and regroup my brain before having to plunge into more conversations, but, of course, Jimmy was right next to me as I headed out onto the balcony. So much for trying to speak *in italiano solo stasera.* Nicola soon joined us and that is when the conversation got interesting—he and Jimmy spoke to each other in French, while Jimmy would only speak to me in English, which forced me to answer him in English and in as much Italian as I could muster to Nicola, since he only speaks French and Italian. Between the three of us, I think Nicola got the short end of the conversation.

"So, Mark, why are you here? How come you can be here for so long? Where is your wife?" Jimmy asked, in his usual style of multiple questions.

His questions were completely out of the blue. Obviously, my stay with the family for a month had piqued his curiosity, but what I couldn't tell was if he trying to give me a hard time by questioning my sexuality. Jimmy is something of a smart ass, so it seemed possible that he was trying to push my buttons by asking me that question. My immediate instinct was to answer, "I don't have a wife. I'm gay. Why? Are you interested?" I thought it would be funny to be a smart-ass right back at him and put his sexuality in question. But his questions threw me so completely off guard that I could only look puzzled and laugh as if I couldn't believe that he had asked me those questions.

"Oh, it's ok. I don't mean to ask anything too personal. It's none of my business," he said, retreating from his line of questioning.

"No, it's okay. I'm divorced," I said.

Dammit.

Of all the times that I should have proudly declared, "I'm gay," this was the one. I even knew how to say it in French, "*Je suis un homosexuel,*" so both he and Nicola could have heard it in their native tongue. I think that is the answer Jimmy was looking for, and even if it wasn't, I think it would have taken him aback to hear it directly.

I didn't tell Jimmy and Nicola the truth (well, all of the truth, I mean, I am divorced) because I didn't want this night to be known as the night "Marco came out of the closet." It didn't make any sense to come out now, only three days before I left. Still, it irks me that I didn't answer Jimmy directly, if only to see what his reaction truly might have been. "*Je suis un homosexuel*" would have to wait for another trip, because on this one I am only divorced.

The eight of us found our places at the table on the balcony, which is quite large. It is easy to see how important dining *al fresco* is to the Italians by the size of this balcony. The apartment is modest in size for a two bedroom/ one bath and I have never seen a balcony of this size on any basic apartment in America. All of the apartments in this complex had large balconies, so there is nothing particularly special about this unit. There was room for half of the balcony to be covered, which is where Marco had an outdoor refrigerator and a table large enough to comfortably seat eight, and there was just as much uncovered balcony beyond. We were up high enough not to be bothered by *zanzare*—mosquitoes, and we had a great view of the northern hills toward *Lago di Bolsena*.

Nonna sat herself at the head of the table closest to the sliding glass doors. Nicola sat at her right, followed by Jimmy, Marianna and Marco, who sat himself at the opposite end of the table from Nonna. I sat to Marco's right, followed by Alessandra to my right and Lillo to her right, beside

Nonna. I think we all had safe locations around the table—Nonna was not seated next to Jimmy, Nicola was seated next to Jimmy and I had Alessandra next to me for translating purposes, although she is really testing me by only helping out when I am beyond lost and desperate.

Everyone congratulated Nonna on the *sfincione*, and Marco and Lillo made sure our glasses never ran out of wine.

I don't remember how our dinner conversation turned to the American cartoon series "The Simpsons," but when it did, all hell broke loose. Jimmy started talking about the father character, Homer Simpson, by mispronouncing his name in a thick French accent as "Omar Simpson." I let Jimmy tell his story in Italian, being helped by Nicola when his basic Italian failed him, while Alessandra assisted me in understanding Jimmy. I looked over to Nonna who rolled her eyes at me. I could hear her subtext *"Francia, Francia, Francia"* as Jimmy spoke, so I thought I would tease Jimmy a little and correct him on his pronunciation of Homer's name.

"Jimmy, I'm sorry but the character's name is Homer Simpson," I said, stressing the "h" sound at the top of the name.

"No, Mark, the character's name is Omar Simpson," Jimmy said, correcting me.

"Jimmy, mi dispiace, ma so il nome e lo ha detto HOM-ER Simpson." I spoke in Italian so everyone at the table would know what Jimmy and I were talking about.

"No, it is O-MAR Simpson," Jimmy said, emphatically.

Nonna winked at me, egging me on to not let Jimmy win. She told me long ago that the French are notorious for "French-ifying" everything, including people's names. I didn't quite believe her, but now I was experiencing it first hand.

"Jimmy, the character is American and it is spelled H-O-M-E-R, so it is pronounced "HOM-ER." Of course, I pronounced it in as thick of an American Midwestern accent as I could muster, just to ensure that it sounded REALLY American. Alessandra translated for the table. Nonna winked at me again.

"No, you are saying it wrong. It is Omar Simpson."

Marianna now chimed in on the subject. Marianna does speak a little English, so she understood what I was saying and took my side in defending Homer. It was great fun listening to her explain to Jimmy, in Italian, that since I am an American and the character is American, I would logically know how to pronounce the name correctly. She said that even in Italian it is pronounced "Homer".

"No, no, no. Est Omar," Jimmy said in French.

Everyone laughed at how stubborn he was, and Marianna even hit the table with her hand—I know where she learned that.

Again she tried to explain herself and correct him, but he would not change his mind. It was Omar Simpson. Period.

We all laughed as Marianna threw her hands up in disgust.

"Viva la France!" I shouted and raised my glass to toast Jimmy.

"Viva la France!" everyone saluted by raising their glasses, including Nicola.

Jimmy half-heartedly raised his and we all drank.

"Grazie, grazie, grazie," Jimmy said, sounding only somewhat courteous with his French accent thickly applied to his Italian apology.

Nonna discreetly gave me the thumbs-up.

We all reverted to smaller conversations and there was no ill will hanging on about the "Homer vs. Omar" debate.

Marianna served the tiramisù and I have to say that it was indeed better than Silvia's. It is one of Lillo's favorite desserts, and he gave his seal of approval by declaring, *"Molto buono!"* For me, the success of tiramisù lies in the texture of the dessert as you eat it. It should melt in your mouth all of a piece—the same texture throughout the bite—from the dark cocoa top, through the *mascarpone* filling, past the espresso-drenched ladyfinger layers; it should all melt together as one creamy, chocolate, espresso-enriched bite. When done incorrectly, the taste gets interrupted by cake that is too dry, or cream that is too thin, or the liqueur flavor overpowering the espresso, but Nonna's version was *buonissimo!* It was perfectly balanced.

As the ladies cleared the table, Marco brought us guys into the living room to hang out. I was a little unsure of what was going on until he came out of the bedroom carrying a hookah. "Well, here we go," I thought to myself. Whenever I see a hookah I immediately think of the Caterpillar from *Alice in Wonderland* sitting on his mushroom cap blowing colorful smoke letters into the air instead of simple smoke rings. That is the Disney memory I have from my childhood—and not drawings from any book. I don't know anyone back home who owns or uses a hookah, and the ones I have seen in my adult life were either in an antique store, a theatrical properties department or on a TV program.

The ladies joined us in the living room as Marco was loading the hookah. Marianna brought individual plastic smoking tips to hand out to everyone. Oral hygiene is important when passing around the nozzle of a hookah pipe. I declined to take a tip when they were passed to me.

"No, Marco, it is ok," Marianna said, as if assuming I thought that they were going to be smoking hashish or something illegal with the hookah.

"*Grazie, Marianna, ma sono buono,*" —"Thanks, but I'm good,"— I replied, declining her second offering.

She looked at Alessandra for help in explaining to me what was happening.

"Marco, it is pipe tobacco. Nothing harmful," Alessandra said, trying to reassure me.

I was in a jam. I knew from the beginning that they were only going to be smoking pipe tobacco. I could smell cherry and wood when Marco opened the tobacco bag. It smelled exactly like the pipe tobacco my grandfather used to smoke. I wasn't opposed to what they were smoking; it was the fact that I don't like to smoke that made me turn them down. My father smokes, and growing up with that smell in the house and on everything has kept me from ever trying to smoke anything—ever. I'm not opposed to what people are smoking, legal or not; it is the action of smoking that I don't like. Smoke from pipe tobacco doesn't bother me as much. There is something sweet and aromatic about it. Cigarette smoke, on the other hand, gives me a headache and upsets my stomach.

"Alessandra, it is ok that everyone is smoking. I just don't like to smoke."

"It is not drugs," she said.

"Oh, I know. Really, it is ok for everyone and I understand, but I just don't like to smoke. I have never smoked anything in my life." I was trying to think of how many different ways to say that I didn't have a problem with the hookah. I was starting to feel like a wet blanket and I really wasn't one. I wanted them to use the hookah—I thought it would be cool. I just didn't want to smoke, or try smoking, for the first time here and ruin it for everyone. "Alessandra, I will feel very bad if no one smokes because of me—*per favore, va bene!*" I said, putting my palms together in prayer position, crossing my thumbs and pleading with her. She understood and explained to everyone how I felt.

Everyone had a tip, except me, and waited as Marco tried to light the hookah. Marianna held the lighter and Marco inhaled, but to no avail. Marianna tried next, while Marco held the lighter. No success. Jimmy said he could light it—he failed, too. *"Per favore,"* Nonna said, as she took the nozzle from Jimmy and put her plastic tip on it.

Marco held the lighter and Nonna took one deep inhale, paused—and exhaled a smoke ring.

"Brava, Nonna. Brava!" we all cheered and applauded. Even Jimmy laughed and clapped.

"Nonna, davvero?" I said, in disbelief and laughing.

She winked at me and passed the nozzle to Lillo.

"Nonna and my father took a month-long vacation to Turkey one time. That is where she learned how to light and smoke a hookah," Alessandra explained, before taking the nozzle from Lillo.

The room filled with the sweet smell of cherry and wood, and after a while it got to be too sweet for me. I took my glass of wine and headed out onto the balcony to get a little fresh air.

Nonna joined me after a while. The others were inside telling stories and laughing.

"*Brava, Nonna. Stupefacente!*"

"*Grazie, Marco.*"

And standing down wind of me, she lit a cigarette.

Nonna and I leaned on the balcony railing while she smoked and watched *i pipistrelli*—the bats—fly around the parking lot lights below, feasting on moths and bugs attracted to the light. I pointed out the Big Dipper, which I have already forgotten how to translate, and far off in the distance, a lightning storm entertained us.

———

Penne all'Arrabbiata con Panna

"Mad Dog" Penne with Cream

I love it when the Italian language takes the meaning of one word and uses it to explain another. The "spicy heat" in this dish is reflected in the word "arrabbiata," which means "to go mad" when applied to dogs and "to be angry" when applied to people. To increase your "rage" or the "foaming of the dog," add dashes of pepper sauce to your plate at the table until you scream or howl at the moon!

1 tablespoon extra virgin olive oil

2 ¼-inch-thick slices (approx 5 ounces) pancetta, cut into ¼-inch cubes (smoked pancetta is preferred)

1 small onion, thinly sliced into half rounds

1 teaspoon crushed red pepper flakes

1 (28-ounce) can whole peeled Italian plum tomatoes (preferably San Marzano), placed in a bowl and crushed by hand, reserving all of the liquid

½ teaspoon salt

1 pound penne rigate

1 cup heavy cream

½ cup grated Parmigiano-Reggiano, Grana Padano or pecorino cheese, for garnish

Heat oil in a large saucepan over medium heat. When the oil is hot, add the cubed pancetta and cook until browned, 4 to 5 minutes. Add the onion and sauté until soft and translucent, about 3 to 4 minutes, stirring occasionally. Once the onions are translucent and starting to turn golden, stir in the red pepper flakes and cook for 1 minute. Add the crushed tomatoes, their juices and salt, stirring until well combined, bringing the tomatoes to a boil. Once at a boil, reduce the heat to low and simmer until the sauce thickens, 18 to 20 minutes.

Meanwhile, cook the penne pasta in boiling salted water. Remove and drain the pasta just before it is *al dente*, a minute or two less than the package's recommended cooking time. Add the slightly undercooked pasta to the finished sauce over medium heat, stirring until well mixed. Stir in the cream and cook until the pasta is *al dente*—firm but tender to the bite—and the cream has cooked into the sauce, 2 to 3 minutes. Serve hot, garnished with the grated cheese.

This makes 8 servings.

IL GIORNO VENTISEI

We had our first mishap in the kitchen today.

"*Disastro, Marco. Disastro,*" Nonna said, looking at the baked, gooey mess in front of her.

The *amaretti* cookies did not turn out as expected. They tasted great, but they would not hold their shape. Nonna blamed it on the woman she got the recipe from, saying that the woman was not quite right in the head—a good thing to find out now! This was Nonna's first attempt at making *amaretti*, so she didn't have any trade secrets stuffed in her back pocket.

Amaretti cookies are the Italian version of a macaroon—a cookie whose dough is made from egg whites and sugar, using no flour. I thought that the cookies were made with *amaretto*—an almond-flavored liqueur, but the cookies do not have any kind of liquor in them. The name *amaretti*, loosely translated, means "little bitter things" and is derived from the Italian verb *amareggiare*, meaning "to make bitter." The bitter in the name comes from the use of bitter almonds—*mandorle amare*—in combination with sweet almonds—*mandorle dolci*. I had never heard of bitter almonds before now. I find it fascinating that the verb for "to love" and the word used to describe almonds as "bitter" is the same word—*amare*. It wouldn't surprise me if the Italians had linked together the juxtaposition of "love" and "bitter," as they seem to do with other things—life and death, or joy and sorrow.

When made correctly, the cookies should have a crunchy outside with a soft, chewy inside and the flavor of the bitter almonds should not overwhelm the sweetness of the cookie or vice versa. We didn't throw away the failed cookies; we just agreed that we could not call them *amaretti* because there was nothing crunchy about them. Nonna immediately called Lillo and asked him if he could again stop on his way through Blera toward the farm today and buy more *mandorle amare*. Yesterday, Lillo went to two different shops in his hometown of Blera before finding the bitter almonds in a third. They are not an easy item to find nor are they inexpensive. We are going to try making *amaretti* again tomorrow—Nonna will not be defeated.

I am glad we had this failure in the kitchen. It made Nonna, Alessandra and me put our thinking caps on to figure out what went wrong. Listening to Nonna and Alessandra discuss what the problem might be and how to solve it was a great learning experience for me. As they agreed and disagreed with each other, I got to witness the collaboration between two experienced cooks. Alessandra and Nonna suspect the *"disastro"* had something to do with the amount and ratio of sugar and egg whites. I'll trust their instincts.

This morning's recipes are all about Blera. Even though *amaretti* are attributed to northern Italy, I considered them to be from Blera today— the bitter almonds were purchased there and we were using a recipe from a woman in Blera, even if she wasn't right in the head. Lillo is as passionate and proud of his hometown as Jimmy is of France, and there have been days when one of us will chant *"Blera, Blera, Blera"* whenever it seems that Lillo has gone on *ad nauseam* about everything Blera. He has a standing bread order with a Blera bakery for a loaf of their unleavened bread made with *semolina*, which he picks up every Friday. *Semolina*—yellow durum wheat flour—has a slightly coarser grind to it, so its texture is not as fine as standard all-purpose white flour. This is the only bread—*il pane di Blera*—that Lillo will eat at the house. For every meal, slices are cut from *il pane di Blera* for Lillo, and additional slices are cut from a white flour loaf that Nonna and I have purchased from one of the grocery stores. Lillo isn't selfish about *il pane di Blera*; anyone can eat it and he is always eager to share it. I enjoy it, because it is denser than bread made with a leavening agent.

Fettuccine di Blera was the fresh pasta that Alessandra showed me how to make today and it is made with *semolina*, too. Yesterday, Lillo bought a large bag of *semola di grano duro (panificazione)*—durum wheat flour (for bread or pasta), while he was in Blera getting the *mandorle amare*. He was very proud of his purchases yesterday and made a special point of telling me all about them, since they were from Blera.

Fettuccine di Blera is Lillo's mother's recipe, and in Blera this flat pasta is simply called *macaroni*, even though traditionally *macaroni* is a tube-shaped pasta with a hole in it larger than the one in *bucatini*. Lillo's mother has been talked about several times over the course of my stay here in Viterbo. I think I am correct in understanding that she passed away only a couple of years ago and that she was a real "firecracker" of a woman. She has been described as a very small woman with a very large attitude and zest for life. I have gathered that she must have been very short—so short, in fact, that every time she is described to me by anyone in the family, including Lillo himself, she gets shorter and shorter. Before I leave Viterbo she will be the height of a garden gnome.

Alessandra says that Lillo's mother could not read or write and only knew how to sign her name, but out of all the things she taught Alessandra, how to roll out pasta dough has been the most valuable. Alessandra is the master at rolling out large sheets of pasta and she showed me her technique. Because *semolina* is a coarser grind, it takes a little more muscle to roll it out by hand than pasta made with standard, all-purpose, white flour. We have yet to use a pasta machine to roll out pasta. Here, everything is mixed, kneaded and rolled out by hand—*a mano*. Alessandra says that the secret to really good *fettuccine di Blera* is to get it the correct thickness. The pasta should be rolled out thin enough that one should be able to see through it, and, in keeping to her word, the first sheet of pasta that she rolled out was perfect—when she placed it on the kitchen table to dry, I could see the pattern of the tablecloth through the large, round sheet of pasta.

With the first sheet rolled to perfection, it was time for me to roll the second sheet. I have to admit that I am no longer scared of making fresh pasta and rolling it out. My mother makes the best piecrust from scratch, and I was always a little scared of fresh dough and a rolling pin. I was also a little intimidated by my mother's ease and expertise with dough, and although she is a great teacher, I have never made pie dough with my mother. Being here with Nonna and Alessandra has certainly helped me overcome my irrational fear of ruining a couple of eggs and flour with a rolling pin. My sheet wasn't as large as Alessandra's, but I easily got it to the correct thickness and laid it next to hers on the table to dry before we cut it.

While Alessandra and I were making the pasta, Nonna went out and ran the morning errands without me. When she returned, she walked in carrying an olive oil-stained bag—*pizza bianca*—and something wrapped in butcher's paper. *La macelleria*—the butcher shop—that made Nonna's favorite sausages had reopened from their summer vacation, and she stopped there to buy *le salsicce*. I wouldn't exchange my rolling lesson with Alessandra for anything, but I was pretty disappointed that I didn't get to go with Nonna to *la macelleria*. I really wanted to see the butcher shop and check out what other divine things they had there.

Nonna bought a lot of sausages and I realized that we had also made a lot of pasta. *"Qui viene per il pranzo oggi?"* —"Who is coming for lunch today?"— I asked Alessandra. I wished I had learned a little of future tense because what I was really asking was, "Who will be coming for lunch today?" My original question was correct enough because I used a time qualifier with it—"today"—so that allowed me to speak in the present tense, although Italians more commonly use the future instead of the present with a qualifier. Regardless of whether I know the future or not, the fact that I recognize the difference in usage is some kind of sign that I have learned something about the language while sitting in the den.

"*Marianna, Marco, Jimmy e Nicola verranno a pranzo oggi,*" Alessandra answered.

"*Mamma mia! È una grande festa,*" —It is a big party,"— I said.

"*Si, si. Nicola e Jimmy tornano a casa loro in Francia dopo il pranzo.*" —"Yes, Nicola and Jimmy are driving home to France after lunch."

"*Ciao, ciao—Francia, Francia, Francia!*" Nonna said, waving her handkerchief as if she were seeing them off from a dock.

After my language lesson, Alessandra showed me how to cut the pasta into noodles. She rolled up the sheets of pasta, and using a very sharp knife, started at one end of the roll and cut the pasta into thin pieces. She cut a few pieces and then handed me the knife to cut the rest. I started off by cutting them about a ¼-of-an-inch wide—"*Marco, troppo grande. Attento,*" Alessandra said, as she demonstrated again, cutting pieces just under a ¼-of-an-inch wide. I watched and tried again—focused on keeping the slices exactly as wide as hers.

"*Buono, Marco,*" she said, giving me her seal of approval.

Once the dough had been sliced, we unrolled all of the individually cut pieces, some at least 3-feet long, and floured them again on the tablecloth, which helped them to keep from sticking together as they continued to dry.

Lunch was really pleasant and we had a wonderful time around the table. *Le fettuccine di Blera* plumped up a little when cooked, and the *semolina* gave wonderful mouth texture to the pasta, so the noodles were as fun to eat as they were great tasting. Nonna's sausages, although cooked in the *sugo,* were served separately as the second course—remember that in Italy meat is usually cooked in the sauce and then removed before the pasta is added.

The only time I noticed Nonna roll her eyes about Jimmy was when he refused to have any wine with lunch. He will only drink French wine and refuses to drink anything Italian, so he drank Coke—room temperature, no ice. His loss. I later found out that the night before he had been drinking his own bottle of French wine that he had brought with him to Marianna and Marco's. Oh well, Jimmy is going to leave as true to form as when he arrived, and that's okay. We are all peculiar in some way. Maybe at some point in his life not everything will be compared to life in France. Moments will be enjoyed for what they are and where they are and will be judged only in the context in which they exist. And if not, well, then, it will be his loss indeed.

I woke up from my siesta today craving a hamburger. I have no clue why. It certainly wasn't because I didn't have enough to eat at lunch today. Maybe it is because I am starting to think about heading home, and if there is one food that is truly American, it is the hamburger.

We started dinner tonight with a simple soup of potatoes, pasta and sautéed onions in a light chicken broth—nothing complicated or heavy. For the main course, Nonna made what I would call "individual eggplant pizzas." She grilled slices of eggplant, and then using a single grilled slice as an individual crust, topped it with a slice of fresh mozzarella, an anchovy, a spoon of chunky tomato sauce, sea salt, black pepper and dried oregano. She put the eggplant pizzas on a baking sheet and popped them into the toaster oven. Ten minutes later, we were eating smoky, cheesy, chunky, slightly salty slices of eggplant.

Alessandra made dessert tonight by taking slices of watermelon and drizzling them with her homemade *arancello* liqueur and a little sprinkle of sugar—nothing like having some spiked watermelon to finish off a meal. Nonna brought out the failed *amaretti*, something she would not and did not serve at lunch today. There is no way she would serve something failed to Marianna, Marco and Nicola—let alone to Jimmy, but since it was only the four of us tonight she was safe serving it to me, Lillo and Alessandra. I missed not having Francesca with us today for both meals. She is still calling with daily reports, although there aren't as many calls per day as there were on the day she left. She is having a wonderful time with Stefano and his parents, but it would have been great to have here with us today.

⋘∿⋙

Pizzette di Melanzane

Eggplant Pizza Slices

This is not your typical pizza recipe—there is no dough. The slices of eggplant are the crusts of these small "pizzas," and you can easily turn them vegetarian by omitting the anchovies.

2 medium eggplants

Salt

¼ cup extra virgin olive oil

Freshly ground black pepper

1 (8 ounce) ball fresh mozzarella, cut into ¼-inch-thick, half-round slices.

8 anchovy filets (optional)

½ cup Nonna's Simple Sauce *(see page 32)*

1 tablespoon dried oregano

Remove and discard the stem end of the eggplants. Cut a ¼-inch-thick lengthwise slice from the side of the eggplant to expose the flesh. Now cut the eggplant into ½-inch-thick lengthwise slices, removing an additional ¼-inch-thick slice from the last slice to expose the flesh on both sides of that last piece. Repeat with the second eggplant. Each eggplant should yield four slices. (Note: depending on the size of the eggplant, if more than 4 slices are yielded per eggplant, adjust the toppings accordingly.) Generously salt both sides of each slice, place the slices in a colander and set in the sink or over a plate, allowing them to weep for 20 minutes.

Preheat the oven to 400 degrees.

Using a paper towel, remove the salt and moisture off both sides of each slice, discarding any liquid from the eggplant. Brush both sides of each slice with olive oil (reserving any unused oil) and place onto a hot grill pan over medium heat. Grill the eggplant, turning after 4 to 5 minutes to grill the other side for 3 to 4 minutes. The slices should have dark brown grill marks and should be tender, but not mushy. Transfer the grilled slices to a parchment–lined baking sheet. (The eggplant can be prepared up to this point a day in advance. Place in an airtight container and refrigerate.)

To assemble the *pizzetti*: Top each grilled eggplant slice with two evenly spaced half-round slices of mozzarella. (Note: If not using the anchovies, season the eggplant with a pinch of salt before adding the mozzarella.) Place an anchovy filet on top of the cheese. Next, drizzle 1 tablespoon of sauce in a zigzag motion down the length of the slice. Sprinkle with a pinch of black pepper and evenly top with the oregano. Drizzle the reserved, unused oil over the slices.

Bake until the cheese is melted and just starting to turn golden, 18 to 20 minutes. Allow to rest 2 to 3 minutes after removing from the oven before serving. Serve hot.

This makes 8 *pizzette*.

*Eggplant has a tendency to be bitter. By salting the slices, the bitter flavor is pulled out of the eggplant during the weeping process—the salt causes the moisture to bead up like tears on the surface of the slices. Do not rinse the salt off with water or the eggplant will become soggy. Remember, eggplant are like sponges and you want them to absorb the flavor of the olive oil after the salt as been wiped away with a paper towel—not water, which has no flavor!

IL GIORNO VENTISETTE

Technically, today is the last day of my "Italian and Cooking" course here with the Stefanis in their home. Where has the time gone? Tomorrow after lunch, I leave Viterbo for Rome and then fly home on Sunday.

Our first task this morning was once again to tackle *amaretti*. We reduced the amount of egg whites and sugar and tried again. The second batch was better, but still not perfect. Ugh! Alessandra called someone she knows in Blera to find out how she makes them, but didn't get much help. The women of Blera seem to be as protective of their *amaretti* recipes as Nonna is of her recipe for Marianna's birthday *torta*. No one in Blera was about to give away her top-secret *amaretti* recipe, but we were determined to crack the code. Nonna was really frustrated about the whole thing and decided to stop worrying about it and solve the problem later. She wanted to move from failure onto something we would be successful at—*gnocchi di patata*.

Potato *gnocchi* are made the same way as *gnocchi di zucca*—pumpkin *gnocchi*. Cooked and riced potatoes are combined with flour, a pinch of salt and an egg to form soft, pillow-like dumplings. *Gli gnocchi di patata* were not as soft as the pumpkin version, so we could actually roll each individual dumpling down the backside of a fork, letting the tines create *gnocchi*'s signature grooves.

I was a bit of a brute on the first couple of dumplings I rolled down the fork, after Nonna had demonstrated her technique on the first three or four. Of course, she whipped right through hers making it appear effortless and, true to my previous pasta making technique of making things too large or using too much force, I pressed the dumplings straight through the tines, completely destroying them.

"Sei troppo duro," —"You're too hard,"— Nonna said, as if I couldn't tell that from the mashed potato mess on the board in front of me. *"Morbido, morbido, morbido,"* —"Soft, soft, soft,"— she continued.

I was so soft with the next two or three that no there were no marks at all on the dumplings—not even an indentation from my thumb on the reverse side of where the grooves should be. Again, Nonna demonstrated, but going slower this time. Holding the fork in her right hand with the tines against the pasta board and the back of the fork facing up, she took a dumpling in her left hand and using her thumb, gently pushed it down the tines of the fork—effortlessly leaving a slight indentation from her thumb on one side and four grooves from the fork's tines on the other. Perfect. Naturally, the dumplings aren't perfectly identical, which is what gives homemade *gnocchi* their beauty—a collective uniqueness.

I improved as I went along. I re-rolled any that were not indented enough and steered clear of mashing them through with my thumb. I reminded myself that Nonna has been doing this for decades, whereas I had only been at it a couple of minutes. When I looked down at the rows of *gnocchi* lined up on the cutting board, I could tell which ones were formed by Nonna and which ones were mine. Mine are a little more *rustico* than hers. As with the *orecchiette*—little ear pasta—that I made weeks ago, only practice will make me more comfortable, and with comfort comes perfection.

Il sugo for *gli gnocchi* was made with chicken today. She seasoned and browned pieces of chicken—a whole fryer that she had cut into her usual 10 pieces—removed them from the pan, and used the residual brown bits and fat to sauté onions before adding the carton of strained tomatoes and a couple of minced garlic cloves. Once the strained tomatoes had cooked a little and the flavors started to blend, she returned the chicken to the sauce, covered the pot and lowered the heat to let the chicken finish cooking in the *sugo*.

When Alessandra and I came out of the den after our morning lesson, Nonna presented us with a plate of perfect *amaretti*. While I had been reviewing what I had learned over the past month, Nonna had been in the kitchen alone, tinkering with the recipe. She had cracked the code, or at least, had created her own secret recipe. We each took a cookie and taste-tested them. *"Mmmm, buono." "Molto buono." "Brava, Nonna!"* They were crunchy on the outside and still tender on the inside with just a hint of the bitter almond flavor balanced by the sugar and the sweet almonds.

"Marco, porti questi amaretti a casa domani," —"You can take these *amaretti* home tomorrow,"— Nonna said, proudly.

"Anche la ricetta?" —"And the recipe, too?"

"Certo!"

We went into the kitchen and Nonna told me the amounts she used in the final batch and explained her process. We sat together at the kitchen table— me writing the recipe in my red notebook and her writing it in a thick, small, white fabric-covered book that Marianna and Francesca had labeled, in gold cursive text, *"La Bibbia di Cucina di Nonna."* —"Nonna's Kitchen Bible." There were hundreds, if not thousands, of recipes in this bible. She paged through it, stopping on various recipes, telling me that I would have to come back so we could make this one or that one.

I watched as Nonna dropped a handful of *gnocchi* into boiling, salted water. They immediately sank to the bottom, but after a moment or two floated to the surface. *"Quando nuotano, hanno finito,"* —"When they swim, they are finished,"— Nonna said, as she strained off the first handful and placed them directly into the *sugo*. *Gli gnocchi* were boiled in batches and added to the red sauce after they had come up for air and floated in the slowly boiling water. Nonna said if the salted water boiled too hard or too fast it would destroy the *gnocchi*, so the heat was adjusted to maintain a gentle boil for the swimming dumplings.

True to form, the chicken had been removed from *il sugo* to a covered platter before we added *gli gnocchi* to the sauce. We skipped having an *antipasto* with lunch today; we started with the pasta course—*gli gnocchi nel sugo rosso*. Our handmade dumplings were soft and delicate, chewy but not tough, and the grooves and indentations collected and held the red sauce on the surface of each pillow of potato perfection.

Instead of taking a siesta today, I walked to Le Clerc to do some final shopping. I wanted to buy Nonna, Lillo and Alessandra a little token of my appreciation for everything they have done for me and with me this past month. I wasn't sure about what to get them before I left the house, but once I got to Le Clerc I had some ideas.

I returned to the house just in time to have a glass of water, a couple of *amaretti* and go into my last language lesson with Alessandra. It definitely felt like the last day of school, even though I really wasn't looking forward to leaving. There wasn't a lot of serious work on a particular subject. We mostly talked about ways I could keep pushing myself to learn and improve my Italian. She recommended a couple of language books that she really liked and thought would be helpful and also gave me some paperwork from the school in Siena through which this course is affiliated. I can fill out and submit the paperwork from home and receive a certificate saying that I completed this course. Maybe I should frame it and put it on my wall as if I were a doctor.

There was no end-of-class or university exam to test my proficiency, which means there is no pressure here at the end to perform at one's best, except that Alessandra has given me a guest book to sign. Every student who comes to live with the Stefanis has made an entry in this guest book. Page after page, the entries vary from simple single-line statements to full-page stories. Some people included postcards from their native country or personal photos taken while on vacation in Italy. Some are written in English, or Italian or the person's native tongue—or a combination of all three.

Now I have been given the book—the student who has spent the longest single period of time with the family. Some students have returned multiple times, but no one has spent four weeks in a single visit. I alone hold that honor, and with that honor comes the pressure of writing the perfect entry. The pressure comes from myself and not anyone else—well, maybe from seeing the writings of all the previous students as I leafed through the guest book. On some level, this is the biggest exam I have or will ever take.

"Alessandra, devo pensare. È molto difficile per me scrivere qualchecosa a questo momento." —"Alessandra, I must think. It is very difficult for me to write something at this moment."

"Naturalmente, ho capito."

"Posso portare questo su alla mia camera e scrivo stasera?" —"Can I take this up to my bedroom and I'll write tonight?"

"Si, si, si," Alessandra said, nodding her head, and continued, *"È ok se non voui scrivere niente."* —"It's okay if you don't want to write anything."

"No, no, no. Io voglio scrivere nel libro, ma dopo la cena stasera." —"No, no, no. I <u>want</u> to write in the book, but after dinner tonight."

The highlight of dinner tonight was *suppli*—the Roman version of the Sicilian *arancini*—the stuffed and fried rice balls that I made my second week here. *I suppli e gli arancini* are made in a similar fashion but *i suppli* are not identical to their Sicilian counterpart. The cooked rice is mixed with tomato sauce made with basil and sautéed onions, and then formed into an elliptical shape instead of a ball. While forming by hand, small cubes of mozzarella are inserted into the center of the *suppli* before they are battered with bread crumbs and fried in sunflower oil.

I had my camera close by, so I took lots of pictures of Nonna forming *i suppli* by hand. She said that she was going to have the most famous hands in America because I am always taking photos of her hands making something. I showed her the *suppli* photos and she was not amused.

"*Marco, le mie mani sono brutte,*" —"Mark, my hands are ugly,"— she said, staring at the image on my digital camera.

"*No, Nonna.*"

"*Si, si, Marco.*"

"*Nonna, è ok perchè le tue mani sono famose brutte mani,*" —"Nonna, it's ok because your hands are famous ugly hands,"— I said. That made her laugh.

Anna and Giulio came over last night after dinner, bringing with them a huge basket of vegetables from their garden, including more of the sinister-looking tomatoes. There were "ohs and ahs" over the produce, and I complimented them by saying that I wished I could have tomatoes like theirs in America. Giulio said that I should grow my own. I told him that I had never seen tomatoes like this before, so I doubted I would be able to find plants.

"*Prendi dei semi a casa,*" —"Take some seeds home,"— he said.

I never thought of that. It's true; I could just grow my own that way. There was a huge discussion amongst the Italians about where I could get San Marzano tomato seeds before I left town tomorrow. It was decided that Nonna would take me in the morning to buy some. Tomorrow is going to be a very busy day.

Alessandra made *caffè* and Lillo grabbed the *grappa* and the homemade *arancello* from the liquor shelf by the phone. Lillo poured shots of the *grappa* for us men, while the ladies decided to have the coffee—although Alessandra did pour herself a shot of her orange liqueur at one point. I joined her with my own shot of the *arancello*, too. Nonna passed around the *amaretti*, stacked in a bowl.

The six of us sat around the kitchen table drinking, eating, laughing and reminiscing about my time here in Viterbo. We toasted to the memory of Anna and Giulio's pizza party, and then to the success of Marco and Marianna, to America and to Italy.

When I got upstairs, my hardest Italian assignment was glaring at me from the nightstand—the guest book. Even after four weeks, I was terrified to attempt any long, complicated thoughts, so I kept my entry to simple sentences highlighting my time with the Stefanis:

"Mi piace gelato molto!"

"Francia, Francia, Francia!"

"Zuppa di gatti."

"Disastro!"

"GOOOOOOOL!"

"Non c'è problema—il gelato è liquido!"

"Ciao, ciao." "Ciao, ciao, ciao."

"Grazie per tutti! Con affetto, Marco—una persona molto importante dall'America."

Pollo con Farfalle

Chicken with Bow Tie Pasta

In Italy, the main course meat is often cooked in the pasta sauce to flavor it. Just before adding the pasta to the sauce, the meat is removed, allowing the pasta to be easily sauced and served alone as the first course. Here, the chicken would be plated and held stoveside until it was time to be served as the second course, after Nonna had cleared the pasta plates from the table.

1 (4 to 4½-pound) chicken, cut into 8 or 10 pieces (cut into 10 by dividing the breast into quarters)

Salt and freshly ground black pepper

1 tablespoon extra virgin olive oil

1 medium onion, finely minced

¼ cup water

2 large cloves garlic, finely minced

½ cup wine (Nonna used either red or white, whatever was left from the previous night's dinner)

1 (28-ounce) can whole peeled Italian plum tomatoes (preferably San Marzano), placed in a bowl and crushed by hand, reserving all of the liquid

1 cup strained tomatoes, such as Pomi brand *

Serve with:

1 pound *farfalle* (bow tie pasta)

10 basil leaves

1 tablespoon chopped fresh Italian flat-leaf parsley

½ cup grated Parmigiano-Reggiano or Grana Padano cheese

Using paper towels, pat any excess moisture off of the chicken and generously salt and pepper each piece.

Heat the oil in a large pan over medium-high heat. When the oil is hot, add the chicken, skin side down, and cook until the skin is golden brown on both sides, 3 to 5 minutes each side. Remove the chicken to a platter to rest.

Add the onion to the hot oil and chicken drippings and sauté for 1 minute, stirring constantly to remove the brown bits from the bottom of the pan. Add the water and garlic, cooking until the water has almost evaporated, 2 to 3 minutes. Stir in the wine and cook until it has almost evaporated, stirring occasionally, another 2 to 3 minutes. Add the crushed tomatoes with their juices, strained tomatoes, ½ teaspoon salt and ¼ teaspoon pepper, and mix until well combined. Bring to a boil and then reduce the heat to low. Simmer for 5 minutes.

Add the reserved chicken, with juices, back to the pan and stir into the sauce. Cover the pan with a lid set slightly ajar, and simmer on low for an additional 20 minutes, stirring occasionally.

Meanwhile, bring a large pot of water to boil. Once boiling, add 2 tablespoons salt and the *farfalle*, and cook following the directions on the package. When the pasta is *al dente*—tender but firm to the bite—remove the chicken to a plate and cover with foil to keep warm. Drain the pasta and add it to the sauce, stirring until the pasta is thoroughly covered with sauce. Cook for one minute until the sauce starts to bubble. Remove the pan from the heat, add the parsley, then tear the basil leaves by hand into pieces and stir with the parsley into the sauced pasta. Drizzle each serving with extra virgin olive oil and a tablespoon of grated cheese. Serve the chicken as the second course.

This makes 8 servings.

Note: Strained tomatoes can be readily found in most supermarkets in either the canned tomato or pasta aisles. Sometimes it may be referred to by its Italian name "passato" and it can be found either bottled or cartoned, as is the case with the Pomi brand.

IL GIORNO VENTOTTO

"*A ndiamo!*" Nonna said, holding her purse and car keys, as I put my cereal bowl in the sink. "*Prendi le bottiglie,*" —"Take the bottles,"— she continued, pointing to the two plastic bags of recycling on the floor next to the fridge, as she turned and headed toward the front door. Today was going to be a very busy day, indeed.

We ran our usual errands—newspaper stand, grocery store and recycling bins, but then we headed toward *il centro di Viterbo* for tomato seeds. We passed the cemetery, whipped around the roundabout and headed straight toward the *Porta Fiorentina*. Once we passed through the *porta* we took a hard right at *la Fontana della Rocca*—the Fortress Fountain, driving to the far end of *la Piazza della Rocca*, before finding a vacant parking spot.

I followed Nonna into a small hardware shop that had racks of seed packets on display just inside the front door.

"*Prego?*" asked a burly, middle-aged Italian man as he approached me.

"*Cerchiamo per i semi di San Marzano ... i semi di pomodoro,*" —"We are looking for San Marzano seeds ... tomato seeds,"— I said.

"*OK,*" he said, pointing us to a seed rack tucked behind some others. He asked me several rapid-fire questions and I stood there dumbfounded. Nonna jumped in and explained that I had been in Viterbo for a month and I was going home today and wanted to take some seeds with me so I could grow my own authentic Italian tomatoes.

"*Di dove sei?*" he asked.

"*America. Abito a Alabama,*" I answered.

"Eh, sweet home Alabama," he said in a thick Italian accent.

"*Si, si,*" and I laughed with him.

There were several types of tomato seeds to choose from and so, with Nonna's help, the three of us figured which ones would do best in Alabama's climate zone. I bought a couple of packets each of two different varieties. By the time he rang me up at the cash register, two other employees had joined us, and for a moment this Italian hardware store felt like any other small-town store back home where the owner or employees stand around chatting with their customers.

Back in the car, we zipped back around the *fontana* and through the *porta*, headed toward the house. Halfway home, Nonna pulled into the parking lot of the bakery and made one last purchase of *pizza bianca*. Nonna insisted on buying enough for us to eat now and for me to take to Rome and home. Sadly, there is no way it will last that long—I know I'll eat it all before Sunday. We each ate a piece back in the car.

Last night I had been asked what I wanted to eat for my last lunch here in Viterbo. My immediate response was "*Tutti!*" An impossible task, but there were so many things that I would love to taste again—octopus salad, spinach and ricotta crepes, mozzarella in carriages, *fettuccine* with truffles, *rigatoni* with cauliflower, veal tips with polenta, the secret recipe *torta*, let alone all of the various salamis, cured meats, bread, cheeses and wines. I decided that it should be a simple lunch of easy-to-prepare food—*penne* pasta with sauce made from Anna and Giulio's tomatoes followed by grilled turkey cutlets.

Nonna and I put the tomatoes through the food mill and prepared her simple sauce using onions and garlic. It was assembled in no time, which gave me some extra time to go upstairs and finish packing, while the sauce simmered on the stove.

Marco and Marianna stopped by before lunch on their way to the farm to ride the horses and feed the cattle. They had a busy day so they were not going to join us for lunch and had only stopped to tell me goodbye. There were hugs, kisses and handshakes by the back door and I handed Marianna the *zuppa di gatti* jar from the stovetop so she could feed the cats.

"*Ciao, ciao.*"

"*Ciao. Buon viaggio!*"

"*Grazie. Ciao!*"

"*Ciao, ciao, ciao!*"

"*Ciao, ciao!*"

"*Ciao, ciao, ciao, ciao,*" as they disappeared out the backyard gate.

It wasn't even 10 minutes later when Lillo came walking in the back door. He had been at the farm and said he had passed Marianna and Marco on the road. We were still about an hour away from lunch and there really wasn't much to do. I had finished packing, so while Lillo went upstairs to get cleaned up, Nonna, Alessandra and I hung out around the kitchen table and chatted.

When Lillo came back downstairs he wanted to show me something out in the backyard. We went out the kitchen's back door and walked toward to back gate. I thought maybe there was something out in his car so I was a little surprised when he stopped me as I was opening the gate to go out to the street.

"*No, no, Marco. Qua,*" he said, pointing to the driveway in the backyard. I had never noticed the driveway before, since no one ever parks in the backyard. There is a set of car gates but I have never seen them used.

He kicked a couple of stones away and cleared a little bit of sand from the driveway and pointed down. *"Qua."*

I looked down and there, embedded in the surface of the driveway, was a map of Italy. He had brought stones from the farm and had arranged them into the shape of the country—including the islands of Sicily and Sardinia. Some of the stones were quite large, but all of them were flat on the surface, so unless pointed out, the map would go unnoticed. It was a subtle map of Italy, but I appreciated the time and effort it must have taken to place it into the driveway.

"Bravo, Lillo! La tua mappa è stupefacente!" I said, as I kneeled down to feel Sardinia.

"Lillo, Marco ... mangiamo!" Alessandra called from the kitchen door.

Nonna was just placing the *farfalle* pasta into the sauce as we came through the door.

"Seduto!" —"Sit!"— Nonna said, as we passed by her on our way to the table. In Italy, the pasta waits for no one.

Lillo and I sprinkled pepper sauce and grated pecorino cheese on our bowls of pasta. Lillo was happy to see me join him in a little spicy pasta and slices of his favorite *il pane di Blera*. Before we had completely finished our pasta, Nonna and Alessandra got up from the table to prepare and grill the turkey cutlets. Again, it is better if we wait for the cutlets than it is to have the cutlets done and waiting for us. They need to be eaten straight from the grill pan while they are still hot and crunchy. It does not take long for the meat to cook while the bread crumb and Parmigiano-Reggiano crust browns. Using a grill pan puts darkened grill marks on the cutlets by slightly over-toasting the crust, which gives the cutlets a smoky, grilled flavor.

"Nonna, buonissmi! Grazie. Grazie tanto!" I said. The meal was so good I never wanted it to end.

The cutlets were followed by the usual salad of romaine lettuce dressed with extra virgin olive oil, balsamic vinegar, salt and black pepper, followed by pineapple—*ananas*, then some *amaretti*, and finally, *caffè*. It was a simple but filling lunch. I will not be leaving Viterbo on an empty stomach.

"*Marco, qua,*" Nonna said, handing me a quart-sized jar of her plum *marmelata*, the remaining *pizza bianca* and *amaretti* cookies, and in addition to the tomato seeds already packed in my suitcase, I am leaving Viterbo a rich man—a very rich man.

"*Un momento,*" I said, "*Ho dei regali per voi, anche.*"—"I have some gifts for you, too." I ran upstairs and grabbed the three gifts and came bounding back down to the kitchen table.

"*Per Nonna,*" I said, handing her a simply wrapped box bound with curly ribbon.

She opened the gift gingerly as if she were handling a most precious and delicate object.

"*Ah, grazie, Marco, grazie!*" she said, as she revealed a digital kitchen scale. We measure everything by weight when we cook, and Nonna's plastic kitchen scale was so old that most of the time its red needle would spin and land on a number that was almost worn off, making it difficult to read. Also, when trying to zero out the scale before weighing anything, Nonna and I could never agree on exactly where "0" was. We would each hunch over at the kitchen counter to look directly at the face of the scale and depending on our vantage point say, "*Più, più*"—"More, more"— or "*Meno, meno*"—"Less, less". It took minutes to zero out the scale.

Nonna immediately had to take the new scale out of the box and weigh something. I turned the digital scale on, placed a plate on the pad, hit the "0" button and placed a tomato on the plate. Immediately the weight came up and we all applauded. Nonna was thrilled.

"*Per Alessandra.*"

For Alessandra, I had found David Sedaris' book, "Me Talk Pretty One Day," translated into Italian. It is a collection of his writings centered on his time in France, his lack of command of the French language and his many encounters with the locals. I hope Alessandra will enjoy his humor and the fact that it takes place in France—*"Francia, Francia, Francia!"* It certainly speaks to me of my command of the Italian language—"I am a meat!"

"Marco, mille grazie! Mi piacciono libri. Leggo ogni notte." —"Mark, thanks! I like books. I read every night."

"Ed ultimo, per Lillo," I said, handing him a gift bag.

He untied the ribbon securing the bag's handles and pulled out a very nice bottle of *grappa* that I found at Le Clerc. This *grappa* was produced from the Sangiovese grape solids that remain after the juices are extracted in the process of making *il Brunello di Montalcino,* a very famous style of Tuscan red wine.

"Ah, Marco. Buonissima! Grazie, grazie, grazie!" Lillo said. He knew that this was the "Cadillac" of *grappa.*

"Lo bevi domani sul tuo compleanno. Tanti auguri!" —"You can drink it tomorrow on your birthday. Congratulations!"

There were hugs and kisses all around as we thanked each other all over again for the gifts. Of course, Tequila and Brighitta, not wanting to be left out, managed to wiggle in and join the excitement.

"Andiamo," Alessandra said, tapping her watch. It was time to get me loaded out of the third floor and off to the train station.

Lillo helped me get my bags down the stairs and out to the car. Alessandra climbed in the back, while Nonna put her sunglasses on and got in to drive. I stood at the opened passenger door as Lillo and I said our goodbyes with a quick handshake and the customary kiss on each cheek.

"Ciao, ciao, ciao," Lillo said, as he closed my door for me.

"Ci vediamo anno prossimo," —"See you next year,"— I said through my opened window.

Lillo laughed.

"OK, anno prossimo!" he replied, and with that, Nonna drove away.

We chatted in the car about all different kinds of things on the drive to the Orte train station. My leaving was not the pervasive topic. We chatted about Rome, Francesca's trip, Jimmy and Nicola—that made us laugh—the farm, what Nonna was going to make for dinner and the arrival of the next student tomorrow—a middle-aged American woman who was already in Italy, coming from a week's vacation in Venice.

"She will not be as fun as you," Alessandra said, holding her hairstyle in place.

"*Guardato!*" Nonna said, pointing to my right, "*Il picnic.*"

We were passing the exit off the highway that led to the mountains where we had had our picnic last weekend.

"That was a lot of fun. Marco, did you enjoy that?" Alessandra asked, touching me on the shoulder from the back seat.

Silenzio.

I could not speak. The moment Alessandra touched my shoulder, suddenly, all of the emotions and events of my trip—my arrival, the food, the parties, the laughing, the fights, the newfound friends and my leaving— came flooding over me. If I would have uttered one word, or even a syllable, I would have broken down and cried. I just couldn't speak.

Silenzio.

Alessandra patted my shoulder and I remained looking out of my window at the mountain, silent, for several kilometers.

Eventually, I regained composure and we returned to chatting about this and that all the way to the station.

Alessandra and Nonna insisted on helping me with my bags and made sure I purchased the correct ticket and waited with me on the platform. It wasn't long before the train came into sight, appearing from a grove of distant trees.

I turned to say goodbye, and Alessandra started to speak, "Marco, we have had such a good...."

I held up my hand, smiled and shook my head to stop her. Again, I had become emotional and had to stop her before she went any further. My eyes were starting to well up. I couldn't bear any words at that moment.

Smiling, we kissed each cheek—first with Alessandra, then with Nonna. We all nodded, I picked up my bags and walked alone down the platform. There was no "*Ciao, ciao, ciao*" game here; emotionally, I never would have made it. I turned back every now and then to nod goodbye, since my arms were full of luggage. They smiled and nodded, too.

As I boarded the train, I glanced back one last time to see the ladies start waving goodbye. I could take no more—the floodgates broke, and I stepped up into the train.

✺

Arrosto Pannato

Breaded Turkey or Veal Cutlets

This is a quick and easy way to cook thinly sliced cutlets without coating them with egg or frying them in oil. It is simple, straightforward and to the point—very Italian.

½ cup plain dried bread crumbs

2 tablespoons grated Parmigiano-Reggiano cheese

½ teaspoon salt

¼ teaspoon freshly ground black pepper

1 pound turkey or veal cutlets (8 slices)

2 tablespoons extra virgin olive oil

In a shallow dish, combine the bread crumbs, grated cheese, salt and pepper, stirring until well mixed. Brush both sides of a cutlet with oil and place in the shallow dish on top of the bread crumb mixture. Spoon mixture on top and, using your fingers, press the coating onto the cutlet. Turn the cutlet over and repeat until the entire piece is breaded. Shake off any excess coating and place the breaded cutlet on a plate to hold while breading the rest of the cutlets.

Place a medium non-stick sauté pan over medium-high heat and when hot, add the breaded cutlets to the dry pan, cooking (in batches if necessary) until the coating starts to crisp and turn golden brown, 2 to 3 minutes. Turn the cutlet over and cook the second side for an additional 1 to 2 minutes, until crisp and golden. Serve warm.

This makes 4 servings.

*Even though the cutlets are thin and will take no time to cook, if your pan is too hot the bread crumbs and cheese will overcook and start to burn before the cutlet is done on the inside. Turn down the heat under the pan if you feel that they are cooking too fast, but also know that, like good Italian pizza, it isn't a bad thing if the edges get a little dark or blackened.

Sometimes Nonna would squeeze fresh lemon juice over the cutlets as she plated and served them—and a little chopped fresh Italian flat-leaf parsley sprinkled over the top made them special, too.

A CASA

C iao tutti!

I am safely home in Alabama.

My last night in Rome was pretty uneventful, although I did manage to have gelato three times over the course of Saturday night—*Mi piace gelato molto!*

I landed late into LaGuardia Sunday, which bumped me from my original late afternoon flight to one even later in the evening from JFK to Atlanta. Transferring between the two New York airports was easy, and by the time I got to JFK I was really hungry.

I know that the food choices at airports can be slim, but after being out of the country for a month I forgot how slim. My choices were all fast food. I hadn't eaten fast food in four weeks. During my entire stay in Italy I only saw two fast food restaurants, one set of golden arches was in Rome and the other was in the mall in Viterbo. Those two fast food establishments were it—there was no other fast food competition. Less than 24 hours earlier I was eating Nonna's cooking, and now in JFK my only option was fast food. I had the choice between "burger doodle" fast food and "Italian" fast food.

I couldn't bring myself to attempt anything "Italian." I knew I would only be disappointed—nothing about their menu was truly Italian, including the large image of a bonneted peasant woman picking grapes by hand in a vineyard. *Mamma mia!* No, thanks. I defaulted to the "burger doodle." "Welcome home," I thought, as I swiped my fries through a puddle of ketchup, desperately craving a *panino*. I drowned my culinary sorrow in a large Coke—at least there was plenty of ice.

"So, what did you learn over in Italy?" Richard asked, as I climbed into the car at the Atlanta airport.

"Where do I begin?" I said, laughing at the prospect of trying to explain the past month to him. "You got my e-mails, right?"

"I mean, of everything that you experienced, what is the one thing that you will take away from your month as an Italian?"

I had to stop and think for a moment.

"I am so tired from the trip that I don't think I have an answer. I need to sleep on it."

This morning for breakfast I opened Nonna's *marmelata* and smeared a large spoonful on my toast. I am missing the bread in Viterbo already. I brought out the *amaretti* cookies for Richard to try, since I know they are one of his favorites. "Hmm, good," he said. I think I was expecting a bigger reaction. If he only knew how much drama and turmoil there had been over these *amaretti*. Maybe that is why they tasted so good to me.

Richard's question has been floating around in my head all day today: "What is the one thing that you will take away from your month as an Italian?" There are a million things, tangible and intangible, that I have taken away from this experience. I went over to study the food and language of Italy, and beyond the recipes and verb forms, I really ended up taking a course about life, or as the Italians would say, *La Dolce Vita*. The literal translation into

English doesn't quite convey the essence of this very famous Italian concept.

For me, the "Sweet Life" is going into the kitchen, preparing food and serving it to the people I love and cherish. *La Dolce Vita* is found in those moments of life around a table where stories are told—old memories are relived and new memories are given life. It is where food ultimately unites us through the juxtaposition of laughter, tears, joy, sorrow, happiness, pain and ecstasy.

I am not sure which recipe I'll cook first for Richard from my red folder, "*La Mia Bibbia di Cucina*," but the recipes' secret ingredient will be the most important thing I took away from Italy—*La Dolce Vita*.

Ciao, ciao, ciao…

NOV · 2008

EPILOGO

The Stefanis and I have remained in contact since my stay with them in 2005. Alessandra and I e-mail each other every couple of months and when I have a question about a recipe or feel the need to check in, I call them.

"Pronto?" —"Hello?"— Nonna always answers the phone.

"Ciao, Nonna. Io Marco, in America. Come stai?"

"Marco, ciao, ciao, ciao!! Sono bene, grazie. E tu?"

"Io bene. Bene, bene."

"Alessandra, Marco è al telefono! Marco è al telefono!!"

Instantly, I am right there with Nonna—she is holding the receiver of the green house phone, sitting in the chair next to the telephone table under the shelving filled with liquor bottles, and shouting upstairs for Alessandra to come down. In the distance, Alessandra is repeatedly yelling, *"Marco, Marco"* as I hear the second story door open and her shoes clicking down the tiled staircase.

Tequila and Brighitta are never far behind her, and at some point, while she descends, they start barking. It is a cacophony of sounds—Alessandra and Nonna taking turns yelling *"MARCO, MARCO,"* while the dogs howl, growl and bark until Alessandra arrives, breathless and panting, at the phone.

"Ciao, ciao … ciao … ciao, ciao, Marco!"

I almost weep every time I call because the love coming back at me through the phone is so tangible.

Richard and I have been to Italy for vacation every year since 2005 and we always make a point to stop and have lunch with the whole family regardless of where we are vacationing in the country. I have never told the family that Richard is my partner, although I am sure they have figured it out. They absolutely love him, and whenever we ring the bell at the back gate and all four dogs start to bark, Richard gets a big, goofy grin on his face. He knows the minute we walk through the kitchen door he will be greeted with the same love, hugs and two-cheek kisses as I am.

We spent Thanksgiving Day with them in 2008 and, although that isn't an Italian holiday, it certainly felt like one. Marianna was there with her husband Eric (a tall, handsome Brazilian horse trainer) and their three-month-old daughter. Alessandra is now a *nonna* herself and there is no prouder *nonno* than Lillo.

Francesca and Stefano are no longer dating and she is attending the university in Viterbo, while still living at home. Nicola and Jimmy are no longer friends, and I ran into Nicola in 2006 when Richard and I were in Viterbo for *La Macchina di Santa Rosa*. Seeing *i Facchini* carry the brightly lit tower through the streets of Viterbo was truly an amazing sight and I would give anything to be able to join them in carrying it one day myself.

Nonna has not changed in the least and she still uses the scale I gave her. She always prepares her secret-recipe *torta* for our visits and I always eat more than my share—Richard scolds me and the family laughs when I ask for more; Nonna smiles with pride. Alessandra makes *fettuccine di Blera* and the two large, round sheets of it are always drying on the table when we arrive.

I haven't had the time to go back as a student yet, but every year Richard and I, together, get to spend a glorious day eating, laughing and learning with our Italian family. *Bellissima!*

ACKNOWLEDGMENTS

The journey of this book to publication has been a lot like my travels to Italy; each step along the way has put me in contact with a wide array of people, both American and Italian, all of whom have inspired me—and enriched my life.

To "Big Gram," Erma Reister, my paternal great-grandmother, whose memory reminds me daily, to the very core of my being, that there is nothing as profound as a homemade meal.

To my mom and in loving memory of Richard's mother, both named Pat, whose enthusiastic companionship on our first trip to Italy started it all.

To the Stefani family, to whom this book is dedicated, for sharing the life that fills these pages.

To the persistent Dodgie Shaffer whose "skull and cross bones" note threatened me into writing my first word about Italy.

To the tireless "Team Viterbo"—Tanya Searle, Susan Willis and Sylvia Gregory—whose friendship, coupled with insightful and truthful notes, guided me through every textual variation imaginable. I have used and abused all of my brownie points!

To Biba Caggiano whose words of encouragement are still saved on my cell phone.

To Shana Kelly for convincing me that I was a writer by supporting me through every worried phone call and rewrite.

To Anna Brown and Maria Luisa Ardon for making sure that I did not destroy their native Italian tongue. *Grazie, grazie, grazie! Mille grazie!*

To Jason Enterline for his masterful and creative eye.

To Sally and "Ron" Carr for the mad push to edit at the eleventh hour—and for *"theatre."*

To Kari Hock, my publisher at Gemelli Press and a kindred Italian soul, who read my blog, then my manuscript, and believed that my joyful and heartfelt food memoir/cookbook had a rightful place on the bookshelf.

And to Richard, my partner for over 23 years, who from day one has made my life one hell of a roller coaster ride ~ *mio marito, il mio amore, il mio disastro!*

RECIPE INDEX BY COURSE
Indice delle Ricette ai Piatti

LaVergne, TN USA
01 September 2010
195559LV00002B/2/P